Legal Concepts and Issues in Emergency Care

Legal Concepts and Issues in Emergency Care

N. Genell Lee, RN, MSN, JD

Nurse Attorney

Birmingham, Alabama

W.B. SAUNDERS COMPANY

A Harcourt Health Sciences Company

Philadelphia   London   Montreal   Sydney   Tokyo   Toronto

W.B. SAUNDERS COMPANY
A Harcourt Health Sciences Company

The Curtis Center
Independence Square West
Philadelphia, Pennsylvania 19106-3399

Vice President, Nursing Editorial: Sally Schrefer
Managing Editor: Lisa Potts
Developmental Editor: Billi Sharp
Project Manager: Deborah L. Vogel
Project Specialist: Jodi M. Willard
Design Manager: Bill Drone
Cover Designer: Liz Young

Library of Congress Cataloging-in-Publication Data

Lee, N. Genell.
    Legal concepts and issues in emergency care / N. Genell Lee.
        p. cm.
    Includes bibliographical references and index.
    ISBN 0–7216–8324–X
        1. Emergency medical services—Law and legislation—United States.   I. Title.
KF3826.E5 L44 2000
344.73′03218—dc21

00-041267

Legal Concepts and Issues in Emergency Care   ISBN 0–7216–8324–X

Printed in the United States of America.

Last digit is the print number: 9   8   7   6   5   4   3   2   1

To Jordyn Nicole Lee, whose natural curiosity, intelligence, humor, and beauty are beacons of light that fill my spirit . . . .

N. Genell Lee

Contributor

James T. Noland, RN, MSN, CRNP
Pediatric Certified Nurse Practitioner,
Huntsville Hospital;
CNS Pediatric Intensive Care Unit,
Huntsville, Alabama

Preface

Legal Concepts and Issues in Emergency Care began as a vision for a reference text on critical legal issues facing emergency health care professionals "in the trenches." The vision also included the combination of standard reference materials from journals, case law, and the burgeoning materials available on the World Wide Web. The implementation of the vision is before you. Federal and state laws and regulations are housed in volume after volume of constitutions, statutes, codes, and case law. The intent was not to compile all the applicable laws in one book but to highlight those laws specific to emergency care. Although the format of each chapter differs, specific cases are used throughout to integrate the legal processes and cases with emergency care realities.

This book is divided into four major sections. Section I addresses general legal concepts and serves as the foundation for the remainder of the book. A division of federal, state, and administrative law describes how laws are made and the roles of the three branches of government. This section also covers the components of a civil lawsuit, types of witnesses, and a brief discussion of preparing for whatever role individuals find themselves in during a civil lawsuit. Law and ethics in emergency care are also addressed in Section I.

Section II is the foundational section of the book related to emergency care laws. Chapters on consent, refusal to consent or withdrawal of consent, managed care, and confidentiality, as well as privacy issues, comprise the second section. Actual legal cases are presented and discussed to integrate legal concepts with emergency care issues. Charts of state law requirements are used to illustrate variances in legal parameters. Website references are used throughout in addition to traditional reference materials.

Section III addresses unique circumstances in emergency care. Topics in this section include chapters on forensics, psychiatric emergency care, special treatment centers, EMTALA (Emergency Medical Treatment and Active Labor Act), advance practitioners, prehospital care, and aeromedical transport.

Forensics is found in few other areas of health care. In the emergency department and in prehospital care the health care professional often becomes an evidence collector for law enforcement agencies. EMTALA replaced COBRA/OBRA as the law governing transfers. The law is quite complicated, and there are numerous cases in this section that address the responsibility of the emergency health care provider.

Section IV contains chapters related to tort law or injury to the person. This section contains chapters on intentional torts, professional negligence, and other torts. Actual cases from different sections of the United States illustrate both the legal concepts and typical fact patterns. The book concludes with a chapter that covers other tort actions such as defamation, violation of the right to privacy, wrongful death, and negligent infliction of emotional distress.

The law is conservative in its approach to societal issues. Changes in society, the practice of emergency care, or other changes can occur before the law changes. Laws may change to impose a standard of conduct on the public. Laws aid society in knowing what is and is not acceptable. There is also a school of thought that regulation in particular aids the regulators more than the public and adds costs to the regulated industry. Those are debates for a different book.

Lawyers always have disclaimers, and this lawyer is no exception to that general rule. This book is not a substitute for legal advice and counsel for a particular factual situation. Every attempt was made to provide the current state of the law in multiple jurisdictions. However, I am not licensed to practice law in any state other than Alabama and do not hold myself out as an expert on any state's health care laws. Should the reader find that he or she is in need of legal counsel, do not attempt to use this text as a "self-help" guide to law. My knowledge and understanding of the law continue to grow, and I encourage those who need legal counsel or advice to seek it from a competent, practicing attorney in their own jurisdiction.

N. Genell Lee

Acknowledgments

Robin Carter, nursing editor at W.B. Saunders Company, has been a wonderful mentor, visionary, and colleague for a number of years. Her advice and counsel, and unfailing sense of humor, added to my completion of this exciting task. Lisa Potts ably responded to the re-assignment of the project to her care and management. I appreciate both their efforts.

James T. Noland aided me in using his expertise to write two chapters. His commitment to the process of time deadlines and constant re-editing added to the process and the product. His invaluable contribution is appreciated.

My development as a writer progressed with my development as a registered nurse and now nurse attorney. I had opportunities, relationships, and experiences with nursing colleagues, mentors, and friends. My legal reasoning, honed to a fine tune by the faculty at the Cumberland School of Law at Samford University, serves me well. To the faculty who started me on the path of excellence in nursing at the University of Alabama School of Nursing at the University of Alabama at Birmingham and the law school faculty at Cumberland, I am eternally grateful.

Education is not just formal study but a lifelong process of learning. My parents, Elmer and Edna Lee, are exceptional examples of lifelong learning. Their emphasis on formal and informal educational opportunities led me to the process of learning and love of the written word. I am grateful to them for their examples and sacrifices that made my opportunities all the more meaningful. My brothers and sisters, in-laws, nieces, nephews, great-nieces and nephews, aunts, uncles, and cousins also set examples for me. I appreciate their contributions to the person I am today.

Finally, my friend since nursing school days, Shirley B. Young, keeps my feet planted firmly on the earth while encouraging me to explore the unknown. Thank you to you all.

N. Genell Lee

Contents

CHAPTER 10
Psychiatric Emergency Care 117

CHAPTER 11
Laws and Regulations for Special
Treatment Centers 131

CHAPTER 12
Emergency Medical Treatment and
Active Labor Act (EMTALA) 137

Section IV
Torts: Injury to the Person

Legal Concepts and Issues in Emergency Care

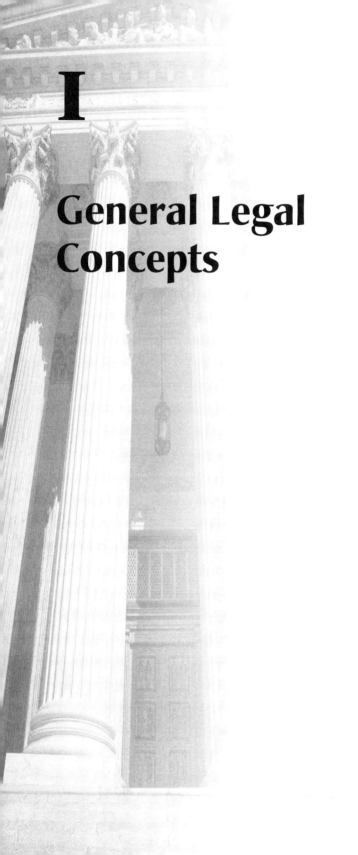

I

General Legal
Concepts

1

Introduction to the Legal System and Its Processes

CHAPTER OUTLINE

The United States has a democratic form of government. The founding fathers incorporated key legal concepts into the U.S. Constitution, the document that serves as the foundation for the democratic system. Many of the legal concepts incorporated into the U.S. Constitution reflected English law, whereas other important changes were written into the Constitution to reflect the freedom the founding fathers intended for the newly formed United States of America. The founding fathers envisioned a limited government, and although health care is a heavily government-regulated industry with unlimited challenges, it is possible to survive and thrive in the industry. Although a discussion about the reasons and rationales for government regulation is beyond the scope of this book, an understanding of the infrastructure of the government and law will aid in coping with and strategizing anticipatory changes in the industry of health care.

BRANCHES OF GOVERNMENT AND THE LAW

Federal Government

To understand general legal concepts in the United States system of laws, it is first necessary to understand the basic structure of the legal system and the processes involved before applying specific data to a factual situation. The infrastructure of the government was first set out in the U.S. Constitution (Box 1-1). The federal government structure is constitutionally based. The founding fathers set up three independent, interdependent branches of a federal government. The U.S. Constitution delineates separation of powers of the three branches with a system of checks and balances. The checks and balances ensure that no one branch, individual, or political party can rule unfettered.

BOX 1-1   Overview of the Articles of the United States Constitution, 1789

ARTICLE I	Established Congress; defined qualifications and duties of the House of Representatives and Senate; specified certain powers (including taxing and spending, regulation of commerce, declaring war)
ARTICLE II	Established Executive branch; offices of president and vice president; identified methods of election, qualifications, and duties; specified certain powers of office (commander in chief, appointment of Supreme Court judges); identified removal requirements
ARTICLE III	Established Supreme Court and granted Congress power to establish other courts; identified jurisdiction and responsibility of Court and specific types of cases
ARTICLE IV	Established relationship among states; established guidelines regarding admission of new states to the union; established Republican form of government
ARTICLE V	Identified process for amending U.S. Constitution
ARTICLE VI	Established U.S. Constitution as the "Supreme law of the land"; bound state and federal officers by oath or affirmation to support and uphold the U.S. Constitution
ARTICLE VII	Specified establishment of U.S. Constitution by ratification of nine states

Amendments to the United States Constitution

AMENDMENT I (1791)	Congress prohibited from making laws infringing on, or establishing, religion; freedom of speech; freedom of press; peaceful assembly; petition government
AMENDMENT II (1791)	Right to raise militia; keep and bear arms
AMENDMENT III (1791)	Prohibition against housing soldiers in private quarters without owner's consent
AMENDMENT IV (1791)	Prohibition against unreasonable search and seizure; probable cause needed for warrants
AMENDMENT V (1791)	Grand jury required for capital or infamous crimes; prohibition against double jeopardy, self-incrimination; due process required before depriving individual of "life, liberty or property"; compensation required if government takes private property for public use
AMENDMENT VI (1791)	Criminal trials must be with impartial jury, speedy, public; accused has right to confront witnesses against him or her; accused has right to counsel
AMENDMENT VII (1791)	Right to trial by jury
AMENDMENT VIII (1791)	Prohibition against excessive bail, fines, cruel and unusual punishment
AMENDMENT IX (1791)	Rights retained by people even if not enumerated

Box continued on following page

BOX 1-1 Overview of the Articles of the United States Constitution, 1789 *Continued*

AMENDMENT X (1791)	Reserves rights to states or the people for those powers not delegated to United States
AMENDMENT XI (1795)	Restricts suits against states by citizens of other states or foreign states
AMENDMENT XII (1804)	Voting procedure for president and vice president
AMENDMENT XIII (1865)	Prohibition against slavery
AMENDMENT XIV (1868)	States prohibited from making laws that deny equal protection to all citizens; due process required before infringement of "life, liberty or property"; defined citizens; Civil War sections regarding debts, representation in Congress
AMENDMENT XV (1870)	Right to vote not denied because of race, color, or previous servitude
AMENDMENT XVI (1913)	Income tax can be levied and collected by federal government
AMENDMENT XVII (1913)	Senate terms, votes, and vacancies
AMENDMENT XVIII (1919)	Commonly referred to as *Prohibition;* liquor outlawed throughout the United States
AMENDMENT XIX (1920)	Women granted right to vote
AMENDMENT XX (1933)	Terms limit for president and vice president; succession procedures identified
AMENDMENT XXI (1933)	Repeal of 18th Amendment, "Prohibition"
AMENDMENT XXIII (1961)	Electors for District of Columbia in presidential and vice presidential election
AMENDMENT XXIV (1964)	Right to vote—prohibition against poll tax or other tax imposed to limit voting
AMENDMENT XXV (1967)	Succession to presidential office
AMENDMENT XXVI (1971)	Right to vote if 18 or older

The three branches of the federal government, as set out in the U.S. Constitution, are the Executive, Legislative, and Judicial (Box 1-2). The role of each branch is distinct and established by the U.S. Constitution. The Executive branch of the federal government is charged with the responsibility to enforce the laws of the land. The Executive branch includes the president, vice president, cabinet officers, and federal agencies. The Department of Health and Human Services, for example, is organizationally in the Executive branch. The National Institutes of Health is also an executive agency. The president serves as the elected chief executive officer. The executive's power is not unlimited, however, because the Executive branch cannot make any laws. Laws can be proposed from the Executive to the Legislative branch, but only Congress can make statutory law. The agencies of the Executive branch may propose regulations to ensure enforcement of the laws enacted by Congress, but only if Congress provides enabling legislation (specific authority from the Congress) allowing or requiring regulations.

The Legislative branch—Congress—has elected members from all 50 states. Congress has the responsibility to make the federal laws that are enforced by the Executive branch. Congress is made up of two distinct bodies: the House of Representatives and the Senate. The members of the House of Representatives are elected, and the number of representatives for each state depends on the state's population. The Senate members are elected, and each state has two senators. Congress is independent from the Executive branch. Congress has oversight responsibilities, generally through various committees of the House of Representatives and the Senate, over various agencies of the Executive branch (another check and balance). Congress' power is not unlimited though; the president can veto legislation.

The Judicial branch is unique in that it too is independent of the Legislative and Executive branches. The Supreme Court of the United States was established

BOX 1-2   Three Branches of Federal Government

LEGISLATIVE (makes law)

House of Representatives
   Officers, Committees
Senate
   Officers, Committees

EXECUTIVE (enforces law)

President
Vice president
Cabinet officers
   Agencies

JUDICIAL (interprets law)

United States Supreme Court
United States Courts of Appeal
United States District Courts
Specialized Federal Courts:
   Tax Court
   Bankruptcy Courts
   Claims Court
   Court of International Trade
   Court of Military Appeals
   Courts of Military Review

BOX 1-3   Federal Circuit Courts of Appeal

1st Circuit	Maine, Massachusetts, New Hampshire, Rhode Island, Puerto Rico
2nd Circuit	Connecticut, New York, Vermont
3rd Circuit	Delaware, New Jersey, Pennsylvania, Virgin Islands
4th Circuit	Maryland, North Carolina, South Carolina, Virginia, West Virginia
5th Circuit	Canal Zone, Louisiana, Mississippi, Texas
6th Circuit	Kentucky, Ohio, Tennessee
7th Circuit	Illinois, Indiana, Wisconsin
8th Circuit	Arkansas, Iowa, Minnesota, Missouri, Nebraska, North Dakota, South Dakota
9th Circuit	Alaska, Arizona, California, Hawaii, Idaho, Montana, Nevada, Oregon, Washington
10th Circuit	Colorado, Kansas, New Mexico, Oklahoma, Utah, Wyoming
11th Circuit	Alabama, Florida, Georgia
DC Circuit	District of Columbia
Federal Circuit	All federal districts

Information from 28 United States Court of Appeals § 41 (1998).

by the founding fathers in Article III of the U.S. Constitution (U.S. Const., 1789). The justices of the Supreme Court are appointed by the president with the advice and consent of the Senate. The Supreme Court justices are not subject to the vagaries of the political process; all federal judges are appointed for life. However, federal judges can be removed through an impeachment process. The Supreme Court, and the lower federal courts, are charged with the responsibility of interpreting the laws established by Congress and enforced by the Executive branch. Cases may be heard in the federal district court, appealed to the Circuit Court of Appeals (Box 1-3), and eventually appealed to the United States Supreme Court. Congress, under authority of Article III, Section 1, of the U.S. Constitution, established courts. Examples of Article I or adjunct courts are the United States Bankruptcy Court, Tax Court, and Courts of Military.

State Government

Each state has a similar infrastructure to that of the federal government. Each state has Executive, Legislative, and Judicial branches. Each state also has a constitution that establishes the system of state government. Generally, the states follow the federal model in that the Executive branch is responsible for enforcing laws, the Legislative branch for enacting laws, and the Judicial branch for interpreting the laws. Each state retained the right to determine how governance would occur. General legal principles, such as informed consent, are universal, but each state determined the specific characteristics of the principle. Thus consent for medical care varies among states. In addition to statutes and regulations that govern consent, common law or cases determined by the courts of each state establish other parameters for consent (see Chapter 5).

SOURCES OF LAW

Evaluation of the impact a law can have on emergency care requires a determination of the source of a particular law. The U.S. Constitution and its amendments provide the structure of federal government and the principles followed in governance. For example, slavery was included in the U.S. Constitution at the time of its passage in 1789. Subsequently, Amendment XIII, ratified in 1865, outlawed slavery throughout the United States and its territories. The abolition of and prohibition against slavery is a basic principle of governance. The U.S. Constitution and its amendments provide basic fundamental rights to individuals of the United States. A state can provide more rights in its own constitution but cannot provide less than that provided in the federal constitution.

Federal Statutes

Federal statutes are laws enacted by Congress. The president has veto power over laws passed by Congress (one of the checks and balances of the system). Congress can override a presidential veto with a two-thirds majority. The laws enacted by Congress, if not vetoed by the president, become federal statutes that govern a particular area of everyday life. Official federal statutes are published as the United States Code. The U.S.C. is available on the World Wide Web. The Internal Revenue Code, commonly called the *Tax Code,* is an example of a federal statute enacted by Congress. The Department of the Treasury, an Executive branch agency, is responsible for enforcing the tax laws enacted by Congress. The Internal Revenue Service, one of the agencies within the Treasury Department, is assigned the task of implementing the Tax Code and regulations to collect tax revenue.

Federal Regulations

Regulations are guidelines enacted by federal agencies for enforcement of laws (Flaherty, 1998). Regulations have the effect of law. Statutes and regulations are analogous to hospital policies and procedures. The statute is the equivalent of a policy, whereas the regulations are the equivalent of procedures to implement the policies. Regulations are adopted by administrative or executive agencies.

Administrative law is a separate body of knowledge and procedures because of the complexity of the heavily regulated society in which we live. Federal regulations are published in the *Code of Federal Regulations* (CFR). Implementing federal regulations generally requires a notice and comment period before the effective date of the regulations. Such notices and calls for comments are published in the *Federal Register* (FR). The CFR and FR are available online.

State Statutes and Regulations

State law is similar to federal law in that the state constitution establishes the structure of state government. As mentioned previously, a state constitution can give citizens more rights but not less than the threshold established by the federal Constitution. State statutes are laws enacted by state legislatures. Each state has its own set of laws governing everything from consent to medical care to taxation of organizations. State administrative agencies, such as Departments of Public Health, issue guidelines or regulations for enforcement of laws. Thus state administrative law detail is different from federal administrative law. For example, a state statute may direct the Department of Public Health to issue regulations requiring that certain diseases or conditions be reported by health care providers. Such statutory language enables the Department of Public Health to proceed with the adoption of regulations. The decision about which diseases or conditions should be reported may be specified in the statute or the Department of Public Health may be authorized to identify the diseases or conditions in regulations.

There may be an overlap of areas in federal and state laws. Often, an attorney must decide whether a client has state or federal claims, or both, and then decide whether to take a case to federal or state court. If a federal facility, federal employee, or federal property is involved, the case is generally destined for federal court. However, a case that involves a state law may be appropriate in state court or federal court.

Common Law

Another source of law is the **common law.** Common law develops with judicial decisions. In the early stages of development, common law in the United States was often based on English common law (Curran, 1997). The common law is not judge-made law, but it is the law that develops as cases are determined by judges. For example, if a dispute between two parties is not covered by statute or regulations, a judge can look to common law principles, custom, and prior case decisions (precedent) to render a just decision. State common law varies. Federal common law also varies, sometimes between districts and circuits.

CONCLUSION

The system of a limited federal government with separation of powers and checks and balances is unique to the United States. The three branches of the federal government are independent and interdependent. State governments follow a similar model. Health care legal principles are found in individual state statutes, regulations, and common law, as well as federal statutes, regulations, and common law. The source of a particular law is important in understanding underlying foundational principles of legal concepts. Subsequent chapters address specific legal concepts related to emergency care.

References

Curran WJ: Legal history of emergency medicine from medieval common law to the AIDS epidemic, *Am J Emerg Med* 15:658-670, 1997.
Flaherty L, Snyder JA: From the feds: an introduction, *J Emerg Nurs* 24:171-174, 1998.
U.S. Constitution, 1789, as amended.

Suggested Reading

Brent NJ: *Nurses and the law: a guide to principles and applications.* Philadelphia, 1997, WB Saunders.

Suggested Websites

www.thomas.loc/gov	Contains key government links
www.house.gov	House of Representatives main site
www.senate.gov	Senate main site
www.hhs.gov/progorg/	Health and Human Services agencies on the Internet
www.whitehouse.gov/	White House website
www.lcweb.loc.gov/global/executive/fed.html	Executive branch links from the website of the Library of Congress
www.lcweb.loc.gov/global/judiciary.html	Judicial branch links from the website of the Library of Congress
www.lcweb.gov/global/state/stategov.html	Meta-indexes for state and local government information
http://www.lcweb2.loc.gov/const/mdbquery.html	Historical documents (Constitution, Declaration of Independence, Federalist Papers) on Library of Congress website

2

Components of a Civil Lawsuit

Chapter Outline

The components of a civil lawsuit are used for illustration only. Criminal cases have different rules and components. Each state and the federal government, including the military, have specific rules for civil and criminal procedures. This chapter generalizes the components of a civil lawsuit, but should one be involved in a civil or criminal proceeding, specific information should be obtained from an attorney.

NATURE OF THE LEGAL SYSTEM

The legal system in the United States is adversarial by its nature. Each side has a story to tell and a perception of what happened leading up to a lawsuit. The adversarial process results in each side using evidence, including witnesses, to prove its point of view. A judge or jury determines the truth and renders justice in specific cases. The legal system can be intimidating to an emergency care professional (ECP) accustomed to working in collaboration with other health care providers to ensure that patients receive the best care available. Even as a fact witness with no vested interest in the outcome of a case, the ECP will be subject to and experience the adversarial process through cross-examination.

Whether one is a witness or a party to a lawsuit, knowledge about the process reduces the intimidation.

COMPONENTS
Initial Interview

An initial consultation with a lawyer can be invaluable for an individual or organization that needs legal advice. The first step in the initial consultation, after providing demographic information, is disclosure of the facts surrounding the dispute. The individual seeking advice tells his or her story. The potential client may be tempted to omit information he or she does not consider important. However, all the facts of a particular situation are significant. Full disclosure of the facts and circumstances is important. The lawyer will ask questions as the potential client tells the story.

After reviewing the facts and applicable law, the lawyer decides whether to accept the case and client. If the lawyer accepts the case, a written contract outlining the responsibilities of each party, including payment arrangements, is signed by both the lawyer and client. The lawyer's investigation does not generally occur without authorization from the client.

One of the key roles of lawyers is that of counselor. The lawyer counsels the client, or potential client, about the viability of a case, the risks and benefits of filing a lawsuit, and what the client can expect during the process. The lawsuit process may be long and detailed, but it is guided by legal rules. Some of the legal rules are discussed in general terms in the remainder of this chapter.

Jury Trial

One of the first decisions is whether the case qualifies for a jury trial. Jury trials are not always available, and some cases are best suited for a nonjury, or bench, trial. The U.S. Constitution guarantees a jury trial in criminal cases because the defendant risks losing liberty or life (U.S. Const., as amended, 1791). The court system historically was divided between law and equity. Cases "at law" usually involved monetary damages. Cases "in equity" were not generally determined by a jury because there were no monetary damages. For example, a case between parties for breach of a written contract includes monetary damages. In a case of divorce, the parties are legally severing a marital relationship, and perhaps property, thus the case "sounds" in equity. Equity balances interests. Historically, parties in equity cases were not entitled to a trial by jury.

State and federal court systems have rules defining whether jury trials are available for a specific case. In a bench trial, the judge listens to the facts presented, applies the law to those facts, and reaches a judgment. Disputed facts are decided by the jury or judge, and the law is then applied to the particular factual situation.

Jurisdiction and Venue

Before filing a lawsuit, the lawyer will consider jurisdiction and venue issues. State and federal law define the requirements for jurisdiction and venue. **Jurisdiction** refers to the legal authority or power of a court to render a decision. A court must have authority over the subject matter of the lawsuit. For example, the law may require that cases worth a certain dollar amount, as alleged by the plaintiff, be heard in specified courts. The amount of a claim for damages in small claims court is different than a case in circuit court.

The court should also have jurisdiction over the individual or company being sued. Otherwise, the court cannot enforce any orders or judgments. Disputed jurisdictional issues, particularly over the parties, must generally be raised and resolved in the initial stages of the lawsuit for the lawsuit to proceed. Jurisdiction over the subject of the lawsuit may be raised later in the proceeding. State or federal law determines at what stage in the lawsuit jurisdiction must be raised as an issue.

Venue, similar to jurisdiction, relates to the location of the lawsuit. A dispute over ownership of real property, for example, generally must be brought in the state and county where the property is located. Specific venue requirements are incorporated in state and federal laws.

PLEADINGS

Once the lawyer decides the legal theories of a case, jurisdiction, venue, and jury trial issues, the lawsuit begins with the filing of **pleadings.** Pleadings is the term used for a general category of documents that set forth claims and defenses of the parties (Black, 1990). Pleadings provide notice to the opposing side of the facts and legal theories of a particular case. State or federal civil procedure determines what specific items must be included in pleadings documents. Some cases require only general pleadings, or claims, sufficient to provide notice to the defendant about the subject of the lawsuit. Other types of cases may require specific types of allegations of fact or legal theory (sometimes referred to as *pleading with specificity*). The legal theories, facts of the plaintiff's claims, and law direct whether pleading can be general or must be specific.

Complaint

The first document in a civil lawsuit is the **complaint.** The person being sued, the **defendant,** may be unaware of the lawsuit until he or she receives the complaint.

The complaint is drafted by the **plaintiff,** the person suing, or the plaintiff's lawyer. The complaint identifies the facts of the case, proposes legal theories of liability, and asks for damages or an equitable determination of interests. Statutes, regulations, or common law may provide specific items that must be included in the complaint. Along with the complaint is the **summons.** The summons is the notice of the lawsuit to the defendant (the person or company being sued) (Black, 1990). The defendant is directed to answer the complaint within a specified time frame. The amount of time a defendant is given to answer depends to a great extent on the specific court. The amount of time a defendant is given to answer the complaint also depends on whether the case is in federal or state court. If one receives a summons and complaint, hiring a lawyer and finding out what the allegations are in the complaint requires prompt action to ensure that the allocated time does not expire.

Answer

An **answer** is the defendant's response to the plaintiff's **allegations** in the complaint. Usually, if one does not deny the specific facts in a complaint, the defendant is considered to admit the allegation. Along with the answer, the defendant may countersue (counterclaim) against the plaintiff. Complex cases may find multiple allegations in the complaint against the defendant with multiple counterclaims against the plaintiff. The answer may also set out affirmative defenses. An affirmative defense is what the defendant alleges he or she can prove to dispute liability or damages.

If the answer is not filed within the time specified in the summons, the plaintiff may file for, and receive, a **default judgment** against the defendant. A default judgment occurs when the defendant fails to plead, answer, or otherwise defend against the allegations in the complaint (Black, 1990).

DISCOVERY

The **discovery** period occurs between the service of the complaint and up to and including the trial. During this period, each side is allowed to gather evidence (including the other side's evidence) and learn the identity of witnesses. The adversarial process requires a lawyer to develop two cases: the one for his or her client and the one challenging the legal theories and evidence of the opposing party. Various types of discovery techniques exist. **Interrogatories** are written questions directed to a party, or witness, generally answered under oath (Black, 1990). Specific time limits, established by state law or court rules, govern when interrogatories must be answered. **Depositions** are oral testimonies taken under oath (Black, 1990). The questions and answers are recorded, either in written or videotape form, and a transcript of the testimony of the party or witness is available for both sides. Depositions are useful in that they can be used at trial as prior testimony to impeach a witness and may constitute evidence.

Document production is a key component of the discovery process. The time frame to answer a request for production of documents is governed by state law or court rules. Some types of documents that may be requested include policies and procedures, job descriptions, employment records, committee meeting minutes, and medical records. The documents requested by either side will to a large extent depend on the type of case. Internal correspondence, including intraoffice electronic mail, is usually discoverable. States may have specific laws that exempt discovery of peer review or quality assurance materials.

Pretrial Motions

Various pretrial **motions** are available for either party to use to try to resolve the case before it proceeds to trial. A **motion to dismiss** can be filed before the answer or along with the answer. Civil procedure rules in each state, or in federal court, govern some general reasons for dismissal of a case. If the court does not have jurisdiction (authority) over an individual or a particular type of case, the defendant may raise that as an issue in a motion to dismiss. If a judge rules that the court does not have authority over a particular case, then the court grants the motion. If a court grants a motion to dismiss, the case is over unless one of the parties appeals the decision.

A **motion in limine** is filed before or during the trial to try to keep out information about a party or witness that is not relevant, is prejudicial, or has questionable value to the case. There are various discovery pretrial motions. Some types of pretrial discovery motions include **motion for protective order, motion to compel,** and **motion for sanctions.** A protective order may be necessary in the discovery process to protect confidential information. For example, in an employment discrimination case, the employer may seek a protective order to ensure that confidential information about employees who are not part of the lawsuit is protected. A motion to compel may be necessary if an opposing side does not respond to discovery requests (interrogatories, production of documents, deposition). A motion for sanctions may be filed if one side fails to comply with a court order.

Another key component of pretrial practice is a **motion for summary judgment.** Either side can file for summary judgment. Generally, a motion for summary judgment is filed when a party believes there is no genuine issue of material fact and he or she feels entitled to prevail as a matter of law (Black, 1990). The opposing party can file an opposition, and both sides argue the law applied to the specific facts.

TRIAL

Once the pretrial motions and initial discovery is complete, the trial of the case begins if settlement has not occurred. The order of the case is usually that the plaintiff presents evidence first. The **burden of proof** in a civil case can be a preponderance of the evidence, substantial evidence, or clear and convincing evidence. The plaintiff generally carries the burden to prove to a jury, for example, that the defendant was negligent. Once the plaintiff presents his or her case, the defendant presents evidence. Not only does the defendant present evidence to rebut the plaintiff's case, but he or she may be required to present evidence of affirmative defenses alleged in the answer.

Lawyers for both sides present opening statements to the jury or judge; witnesses are then called. After all the witnesses for both sides testify, the lawyers present closing arguments. Closing arguments attempt to persuade the jury or judge to "see it my way." Neither opening statements or closing arguments are evidence in the case. The judge will give a jury instructions on the law before they begin deliberations.

The order in which the witnesses are called is decided by the attorneys in the case. Last-minute surprise witnesses occur on television, not in real courtrooms. Most lawyers know the identity of witnesses long before the trial begins. A witness is subject to both direct and cross-examination. Specific rules govern the way in which witnesses are questioned. Direct examination is usually easy for the witness. The witness likely received preparation and discussion from the lawyer before the deposition or trial. Cross-examination, however, demonstrates the adversarial nature of the process. One of the tools used to decrease a witness' impact is to question the witness' credibility and believability. The cross-examining lawyer may try to show inconsistent statements in an attempt to infer or demonstrate that the witness is less than truthful. Interrogatories and depositions can usually be used at the trial, so if the witness gave one "story" during a deposition and another at the trial, the cross-examiner will likely highlight those differences. Cross-examination attempts to limit the witness' answers to yes or no. Carefully crafted questions can confuse the witness and lead to an answer the witness did not expect. It is vital that the witness comprehend the question being asked.

Motions occur during the trial as well. Motions in limine may occur before or during the trial. A **motion for directed verdict** occurs at the close of one party's case. For example, at the conclusion of the plaintiff's case, the defendant may move for a directed verdict. Basically, the defendant is asking the judge to find in his or her favor because the plaintiff failed to meet the burden of proof. If a judge grants a directed verdict, the case does not go to the jury. If either side is unhappy with a jury's verdict, a **motion for judgment notwithstanding the verdict** can be made. This motion basically asks the judge to set aside the verdict of the jury. The verdict may determine liability and damages or, if liability is not in dispute, damages only.

POST-TRIAL

Numerous post-trial activities can occur. Either side, or both, may file a **motion for a new trial.** An **appeal** can be filed by either party unhappy with the outcome. A settlement may occur after the trial. Once a verdict is obtained, collection activities occur if a money judgment was awarded. Although a plaintiff may win a judgment against a defendant, collecting that judgment can be difficult, if not impossible.

The complexity of the legal system and the court-specific rules are beyond the scope of this book. However, it is helpful to have a grasp of common terms to ensure that one decreases the intimidation factor if involved in a lawsuit. Cases will be used throughout this book to illustrate various legal concepts. It is helpful in reviewing cases to know at what point in the process a decision was reached.

CONCLUSION

The adversarial nature of the system provides a foundation for the presentation of evidence in search of the truth. Understanding the basic concepts and processes involved in a civil trial can aid the ECP who reviews cases, reviews records, or is called as a witness.

Reference

Black HC: *Black's law dictionary,* ed 6. St. Paul, 1990, West.

3

Role of the Emergency Care Professional in a Legal Case

CHAPTER OUTLINE

The role of the emergency care professional (ECP) in a legal case directs the amount and type of preparation needed before the trial. A basic understanding of the various roles is important to ensure that if called upon to function in one or more of the roles, the ECP has the confidence to act in a professional manner. The ECP can either be a witness or be a party in a lawsuit.

WITNESS ROLE

Fact Witness

ECPs are often **fact witnesses** in legal cases. A witness can be called by either side in a legal case. A physician or nurse who provided care to a patient in the emergency department may be called as a *fact witness* in either a civil or criminal case. A fact witness is one who has personal, firsthand knowledge of the facts of a case. Civil cases, and often criminal cases, may not proceed to trial for a long time. As a fact witness, it is difficult to rely solely on memory of events that took place months or years before the trial or discovery period. Documentation of events in the medical record not only provides a record of what occurred but can assist in the testimony of a fact witness.

If contacted by either attorney, the fact witness needs to clearly understand the role he or she is being asked to assume. For example, if a hospital is being sued, the plaintiff's attorney should not contact a current employee of the hospital unless there has been communication with the hospital's attorney. The hospital should have clearly delineated policies and procedures regarding contact with attorneys.

In a civil case, the fact witness is providing testimony that may directly bear on liability and damages. In a criminal case, the fact witness is providing testimony that may have a direct impact on an individual's liberty. Because the liberty of an individual is at stake in a criminal case, the rules governing evidence are more stringent. For example, evidence collected in a rape case must be untainted. One way the integrity of evidence is ensured is through chain of custody. Although the emergency nurse may not understand why she is subpoenaed to testify in a rape case in which everything is documented, she often is needed to verify the chain of custody—and thus the integrity of the evidence. The fact witness has a responsibility to testify truthfully about what he or she knows about a particular case.

Expert Witness

An **expert witness** is commonly used in both civil and criminal cases in which the emergency care of an individual is involved. An expert witness is generally one who, because of education, experience, and training, is qualified to testify as to the standards of care in a particular case. An expert witness is often needed when the scientific or technical information relayed by the expert is outside the general knowledge of an average juror. For example, in a criminal case in which the defendant is charged with an offense involving alcohol (driving under the influence or vehicular homicide, for example), the defendant's serum blood alcohol level may be critical evidence. The procedures and methods used to draw the defendant's blood will be closely questioned by the defendant's attorney. The average juror likely does not know that prepping the skin with isopropyl alcohol does not influence the results of a serum blood alcohol test. An expert witness may be needed to explain the standard of care in prepping skin before withdrawal of blood for alcohol analysis. The prosecutor may qualify the emergency nurse as the expert, based on his or her experience, training, and education. In a professional negligence case, an expert physician witness may be needed to inform the jury what the standard of care is in a particular case and whether the physician treating the patient acted within that standard of care. Expert witnesses generally are not needed if the jury has knowledge common to the average person. For example, an expert is not needed to tell the average lay juror that a sponge or instrument should not be left in a patient during surgery. The legal doctrine for such a case is *res ipsa loquitur,* which means "the thing speaks for itself" (Black, 1990).

PARTY

Civil

The ECP may be a party to the lawsuit. If the ECP is suing someone, he or she is the plaintiff. If the ECP is being sued, he or she is the defendant. In either case, the ECP should retain the services of a lawyer. When the defendant, the ECP should promptly notify his or her insurer (assuming the ECP has insurance that covers the situation). The insurer may decide to hire legal counsel to represent the defendant. Cooperation with the lawyer is vital. Complete **disclosure** should occur, regardless of any sense of embarrassment, guilt, or shame. The communications between the lawyer and client are generally protected by **attorney-client privilege** to encourage such disclosure. It is often difficult to know what the other side knows, and without complete disclosure, the case may be jeopardized. It is important, however, not to talk to third parties. Although conversations between attorneys and clients are protected, if a client talks to a third party and discloses damaging information, the communication between the client and third party may not be privileged and may be discoverable.

Criminal

If the ECP is charged with a crime, legal representation is vital. Suppose, for example, that a patient charges an emergency physician with criminal assault and battery. Seeking legal counsel is important because such a charge not only has implications for one's potential loss of money or liberty but also has licensure ramifications. Complete disclosure of the circumstances surrounding the case are important. The ECP's attorney will also delve into past situations. Has the emergency physician ever been criminally charged and/or convicted in the past? Has there ever been contact with this particular patient in the past, and what were the circumstances of any past contact? Has this patient ever complained about this particular physician?

PREPARATION FOR ROLE

Regardless of the role assumed by the ECP, preparation throughout the process is key. If one receives a subpoena to appear as a fact witness in a criminal case, talking with the prosecutor in the case can be helpful. In circumstances in which one is required to give a deposition or testify at the trial for the first time, role-playing before giving testimony helps reduce anxiety and simulates the anticipated testimony.

If the role is that of witness, one does not have to appear either at the trial or for a deposition unless served a subpoena. A subpoena commands the witness to come to a deposition or trial to offer testimony (Black, 1990). The subpoena generally must be personally served to the person named on the subpoena. State law governs how a subpoena is served, by whom, and the recipient's responsibilities. If, for example, a witness is subpoenaed from another state, whether the witness must comply is determined by law. Courts may decline to enforce subpoenas if the witness lives a certain distance from the courthouse where the lawsuit is filed. In addition, witness fees may be required. One should clarify, in writing, who will pay expenses if long-distance travel is required.

A **subpoena duces tecum** requires the recipient to bring documents or records to a deposition or trial (Black, 1990). Admission of records into evidence is determined by applicable evidence law in both state and federal court. In general, medical records are hearsay testimony—an out-of-court statement used to assert the truth. Medical records may be admitted, according to evidence rules, under the "business record" exception to the hearsay rule. However, the record must be authentic to be used as evidence. The ECP may only be needed to authenticate the record.

Rules of evidence, and case law, specific to state and federal courts determine how evidence is submitted to the court.

CONCLUSION

The degree of involvement of the ECP in a civil or criminal case depends on the role assumed. As the plaintiff or defendant, the ECP will work closely with the attorney throughout the process. Serving as a witness, either to testify about facts or to testify as an expert about the standard of care, requires thorough preparation.

Reference

Black HC: *Black's law dictionary,* ed 6. St Paul, 1990, West.

Suggested Reading

Aiken TD: Depositions. 1998. www.nso.com/dondont.html.
American College of Surgeons: ST-8: statement on the physician expert witness. 1999. www.facs.org.fellows_info/statements/st-8.html. [Accessed 6/17/99].
Baldwin JB: Cross-examination of the lay witness. *From classroom to courtroom: association of trial lawyers of America* 4(1):1-3, 1995.
Perry RK Jr: Deposing witnesses, *Trial* 32:64-66, 1996.

4

Law and Ethics
in Emergency Care

CHAPTER OUTLINE

Ethical dilemmas often occur in the emergency care of patients. **Ethics** is the study of decisions and the bases of those decisions (Veatch, 1997). The urgency of caring for patients in emergency situations rarely allows adequate time for reflection and consideration of how decisions are made. However, if the emergency care professional understands the basic concepts of ethics and how those concepts relate to law, a framework for decision making can enhance the care patients receive (Isaacs, 1998).

GENERAL ETHICAL CONCEPTS

Ethical concepts help define and identify the foundational principles used to analyze choices made by individuals. The concept of **beneficence** means to do good. The emergency health care provider operates from a principle of beneficence if "doing good" underlies the decisions made in the delivery of care (Isaacs, 1998; Veatch, 1997). Another way of evaluating beneficence is to determine what is in the patient's best interests. Closely related to beneficence is the concept of **nonmaleficence,** or avoiding harm. Although risks may be associated with the care provided, an ethical health care provider does not attempt to harm the patient.

Autonomy is fundamental to the patient–health care provider relationship. The autonomous patient has a fundamental, ethical right to control decisions about his or her body. Respect for the patient's right to make choices undergirds other concepts, such as *confidentiality, informed consent,* and *privacy* (Wear, 1993). These concepts are discussed from a legal perspective in subsequent chapters but also serve as ethical concepts. If one has respect for an individual's autonomy and right to make choices, paternalism (or substituting the health care provider's judgment for that of an autonomous patient) is less likely to occur (Veatch, 1997). Paternalism is analogous to the parent-child relationship where the health care professional is the parent and the patient is the child (Childress,

1997). The paternalistic health care professional tells the patient what will be done under the guise of "I know what is best for you."

Justice is another ethical concept important in the emergency care of patients. Health care resources are limited. Justice is fairness in the distribution of those scarce resources (Isaacs, 1998). If the health care delivery system does not fairly distribute available resources, regulation and control by the state or federal government can occur. **Rationing,** or limiting available resources, is closely related to the concept of justice. The failure of the health care delivery system to "fairly" distribute emergency care resources arguably resulted to some extent in the passage of the Emergency Medical Treatment and Active Labor Act **(EMTALA)** (42 U.S.C.A. 1395dd 1998). Initially known as *COBRA* (Comprehensive Omnibus Budget Reconciliation Act of 1986), EMTALA was passed in response to reports of uninsured and unfunded patients, some in allegedly unstable condition, being transferred to public facilities. The patient's financial status or lack of financial resources was perceived to undergird some transfer decisions. From an ethical focus, justice was not served when patients in unstable conditions were placed at risk based on an inability to pay. Of course, the other side of the argument is that EMTALA is an unfunded mandate that places the risks of nonpayment for services on health care providers. Scarce resources are then allocated by the government regardless of whether the health care provider can survive financially. The larger implication is that if the health care provider is subject to sufficient unfunded mandates like EMTALA, justice will not be served when hospitals close their doors to the community. For a more detailed discussion of EMTALA, see Chapter 12.

SPECIFIC ETHICAL CONCEPTS AND THE LAW

In a study of emergency physicians' decisions concerning cardiopulmonary resuscitation, most physicians based their decisions primarily on perceived litigation risks and potential criticism from colleagues (Marco et al., 1997). The law, however, cannot provide an answer for every situation encountered in emergency care. Legal concerns, although valid, do not excuse any emergency care provider from the ethical considerations encountered in emergency care decision making. Some specific ethical concepts and the relationship between those concepts and the law are discussed.

Confidentiality

Confidentiality can also be expressed as the ethical concept of the **right of fidelity.** The patient has an expectation of privacy in the relationship with the emergency health care provider. Even if state or federal law does not specifically provide that an emergency patient's communications with the health care provider are confidential, there is an ethical obligation to maintain the patient's privacy. Each individual desires to control his or her personal information (Brody, 1997). Of concern is the number of health care providers who would not seek diagnosis and treatment in their own facilities because of concerns about the privacy of information. If an emergency physician or nurse would hesitate, what does that say about the lay person who is at the mercy of an institution and health care providers who may talk about patients in elevators, cafeterias, hallways, nurses' stations, and waiting rooms?

Privacy is closely related to confidentiality but implies a broader scope. Even if information is not confidential internally, such as laboratory results uploaded to an institution's mainframe computer, there is an expectation of privacy. Each person who has access to individual patient information has an ethical obligation not to reveal information about the patient to anyone not involved in the patient's care. Privacy may or may not be codified in state law. A federal right to privacy, as opposed to confidentiality, has a basis in the Constitution. In *Roe* v. *Wade* (1973), Justice Blackmun wrote the majority opinion of the Supreme Court and relied on a "zone of privacy" in determining that a woman's decision about whether to terminate a pregnancy is private in the first trimester of pregnancy. Regardless of one's position on abortion, *Roe* stood for the proposition that certain aspects of our lives are private and the government must prove a compelling interest to intercede in these private areas. The Supreme Court has recognized a right to privacy in the areas of contraception, sterilization, marriage, abortion, child rearing, and education.

Informed Consent

Informed consent is another legal and ethical concept. Informed consent as an ethical concept relates to a recognition and respect for the autonomy of an individual. Without an informed consent law, ethical decision making would still recognize the right of an individual to make his or her own decisions about his or her body and treatment.

In a case notable for its nondisclosure, health care providers failed in their ethical obligations to obtain informed consent. The Tuskegee experiments, in which poor African-American Alabama sharecroppers were given bogus treatment during a U.S. Public Health Services' 40-year study of syphilis, demonstrated a glaring failure of the ethical respect for the right of individuals to make their own health care decisions with full disclosure (Jones, 1993). Protections for the rights of individuals to full disclosure in the area of medical research came about because of incidents like the Tuskegee study.

Emergency health care professionals often argue that informed consent is not possible in emergency settings. However, the patient is entitled to as much disclosure about his or her condition as time allows with a discussion, even if abbreviated, about the risks and benefits of certain treatment options. Beauchamp

(1997) suggested the use of seven components to analyze consent issues. Each component is categorized according to where, analytically, the component falls in the process of informed consent. The first category is **threshold elements,** or conditions that must be present before informed consent is valid. The threshold elements are *competence* and *voluntariness* (Beauchamp, 1997). If the patient is unable to understand or decide about the disease, treatment options, and risks (competence), then informed consent is not possible. In addition, if the patient is coerced or unduly influenced, the element of voluntariness is absent and informed consent is not possible (Beauchamp, 1997). The second category of elements is information (Beauchamp, 1997). Information provided to the patient should include a full **disclosure** about the patient's condition, implications, and prognosis (if applicable). The next element of information is a *recommendation* by the health care provider (Beauchamp, 1997). What are the realm of possible treatments, risks and benefits associated with each, and the specific plan recommended by the patient's physician (Beauchamp, 1997)? The last informational element is *understanding*. Does the patient understand the disclosure and the recommendations provided by the physician? Comprehension of the disclosed information and the treatment plan is necessary for informed consent. The elements of actual consent is the last category in Beauchamp's analytical framework. Once the physician determines the patient passes the threshold elements of competence and voluntariness, and comprehends the disclosures about the condition, treatment, and recommendations, then a *decision* is reached by the patient (Beauchamp, 1997). The decision may be to accept or refuse the recommendations by the physician. The final consent element is *authorization* (Beauchamp, 1997).

Before obtaining the authorization of the patient, the physician should ensure that the other elements have been considered and evaluated. Obtaining a patient's written authorization (signing a standardized consent form) without consideration of the other elements involved in the informed consent process is insufficient to meet ethical obligations. There are exceptions to informed consent, both in the law and in ethics. Patients who are incompetent do not meet the threshold condition. In cases of public health emergency, informed consent is not possible because of the overriding state interest in protecting the public. Medical emergencies are another exception to informed consent. If the patient is in a life- or limb-threatening situation, there may not be time to advance through the analytical framework of elements. However, because a patient has a medical emergency does not preclude the ethical responsibility to inform the patient about his or her condition if he or she has the capacity to hear and understand the information. A conscious patient with multiple trauma injuries is entitled to receive disclosure about his or her condition and treatment options even if in an abbreviated form.

Language is important in addressing informed consent issues. Use of medical terms such as *splenic rupture* without verification that the patient understands confuses the issue of informed consent. Patients may smile and nod as their condition is explained, but if common terms are not used then disclosure has been inadequate. If the emergency health care professional and patient speak different languages, the importance of eliminating that communication barrier cannot be overemphasized (Wear, 1993).

EMERGING ISSUES

The emergency health care professional is on the cutting edge of emerging ethical issues. Recent reports concern the postmortem retrieval of sperm for potential future use (Whitney & Mian, 1998). In addition to the ethical concepts discussed previously, larger ethical issues loom when a spouse or family member requests that sperm be retrieved from a man who dies in the emergency department, operating room, or critical care unit. Although the ethical issues have not been resolved, a new dialog is occurring about the role of fathers, consent issues for an individual who died, society's role in such a decision, consideration of financial resources, and other complex issues. Although the emergency health care professional may not be in a position to decide those ethical issues when faced with a request for postmortem sperm retrieval, prior consideration of the issues can be useful.

Other ethical issues commonly seen in emergency departments, especially those serving adolescents, are the use of alcohol and drugs and sexual activity. When a parent brings a 15-year-old teenager to the emergency department demanding a drug or alcohol test for suspicious behavior, not only is the situation itself unpleasant but it also can create ethical dilemmas for the emergency physician and nurse. What is the right of the parent in obtaining data about the teenager? What is the right of the teenager in personal integrity? What is the physician or nurse's role in the family conflict? What other options does a parent have to obtain the information? The law may provide little or no assistance. Consent for health care by minors is discussed in Chapter 5 and refusal in Chapter 6. However, the law cannot and does not address each individual situation that occurs.

Similarly, when a mother comes to the emergency department with her 14-year-old daughter and demands that a rape kit be completed, ethical issues become paramount. The parent wants to determine whether or not the teenager is sexually active and may misperceive that the rape kit evidence collection will answer that question. The teenager wants to maintain private information as well as bodily integrity. The emergency health care professional is squarely in the middle of a family dynamic that probably cannot be resolved in the emergency department. Suppose the teenager admits to the emergency nurse that she is sexually active. Should the emergency nurse relay that information to the parent? If she does, what about the nurse's ethical obligation to maintain patient confidentiality and privacy? Is the teenager respected as an individual with the ability to make decisions about examination of her most private activities? Those health care professionals who work with adolescents can often obtain a more accurate history if the parent(s) are not present. If something is discovered that the parent wants to know about (a pregnancy test for example), is the ethical obligation to the teenager or the parent?

CONCLUSION

The emergency health care professional has both legal and ethical responsibilities and obligations to patients. The law may or may not address a specific issue, such as confidentiality, but it is addressed in ethics. Ethics is the study of decisions and choices. Because of the relationship between patients and providers, the study of decisions is an ongoing process. An understanding of ethical concepts common to the emergency care environment can aid in the delivery of quality, ethical, and legally sufficient care.

References

Beauchamp TL: Informed consent. In Veatch RM, editor: *Medical ethics,* ed 2, Sudbury, MA, 1997, Jones and Bartlett, pp. 185-208.

Brody H: The physician-patient relationship. In Veatch RM, editor: *Medical ethics,* ed 2, Sudbury, MA, 1997, Jones and Bartlett, pp. 75-101.

Childress JF: *Practical reasoning in bioethics,* Bloomington, IN, 1997, Indiana University Press.

Isaacs E: Ethics in emergency medicine, 1998. www.emedicine.com/emerg/topic692.htm. [Accessed 5/28/99].

Jones JH: *Bad blood: the Tuskegee syphilis experiment,* New York, 1993, Free Press.

Marco CA, Bessman ES, Schoenfeld CN, Kelen GD: Ethical issues of cardiopulmonary resuscitation: current practice among emergency physicians, *Acad Emerg Med* 4:898, 1997.

Roe v. *Wade,* 410 U.S. 113, 93 S.Ct. 705, 35 L.Ed.2d (1973).

Veatch RM: *Medical ethics,* ed 2, Sudbury, MA, 1997, Jones and Bartlett.

Wear S: *Informed consent: patient autonomy and physician beneficence within clinical medicine,* Boston, 1993, Kluwer Academic.

Whitney S, Mian P: Life after death? Ethical questions raised after a request for postmortem sperm retrieval in the emergency department, *J Emerg Nurs* 24:492, 1998.

Suggested Websites

www.asbh.org/	Home page for American Society for Bioethics and Humanities; offers links to other sites on ethics
www.afss.com/ethics	Cases regarding end-of-life decisions in Michigan
www.bioethics.gov/	Home page for National Bioethics Advisory Commission

www.aslme.org/ — Home page for the American Society of Law, Medicine & Ethics

www.thehastingscenter.org/ — Home page for The Hastings Center; research in ethics and medicine

www.ethics.acusd.edu/ — Ethics Updates home page; ethical theory and applied ethics

www.med.upenn.edu/bioethics — University of Pennsylvania Center for Bioethics home page; includes reviews of episodes of *ER,* the popular medical show on the National Broadcasting Company network from an ethical viewpoint

II

Consent and Confidentiality

5

Consent

CHAPTER OUTLINE

Consent is a potential minefield of liability in the emergency care area. The emergency health care professional must comprehend state consent laws and apply the laws to specific factual situations, often in the middle of the night when administrative support is minimal or nonexistent. Consent is a process of communication between the health care provider and the patient (Rosoff, 1999). Historically, if a patient did not object to treatment, consent was presumed (Grisso & Appelbaum, 1998). The physician is generally responsible for obtaining consent from a patient for procedures and treatment. If the basis of a lawsuit is absence of consent, the facts and circumstances of the communication between the patient and physician will receive close scrutiny.

In *Medeiros* v. *Yashar* (1991), the patient was admitted with a pericardial effusion. A pericardiocentesis was performed by the physician. During the procedure, puncture of the heart muscle resulted in a cardiac tamponade. The patient became hypotensive. An emergency thoracotomy was performed to relieve the cardiac tamponade. The patient survived and sued the physician on the legal theories of professional negligence and lack of informed consent. The jury found that the physician performed the pericardiocentesis with due care and that the complications were not caused by any substandard care during the procedure. The patient prevailed on the theory of failure to obtain informed consent.

The physician appealed the judgment. The physician testified that his "policy of twenty-one years has been to tell a patient there may be 'risks' to any given procedure and that if the patient has any specific questions, he will be glad to answer them" (*Medeiros,* 588 A.2d at 1039). The physician further testified that two facts he always explains to patients are mobility and mortality. (The appellate court pointed out that the physician likely meant morbidity but mobility was the word used in the transcript of the court testimony.) The physician did not provide detailed disclosure of risks, benefits, or complications unless the patient asked.

The physician lost his appeal of the jury verdict. The Rhode Island Supreme Court stated (*Medeiros,* 588 A.2d at 1042-43),

> We rule that the defendant's confusing and uninformative "mobility and mortality" lecture was insufficient as a matter of law to allow the plaintiff to informedly consent to the test. Our case law clearly mandates that a patient must be informed of the particular material risks of an operation. Stating that risks exist, as the defendant did in this case, is not the same as stating what those risks are. Absent being particularly informed of the known material risks, a patient cannot intelligently ask questions concerning the procedure, nor can the patient informedly consent. Here we rule as a matter of law that the plaintiff did not have *any* information on which an informed decision could have been made.

The court reviewed what the physician said to the patient. The court's characterization of the physician's disclosure as a confusing, uninformative "lecture" demonstrates that how the communication process occurs can also be important. The court did not address whether a consent form was signed. Even if the patient signed a consent form for the procedure, the court can look beyond the form to the substance of the communication.

Effective consent requires that the patient have the capacity to consent, that sufficient material information is disclosed to make a reasoned choice, and that consent be freely and voluntarily given (Grisso & Appelbaum, 1998). The use of coercion, duress, or pressure to obtain consent is not only unethical but in some circumstances may be illegal.

TYPES OF CONSENT

There are four general types of consent: express, informed, implied, and emergency exceptions. **Express consent** can be verbal or written. The patient agrees or provides permission. In many states, written consent creates a presumption of valid consent. In those states, a patient who signed a written consent would have the burden of producing evidence to overcome the presumption of validity. For example, Georgia law provides that an oral consent to procedures does not create a presumption that the consent is valid (Ga. Code Ann. § 31-9-6.1[b][1] [1998]). If the consent is written, a rebuttable presumption exists. Thus, if a patient asserted lack of consent as a basis for liability, he or she would also have to submit evidence of sufficient quality and quantity to overcome the presumption. However, the law in Georgia requires that the patient receive information, in general terms, about the diagnosis, purpose of the procedure, risks associated with the procedure, expected success, alternatives, and prognosis (Ga. Code Ann. § 31-9-6.1[a] [1998]). The written consent must incorporate the disclosures identified in the statute for the health care provider to receive the benefit of a presumed valid consent.

Informed consent is when, after full disclosure of the risks and benefits, the patient provides authorization for the treatment or procedure. State or federal law may specify what elements are required for valid informed consent. Under the Louisiana Medical Disclosure Act (1992), the written consent should specify the nature and purpose of the procedure(s), the known risks, the disclosures made, and all questions satisfactorily answered. Finally, the patient must sign granting authorization (La. Rev. Stat. Ann. § 40:1299.40[A][1] [West, 1992]). If the written consent contains all the elements outlined by the statute, the physician receives protection by presuming validity (*Ardoin v. Murdock,* 1998).

The duty of disclosure is determined by one of two standards. One standard is the professional physician's standard in the community (*Korman v. Mallin,* 1993; Rosoff, 1999). A physician expert witness may be necessary to identify the expected disclosure in a given situation. A more recent standard is that of a reasonable patient—what material information would the reasonable patient need to know to make an informed decision (*Korman,* 1993)? If disclosure is measured by a reasonable patient standard, an expert witness is not required (*Korman,* 1993; Rosoff, 1999).

State law may not require disclosure or may require disclosure but not specify how the disclosure is measured. However, common law in the current legal environment requires some disclosure for informed consent to be valid. A prudent approach is to document any discussion between the health care provider and the patient about the informed consent communication, particularly if a standardized authorization form is used for multiple procedures.

Implied consent is a legal fiction used to protect health care professionals. The law presumes in certain cases that the patient would consent to treatment if capable of doing so. For example, an unconscious patient is unable to consent, but treatment can occur under the theory of implied consent. The law presumes that an unconscious patient would consent to treatment if he or she were awake, so the law implies consent on the patient's behalf. Some states identify circumstances when implied consent will apply. Arkansas (1997) and Missouri (1998) specify that consent is implied in cases of emergency. Some implied consent statutes relate to testing of drivers suspected of driving under the influence (Rozovsky, 1990).

Emergency exceptions consent is similar to implied consent. In life-threatening emergencies, a physician(s) signature(s) may be required, certifying that there is no time to obtain consent from the patient or anyone else before instituting lifesaving treatment.

CAPACITY ISSUES

Although consent is a potential minefield of liability, obtaining consent without consideration of capacity is similar to walking through a minefield without a guide or map. Before obtaining consent, one must determine whether the patient has the **capacity** to consent (Grisso & Appelbaum, 1998; White, 1994). Issues related to capacity to consent in emergency care are addressed in the following discussion.

Minors

Historically, the common law rule was that minors did not, as a matter of law, have the capacity to consent to medical treatment (Kramer, 1998). Changes in society, family structure, and a focus on children's rights led to changes in medical consent laws for minors.

Age

The age of consent varies from state to state (Table 5-1). Age of consent for medical treatment often differs from the legal age of majority. The age of majority is when the state determines a minor has reached adulthood. Generally, the age of majority ranges from 18 to 19 years of age. The age of consent for some types of medical care may be as young as 12 years of age.

Age is not the only consideration in assessing the capacity of a minor to consent. Arkansas, Idaho, Louisiana, and Mississippi provide that an intelligent minor who understands, appreciates, comprehends, or believes himself or herself to be ill can consent to medical care and treatment (see Table 5-1). The standard for evaluating intelligence or comprehension is not defined in these statutes. The Idaho consent statute (1998) specifies that the physician, dentist, or hospital can rely on the consent if the person "appears . . . to possess such requisite intelligence and awareness at the time of giving [consent]."

Emancipated Minor

Legal emancipation allows a minor to consent for himself or herself. **Emancipation** is the legal recognition of adulthood even if the chronologic age is below the age of majority. Another term used, in lieu of emancipation, is the *removal of*

Text continued on page 54

TABLE 5-1   Summary of Consent Laws by State

State	Age of Majority	Age and Conditions of Minor's Consent	Specific Exceptions	Applicable Law(s)	Specific Website(s)
Alabama	19	14 and over: any Marriage High school graduate Divorced Pregnant Borne a child Relief of disability of nonage	12 or over: STD Any Pregnancy Venereal disease Drug dependency Alcohol toxicity Reportable diseases	Ala. Code §§ 22-8-4, 22-8-5, 22-8-6, 22-11A-19, 26-13-5, 26-13-6, 30-4-15 (1997)	legislature.state.al.us/Code of Alabama
Alaska	18	Living apart and managing own finances Marriage Parent	Venereal disease Pregnancy (treatment and prevention)	Alaska Stat. §§ 25.20.020, 25.20.025, 25.20.010 (1998)	legis.state.ak.us touchngo.com
Arizona	18	Emancipated Marriage Homeless 12 or over: under influence of drug/narcotic regarded as consenting for treatment	Any Venereal disease	Ariz. Rev. Stat. Ann. §§ 36-2271, 44-132, 44-132.01, 44-133.01 (1994)	azleg.state.az.us
Arkansas	18	Married Pregnancy, childbirth Emancipated "Of sufficient intelligence to understand and appreciate consequences"	Any Venereal disease Incarcerated	Ark. Code Ann. §§ 20-9-602, 20-9-603, 20-16-508 (Michie 1997)	arkleg.state.ar.us

State	Age of majority	Emancipation conditions	Conditions minor may consent to	Statute	Website
California	18	15 or over, living separate and apart Managing own finances Pregnancy Contraception	12 or over Mental health Infectious, contagious, communicable diseases, STD Rape Drug or alcohol-related problem	Calif. Fam. Code §§ 6922, 6924, 6925, 6926, 6926, 6927, 6929 (West, 1994)	leginfo.ca.gov/
Colorado	18	15 or over: living separate and apart and managing own finances Marriage	Any Addiction to drugs Sexual assault victim 15 or over: mental health	Colo. Rev. Stat. Ann. §§ 13-22-102, 13-22-103, 13-22-106 (West Suppl, 1998)	intellinetusa.com. stat98/
Connecticut	18	Married Borne a child	Any: alcohol, drug dependent Outpatient mental health if 1. Requiring consent of parent would cause minor to reject treatment, 2. Treatment clinically indicated, 3. Serious detriment to minor if no treatment, 4. Minor knowingly and voluntarily sought treatment, and 5. Minor mature enough to participate	Conn. Gen. Stat. Ann. §§ 1-1d, 17a-682, 19a-14c, 19a-285 (West 1997)	cslnet.ctstateu.edu/ statutes/index.htm

STD, Sexually transmitted disease.

Table continued on following page

TABLE 5-1 Summary of Consent Laws by State *Continued*

State	Age of Majority	Age and Conditions of Minor's Consent	Specific Exceptions	Applicable Law(s)	Specific Website(s)
Delaware	18	18, married, minor parent	12 or over: pregnancy, communicable disease Trauma, life- or health-threatening after reasonable efforts to contact parent unsuccessful	Del. Code Ann. tit. 13, § 707, tit. 16, §§ 708, 710 (1995)	lexispublishing. com/resources/ default.htm
Florida	18	Pregnancy	Any STD Venereal disease Incarcerated	Fla. Stat. Ann. ch. 384.30, 743.064, 743.065, 743.065, 766.103 (Harrison 1994)	leg.state.fl.us
Georgia	18	Married Pregnancy, childbirth	Any Venereal disease	Ga. Code Ann. §§ 31-9-1, 31-9-2, 31-9-3, 31-17-7 (1996)	ganet.state.ga.us
Hawaii	18		Any Venereal disease Family planning Pregnancy	Haw. Rev. Stat. §§ 577A-1, 577A-2 (1993)	capitol.hawaii.gov/
Idaho	18	Intelligence, awareness, comprehension	14 or over: infectious, contagious, communicable disease	Idaho Code §§ 39-3801, 39-4302 (1998)	idwr.state.id.us

State	Age			Citation	Website
Illinois	18	Parent Married Pregnant minor	12 or over STD Drug or alcohol abuse Emergency Sexual assault victim	Ill. Ann. Stat. ch. 210, pp. 1-4, ch. 410 (Smith Hurd 1993)	legis.state.il.us/ilcs
Indiana	18	14 or over Emancipated Married Divorced Active military Not dependent on parent(s)	Any STD Emergency	Ind. Code Ann. §§ 16-36-1, 16-36-3 (Burns 1998)	law.indiana.edu/codes
Iowa	18		Any Venereal disease Substance abuse	Iowa Code Ann. §§ 125.33, 135L.1, 140.9 (West 1997)	www2.legis.state.ia.us/iacode
Kansas	18	16 where no parent immediately available Pregnant Married	Any Drug abuse, misuse, addiction	Kan. Stat. Ann. §§ 38-101, 38-123, 38-123b, 65-2892a (1993)	ink.org/public/statutes/ksa.cgi
Kentucky	18	16: outpatient mental health counseling Emancipated Marriage Emergency	Any Venereal disease Pregnancy Drug, alcohol abuse	Ky. Rev. Stat. Ann. §§ 214.185, 222.441 (Baldwin 1988)	lrc.state.ky.us
Louisiana	18	Any minor who is or believes himself or herself to be afflicted with illness or disease	Any Venereal disease Drug abuse Emergency	La. Rev. Stat. Ann. §§ 40:1065.1, 40:1095, 40:1096, 40:1299.54 (West 1992)	legis.state.la.us (statutes not on web as of date of publication)

STD, Sexually transmitted disease.

Table continued on following page

TABLE 5-1	**Summary of Consent Laws by State** *Continued*				
State	**Age of Majority**	**Age and Conditions of Minor's Consent**	**Specific Exceptions**	**Applicable Law(s)**	**Specific Website(s)**
Maine	18		Any Alcohol, drug abuse, emotional, psychological problems	Me. Rev. Stat. Ann. tit. §§ 1501(3), 1502 (West 1998)	janus.state.me.us

Maryland	18	Married
		Parent of child
			16 or over: mental or emotional disorder
			Any
			  Drug abuse
			  Alcoholism
			  Venereal disease
			  Pregnancy
			  Contraception
			  Rape/sexual offenses victim
				Md. Code Ann., Health-Gen. §§ 20-102, 20-104 (1996)	mlis.state.md.us/

Massachusetts	18	Married
		Parent
		Widowed
		Divorced
		Active armed forces
		Pregnant
		Living separate and apart and managing own finances
			12 or over: drug dependent if 2 or more physicians confirm
			Any
			  Venereal disease
			  Emergency
				Mass. Gen. Laws Ann. ch. 111, § 117, ch. 112, §§ 12E, 12F (West 1991)	state.ma.us/legis/laws

State	Age				
Michigan	18		Any Pregnancy and associated conditions Venereal disease Alcohol, drug abuse	Mich. Comp. Laws Ann. §§ 25.444(1), 722.1 (West 1993)	michiganlegislature.org.law
Minnesota	18	Living separate and apart Managing own financial affairs Married Borne a child	Any Emergency treatment Pregnancy and associated conditions Venereal disease Alcohol, drug abuse	Minn. Stat. §§ 144.341-346 (1998)	leg.state.mn.us
Mississippi	18	Married Emancipated "Sufficient intelligence to understand and appreciate consequences"	15 or over: mental or emotional problems related to alcohol/drug abuse Any Pregnancy, childbirth Venereal disease	Miss. Code Ann. §§ 41-41-3, 41-41-7, 41-41-13, 41-41-14 (1999)	mscode.com/free/statutes
Missouri	18	Married Parent	Any Pregnancy Venereal disease Drug or substance abuse	Mo. Ann. Stat. §§ 431.061, 431.063, 431.065 (Vernon 1998)	moga.state.mo.us
Montana	18	Married High school graduate Emancipated Self-supporting	Any STD Pregnancy Reportable communicable diseases	Mont. Code Ann. §§ 41-1-402, 41-1-405, 41-1-406 (1997)	www.state.mt.us/leg/branc/laws.htm.

Table continued on following page

STD, Sexually transmitted disease.

TABLE 5–1 Summary of Consent Laws by State *Continued*

State	Age of Majority	Age and Conditions of Minor's Consent	Specific Exceptions	Applicable Law(s)	Specific Website(s)
Montana *cont'd*			Drug/alcohol abuse Psychiatric care or counseling: urgent and cannot obtain parental consent within reasonable time		
Nebraska	19	Married Divorced	Any STD	Neb. Rev. Stat. § 71-504 (1996)	state.ne.us statutes.unicap. state-ne.us/
Nevada	18	Living apart for at least 4 months Married Divorced Borne a child Serious health hazard Understands consequences	Any: Drug abuse STD Attempt to contact parents Mandated examination and treatment for STD	Nev. Rev. Stat. Ann. §§ 129.010, 129.030, 129.060, 441A.310 (Michie 1998)	leg.state.nv.us
New Hampshire	18		12 and over: drug dependency 14 and over: STD	N. H. Rev. Stat. Ann. §§ 141-C:18, 318-B:12-9 (1995)	state.nh.us/gencourt/
New Jersey	18	Emancipated Married	Any: Pregnancy Drug/alcohol abuse Venereal disease Sexually assaulted	N.J. Rev. Stat. Ann. §§ 9:17A-1, 9:17A-4, 9:17B-3 (West 1993)	ngleg.state.nj.us/

State	Age of majority	Exceptions (minor may consent)	Citation	Website
New Mexico	18	16 or over Married Emancipation Active military duty	N.M. Stat. Ann. §§ 24-10-1, 24-10-2, 32A-213 (Michie 1978)	state.nm.us lexislawpublishing.com/resources/default.htm
New York	18	Married Divorced Parent Any Pregnancy Emergency	N.Y. Pub. Health Law § 2504 (McKinney 1993)	state.ny.us
North Carolina	18	Parent(s) can't be located Identity unknown Delay: serious worsening of minor's condition Emancipated Emergency: 2 physicians Surgical procedure: 2 physicians Any: Venereal disease Emotional disturbance Reportable disease Drug/alcohol abuse	N.C. Gen. Stat. §§ 48A-2, 90-21.1-6, (1999)	ncga.state.nc.us/statutes
North Dakota	18	Life-threatening emergency care 14 or over: STD Alcoholism Drug abuse	N.D. Cent. Code §§ 14-10-01, 14-10-17, 14-10-17.1, 23-12-13 (1997)	state.nd.us/lr/centurycode.html
Ohio	18	Married Incarcerated as adult Any Drug/alcohol abuse Venereal disease Pregnancy 14 and over: outpatient mental health treatment limited to 6 sessions or 30 days and no medications	Ohio Rev. Code Ann. §§ 2317.54, 2907.29, 3719.012, 5122.04 (Anderson)	conwaygreene.com

STD, Sexually transmitted disease.

Table continued on following page

49

TABLE 5-1	Summary of Consent Laws by State *Continued*			
State	Age of Majority	Age and Conditions of Minor's Consent	Specific Exceptions	Applicable Law(s)	Specific Website(s)

State	Age of Majority	Age and Conditions of Minor's Consent	Specific Exceptions	Applicable Law(s)	Specific Website(s)
Oklahoma	18	Married Emancipated Has dependent child Separated from parents and not supported by them	Any Pregnant Reportable communicable disease Drug/substance/alcohol abuse	Okla. Stat. tit. 10, § 170.2, tit. 63, § 2602 (1997)	oklegal.onenet.net/statutes.basic.html
Oregon	18	15 or over Married Emancipated	Any Contraception Venereal disease 14 or over: outpatient diagosis, treatment for mental, emotional disorder or chemical dependency	Or. Rev. Stat. §§ 109.510, 109.610, 109.640, 109.675 (1990)	leg.state.or.us
Pennsylvania	18	Married High school graduate Been pregnant	Any: Determine presence of or treatment for: Pregnancy Venereal disease or other reportable diseases	Pa. Stat. Ann. tit. 35, §§ 521.14a, 5101, 780-114, 1010 et seq. (1993)	legis.state.pa.us/ (no statutes on official site) moonface.com members.aol.com/statutes.PA
Rhode Island	18	16 or over Married	Any: reportable communicable disease	R.I. Gen. Laws §§ 23-4.6-1, 23-8-1.1 (1956)	ww2.riln.state.us/rilinsearch/generallaws.htm

State		Emancipation conditions	Minor consent	Citation	Website
South Carolina	18	Married 16 or over: any health services other than operation	16 or over: voluntary admission for chemical dependency	S.C. Code Ann. §§ 20-7-270, 20-7-280, 44-52-20 (West 1976)	lpitr.state.sc.us
South Dakota	18	Married Divorced Emancipated Active military duty	Any: life or health threatened	S.D. Codified Laws Ann. §§ 20-9-42, 26-1-1 (1990)	state.sd.us/state/legis/lrc.htm lexislawpublishing.com/resources/
Tennessee	18	Married Divorced Emancipated		Tenn. Code Ann. §§ 37-1-401, 37-10-302 (1997)	lexislawpublishing.com/resources/default.htm
Texas	18	Disability of minority removed Active military duty 16 or over, resides separate and apart and manages own financial affairs	Any Pregnancy Diagnosis, treatment of infectious, contagious, communicable disease Drug/chemical dependency use Counseling: suicide, sexual, physical or emotional abuse	Tex. Fam. Code Ann. § 32.003 (West 1996)	capitol.state.tx.us/
Utah	18	Married	Any Venereal disease STD	Utah Code Ann. §§ 15-2-1, 26-6-18 (1998)	le.state.ut.us/
Vermont	18	Married Divorced Emancipated Active military duty	14 or over: psychiatric	Vt. Stat. Ann. tit 18, § 7503, tit. 12, § 7151 (1987)	leg.state.vt.us/statutes

Table continued on following page

STD, Sexually transmitted disease.

51

TABLE 5-1		Summary of Consent Laws by State *Continued*			
State	Age of Majority	Age and Conditions of Minor's Consent	Specific Exceptions	Applicable Law(s)	Specific Website(s)
Virginia	18	Married Divorced	Any Venereal disease Infectious, contagious disease Pregnancy Contraception Outpatient substance abuse Outpatient psychiatric services 14 and over: inpatient psychiatric services	Va. Code Ann. §§ 16.1-336, 54.1-2969 (Michie 1996)	leg1.state.va.us/ 000/src.htm
Washington	18	Married	13 and over: outpatient treatment of mental illness and chemical dependency 14 and over: STD	Wash. Rev. Code §§ 26.28.010, 70.24.110, 70.96A.095, 71.34.030 (1992)	access.wa.gov/ government/ awlaws.asp

State	Age	Conditions	Medical Consent	Citation	Website
West Virginia	18	Emancipated Married if over 16	Any: Venereal disease 12 or over: must consent, along with parent, for inpatient mental health, addiction services	W. Va. Code §§ 16-4-10, 27-4-1(b), 49-7-27 (1998)	legis.state.wv.us/
Wisconsin	18	Emancipated Married Divorced	Any: STD 14 and over: inpatient mental health services if parent or court consents	Wis. Stat. Ann. §§ 252.11, 48.375(2) (West 1997)	legis.state.wi.us/
Wyoming	18	Married Divorced Active military duty Emancipated Living apart and managing financial affairs	Any: STD	Wyo. Stat. §§ 14-1-101, 35-4-131 (1997)	legisweb.state.wy.us/

STD, Sexually transmitted disease.

disability of nonage. Active duty in the military, marriage, and the bearing of a child may be sufficient to provide legal emancipation. Emancipation can be total, partial, temporary, or permanent (Kramer, 1998). State laws establish the procedures for minors to obtain judicial emancipation. Any minor under the age of majority can seek judicial emancipation from the courts in some states. Some states require the minor to reach a certain age before petitioning a court for judicial emancipation.

Minors who seek judicial emancipation must provide evidence that they are living separate from their parents and managing their own finances and that they have visible means of support and desire the emancipation. Judicial emancipation results in a court order granting the petition. A minor who claims judicial emancipation but does not have court papers does not meet the strict legal definition. Some states provide that minors living separate and apart from their parents, who manage their own finances, can consent to medical care even without judicial emancipation (see Table 5-1).

Unemancipated, Unaccompanied Minor

A minor seeking emergency care who is unemancipated and unaccompanied may also be capable of consenting. All 50 states allow minors to consent to diagnosis and treatment of suspected venereal or sexually transmitted diseases (see Table 5-1). Pregnant minors can consent in most states for medical care related to the pregnancy. Minors seeking elective termination of a pregnancy are subject to restrictions in each state. The minor's age and condition may allow him or her to consent to certain types of treatment without parental consent. The emergency health professional should be familiar with specific state laws addressing when consent can legally be given by an unaccompanied, unemancipated minor.

Children at risk include runaways, throwaways, and the homeless. Arizona (1994) specifies that homeless minors can consent to medical care. Arizona law defines a homeless minor as one younger than 18 years of age, living separate and apart from parents, without a fixed or regular nighttime residence. Supervised shelters, halfway houses, or "a place not designed for or ordinarily used for sleeping by humans" are included in the definition. Homeless minors risk increased exposure to sexually transmitted diseases, drug abuse, sexual abuse, and malnourishment. Allowing homeless minors to consent to medical treatment demonstrates recognition of the needs of children in risky situations.

Minors Accompanied by a Nonparent Adult

Proxy, or substitute, consent may be allowed if the parent is not readily available at the time a minor needs medical care (Holder, 1999; Rosoff, 1999). Florida (1994) provides a list of persons who can consent for a minor if the legal guardian cannot be contacted within a reasonable time. Anyone who possesses a power of attorney to consent on behalf of the minor is followed, in order of priority, by stepparents, grandparents, adult siblings, and adult aunts or uncles. Minors in foster care or who are wards of the state rely on agents of the organization to provide consent for treatment (Holder, 1999). The American Academy of Pediatrics (AAP) in 1995 identified ethical concerns regarding proxy consents and the pediatrician's responsibility to the patient separate from consent by a legal guardian or proxy. Mississippi (1972) identifies that "any person standing *in loco parentis*" (in place of the parents) can consent to medical care. New Mexico (1978) requires that the health care provider attempt to obtain consent from the parents using "reasonable efforts . . . under the circumstances" before allowing *in loco parentis* consent.

Minors of Divorced or Separated Parents

Domestic relations, or family, law is beyond the scope of this book. Consent for medical care for minors of divorced or separated parents may present special problems. Custody of children may be a significant issue in divorce, separation, or paternity proceedings. One parent may receive sole custody, or the parents may share joint custody. If the noncustodial parent consents for the minor's emergency treatment, the custodial parent may question the emergency care provider's authority to provide the treatment (usually after treatment occurs). In emergency situations, the parent with legal possession of the child will likely be recognized as the appropriate parent to consent (Holder, 1999).

Emergency Exceptions for Minors

Florida (1994) provides that a minor may receive emergency medical care if parental consent is not immediately available, if the minor is injured in an accident or where delaying care would endanger the minor's health or physical well-being. Notification must occur, and the documentation must reflect a statement by the attending physician that the care was necessary to prevent endangering the child. Oklahoma (1997) specifies that the prevention of pregnancy (contraception) is not an emergency service. Oklahoma (1997) also requires that a second physician must concur with the treating physician if major surgery, general anesthesia, or life-threatening procedures are undertaken (Okla. Stat. tit. 63 § 2604).

Mature Minor Doctrine

Statutes and case law in some states recognize the mature minor doctrine. The mature minor doctrine is an exception to the common law rule that parental consent is required to provide medical care to minors. *Belcher* v. *Charleston Area Medical Center* (1992) involved a physician's failure to obtain the consent of an alleged mature minor before a do not resuscitate (DNR) order. The minor was 17 years and 8 months old at the time of his admission for complications from muscular dystrophy. He suffered a respiratory arrest shortly after admission, was intubated, and was given mechanical ventilation. The physician discussed future resuscitation efforts with the parents 3 days after the minor's admission. Four days after admission, the minor's tube was removed. The physician testified that he told the anxious, apprehensive minor that reintubation could occur, but the minor motioned "no" with his head. Later the same day, the parents decided their adolescent son should not be resuscitated unless he requested it himself.

A DNR order was written by the physician, and the parents signed a progress note indicating their agreement not to resuscitate their son in the event of subsequent respiratory arrest. The next day the adolescent died without resuscitation. The parents filed a wrongful death action 21 months later. The jury returned a verdict in favor of the hospital and physician. The parents appealed the verdict with a legal argument that their son should have been consulted before the DNR order because he was a mature minor.

The hospital argued that the relationship between the physician and the patient prohibited the hospital from interfering in the consent process. Hospital employees were aware of the discussions between the physician and the parents about the DNR order. The court pointed out that the parents retained the physician and could have changed doctors if they were unsatisfied with the care provided. The court noted that the result may have been different if the patient had not chosen the doctor but relied on the hospital's choice of physician. The judgment in favor of the hospital was affirmed.

The court reviewed the mature minor doctrine. The court held that procedures, treatment, or withholding of treatment required the consent of a mature minor. The factors considered in determining if a minor is mature included "age, ability, experience, education, training, and degree of maturity or judgment" of the child (*Belcher*, 422 S.E.2d at 838). Other factors related to the minor's capacity to comprehend and "appreciate the nature, risks, and consequences of the medical procedure to be performed, or the treatment to be administered or withheld" (*Belcher*, 422 S.E.2d at 838). The court recognized that a physician's assessment of a minor under the mature minor doctrine is subject to later review. Whether a minor is sufficiently mature to consent to medical care is a factual determination under the circumstances, and no absolute test exists. The judgment of the circuit court as to the doctor was reversed and the case sent back to the trial court to determine the issue of whether the adolescent was a mature minor.

Emergency health care professionals are in a difficult position when the time to assess all the factors associated with the mature minor doctrine is limited. The AAP recommended in 1995 that the consent of the child be obtained when appropriate. The AAP also recommended disclosure to the pediatric patient appropriate for the child's development, understanding, and willingness to accept care. Obtaining the minor's assent to the treatment enhances the child's role in the decision-making process.

Older Adults

Older adults often encounter a bias when capacity issues are considered. No state has an age when capacity to consent is removed from a patient. A competent 100-year-old person retains the right to consent to health care. Physical deficits such as diminished hearing, decreased visual acuity, and memory loss may be wrongly interpreted as an impairment of the elderly patient's capacity (Rozovsky, 1998). Comprehension deficits may exist that require attention to the method used to disclose information about the proposed treatment but do not inhibit capacity (Rozovsky, 1998). The diagnosis of organic brain syndrome or Alzheimer's disease may impair the elderly patient's capacity to consent. However, the consent communication process should include the patient to whatever extent possible.

INCOMPETENCY/IMPAIRMENT

A person unable to manage his or her daily affairs may need assistance in decision making. **Legal incompetency,** a legal proceeding in which a judge determines that an individual is incompetent, is governed by state law. Each state has laws providing the requirements and setting out the procedures to declare an individual legally incompetent. Legal incompetency may not be absolute. For example, individuals could be declared legally incompetent to manage their financial affairs but retain the right to make decisions about where to live, medical care, and so on. A guardianship generally is appointment of an individual for the purpose of protecting a person and the property of that person. A conservatorship generally is appointment of an individual to manage financial and property affairs of the person requiring protection. An individual may have a power of attorney designating the person who is allowed to make decisions for him or her.

Medical or clinical incompetency is not a legal determination. Most state laws do not address medical or clinical incompetency, and it is a gray area that can cause confusion and concern in the clinical setting. An individual may be seen with a medical problem that affects normal decision making. A young adult with asthma in respiratory distress with hypoxemia may have medical incapacity. The patient's medical condition can temporarily impair the usual legal capacity to consent (Grisso & Appelbaum, 1998; Rozovsky, 1990; White, 1994). The patient is not legally incompetent, but the patient's capacity to make a treatment decision is affected.

Impairment is another daily dilemma in emergency care. Patients whose judgment is impaired by alcohol, drugs, hypoxemia, shock, or other pathophysiologic conditions are commonly seen. Such patients can create conflict between physicians, nurses, emergency medical technicians, hospital administrators, and lawyers. The thought processes behind the conflict are important. One side of the argument is that if the patient is conscious, alert, and oriented, then he or she retains the right to decide whether or not to consent to medical care. The foundational belief is the integrity of the individual's personal freedom. The argument is made that substituting the emergency health care professional's judgment for that of the patient is not only paternalistic but illegal. The opposing argument is that a person who ingested alcohol or drugs or who has an injury or illness that impairs his or her mental abilities lacks the capacity to determine the best course of treatment. For example, a patient who took an intentional drug overdose showed mental impairment in choosing to overdose, whatever the reason, and is therefore in no position to refuse or consent to medical care. Without intervention, the patient may die or suffer long-term negative consequences. An alcohol-impaired individual who drives a vehicle away from the emergency department (ED) could kill himself, herself, or others.

The impaired patient creates one of the most difficult legal, ethical, and moral dilemmas for the emergency health care professional. The issues are the individual's rights versus liability for the health care professional. The individual retains the right to decide about medical care, but does an overt act (e.g., drinking to excess) somehow forfeit that right if it places the individual at risk for serious injury or death? If treatment is forced on a patient impaired by drugs (whether legal or illegal), will the health care professional be liable for battery? If an intoxicated patient leaves the ED and the ED staff know the patient plans to drive away, should the police be contacted? What is the patient's right to confidentiality versus society's right to be protected from the hazards of a drunk driver?

There are no easy answers and the law often provides little direction. In analyzing situations, all interested parties must attempt to understand all the ramifications and concerns on all sides of the issue. At the very least, any health care professional should ensure that any decision to substitute one's own judgment for that of the patient is firmly grounded in doing what is in the patient's *best medical interest.*

What if the patient changes his or her story? It is not uncommon for a patient who initially reports a drug overdose, for example, to recant once the treatment procedures are explained. Is the change in the story the truth or a way to avoid painful, invasive procedures? If the patient reports ingestion of "only one beer" but staggers when he walks, has slurred speech, and aggressively seeks to leave the ED, does the patient's behavior correspond to the history? How do health care professionals protect themselves from liability while protecting the patient, and potentially others, from harm?

Mississippi (1972) addressed the issues by statute. A person affected to the extent that he or she "is unable to understand and appreciate the consequences of the proposed surgical or medical treatment or procedures so as to intelligently determine whether or not to consent to the same" may be of "unsound mind" and unable to consent or refuse treatment (Miss. Code Ann. § 41-41-3 [1972]). The statute addresses the potential temporary or intermittent nature of the individual's state of mind. In addition, conditions such as intoxication, injury, drugs, and shock are specifically mentioned in the statute.

In *Miller* v. *Rhode Island Hospital,* 625 A.2d 778 (R.I. 1993), the patient entered the ED after a motor vehicle crash. The patient did not consent, but the physicians performed a diagnostic peritoneal lavage (DPL). The patient had a blood alcohol of 0.233 and was an unrestrained passenger in the crash. The hospital's policy allowed DPL without consent in situations where the patient's mental status was impaired, and the mechanism of injury suggested internal injury. The patient was restrained for the procedure because of his uncooperative behavior. The patient sued for battery. The appellate court stated that an assessment of the patient's understanding of the risks and consequences was appropriate when mental capacity was altered by intoxication. The court further stated that whether intoxication impairs a patient's capacity to decide about medical procedures or treatment was a question of fact for the jury.

PRISONERS, SUSPECTS, OR DETAINEES

EDs often treat prisoners or suspects in the custody of law enforcement. Although incarcerated patients lose some individual rights because of their status as inmates, the right to consent to medical treatment and procedures remains with the patient and not the correctional facility (Rozovsky, 1990). Missouri (1998) specifies that the Department of Corrections must obtain specific written consent from the offender before authorizing or permitting major surgery or administration of a general anesthetic. An exception exists for emergencies or routine care. However, the emergency care professional in a noncorrectional environment should recognize that incarcerated patients have the same rights to control their bodily integrity as any other member of society.

COMMUNICATION BARRIERS

Consent is ineffective if the patient does not understand the disclosures because of language barriers. According to Rozovsky (1998), interpretive services must be provided when the health care provider and the patient do not speak the same language before obtaining consent. The Joint Commission on Accreditation of Healthcare Organizations requires that a facility have a mechanism to provide interpretive services to patients (Rozovsky, 1998). Consent obtained without needed interpretive services is below the standard of care, particularly in communities with a diverse population.

Cultural barriers may also inhibit communication during the consent process (Grisso & Appelbaum, 1998). The patient's cultural background may prohibit questions even with full disclosure of information. Alternatively, the patient may question every piece of information given by the physician. The genders of the patient and the physician obtaining consent may influence the communication process because of cultural differences.

The communication process may be altered if telephonic consent is obtained. If a minor, for example, seeks emergency care but the parents did not accompany the minor, it may be necessary for the physician to obtain consent for medical or surgical procedures or treatment via telephone. Facilities should have policies addressing telephonic consent. Having a witness to the disclosures and subsequent consent is a prudent approach. The recording of telephonic consent may occur in either tape or written form. If the telephone conversation is taped, the physician and witness should identify themselves on the tape after obtaining confirmation that the other party has the legal authority to consent on the patient's behalf. If time allows, recording the individual's name, telephone number, and relationship to the patient provides vital information should a dispute about consent occur later.

Physical limitations may impair communications. Patients who are deaf or cannot speak present special challenges in the consent process (Rozovsky, 1998). Patients who are blind or have significantly impaired vision can also challenge the physician obtaining consent. The physician or nurse should record the patient's limitation or disability and the method used to overcome the challenge in obtaining consent. If an interpreter is used, the name and telephone number of the interpreter should be recorded, even if the interpreter is a friend or family member. Recording the circumstances surrounding the consent process can prevent liability.

DOCUMENTATION

Documentation is critical. Policies and procedures, standardized forms, and quality improvement monitoring are all useful tools in recording consent issues. If the patient is unable to provide written consent because of physical limitations, verbal consent is usually acceptable. Clear documentation of the verbal consent is required.

Written consent is commonly obtained through the use of standardized forms. A patient's signature on a standardized consent form, without other documentation, may be challenged. For example, often the patient is asked to sign a general consent for treatment or a standardized consent form by clerical personnel. No other documentation of the encounter and consent signature occurs. In most situations, such a procedure is sufficient. However, if a patient raises lack of consent as a theory in a subsequent lawsuit, the procedure used in obtaining consent is scrutinized. Is the patient instructed to "sign by the check marks" or is the patient asked to sign a "consent for treatment by the hospital and doctors?" Although a factual dispute may occur, policies and procedures used by the individuals obtaining the patient's signature on standardized consent forms can assist in clarifying how consent is obtained and by whom. Lack of a policy or an ambiguous policy can result in "he said/she said" conflicts.

Written consent is prudent for invasive procedures. Incision and drainage, use of contrast materials in diagnostic studies, and operative procedures are examples of situations where additional written consent is indicated. Generally, it is the physician's responsibility to explain risks and benefits of a procedure to a patient and obtain the patient's consent. A nurse may witness the patient's signature on the standardized consent form. Before the patient signs the consent, the "witness" (nurse) can ask if the patient understands the procedure explained by the physician. If the patient has further questions, obtaining the patient's signature should be deferred until the physician speaks with the patient again. Verification of the patient's understanding of the procedure is vital to document, separate from the standardized consent form. The nurse or physician should document that the patient received information and from whom and verbalized understanding. Should any issue arise related to consent at a later time, the documentation provides a clear picture of what took place at the time consent was obtained.

Along the same lines, emergency health care professionals should focus on discharge and follow-up documentation. Ensuring that the patient understands discharge instructions completes not only the treatment process but the consent process as well. Patients are often asked to sign written discharge instructions acknowledging that they understand. Such signed discharge instructions can also be viewed as consent to the posttreatment plan. Although having a patient sign documented discharge instructions does not ensure future compliance, it does provide evidence that the patient agreed to the discharge and follow-up plans.

Consent is also required in special circumstances. Photographing or video-taping a patient requires consent because of privacy concerns. Obtaining consent for pictures of a patient protects the patient and ensures that the health care professional does not invade patient privacy. Most facilities have standardized forms for such consent.

CONCLUSION

Consent can be a liability minefield. Ensuring that the patient has the capacity to consent is one of the first steps in the consent process. An incapacitated patient cannot give valid consent. Special circumstances and communication barriers require diligence in the consent process. Obtaining consent for a minor requires adherence to a state's statutes, regulations, and common law. Documentation of the consent process in addition to written authorization by the patient can reduce the risks for the emergency care professional should lack of consent be an issue.

References

American Academy of Pediatrics Committee on Bioethics: Informed consent, parental permission, and assent in pediatric practice, *Pediatrics* 95:314, 1995.

Ardoin v. *Murdock,* 711 So.2d 837 (La. Ct. App. 1998).

Ariz. Rev. Stat. § 44-132 (1994).

Ark. Code Ann. § 20-9-603 (Michie 1997).

Belcher v. *Charleston Area Med. Cntr.,* 422 S.E.2d 827 (W.Va. 1992).

Fla. Stat. ch. 743.0645(2), 743.064 (Harrison 1994).

Ga. Code Ann. § 31-9-6.1 (1998).

Grisso T, Appelbaum PS: *Assessing competence to consent to treatment: a guide for physicians and other health professionals,* New York, 1998, Oxford University Press.

Holder AR: Special categories of consent: minors and handicapped newborns. In Macdonald MG, Kaufman RM, Capron AM, Birnbaum IM, editors: *Treatise on health care law,* vol 4, chap 19, New York, 1999, Matthew Bender.

Idaho Code § 39-4302 (1998).

Korman v. *Mallin,* 858 P.2d 1145 (Alaska 1993).

Kramer DT: *Legal rights of children,* ed 2, Minneapolis, suppl, 1998, Clark Boardman Callaghan.

La. Rev. Stat. Ann. § 40:1299.40(A)(1) (West 1992).

Medeiros v. *Yashar,* 588 A.2d 1038 (R.I. 1991).

Miller v. *Rhode Island Hospital,* 625 A.2d 778 (R.I. 1993).

Miss. Code Ann. § 41-41-3 (1972).

Mo. Ann. Stat. § 431.063 (Vernon 1998).

N.M. Stat. § 24-10-2 (Michie 1978).

Okla. Stat. tit. 63, §§ 2602(A)(7), 2604 (1997).

Rosoff AJ: Consent to medical treatment. In Macdonald MG, Kaufman RM, Capron AM, Birnbaum IM, editors: *Treatise on health care law,* vol 4, chap 17, New York, 1999, Matthew Bender.

Rozovsky FA: *Consent to treatment: a practical guide,* ed 2, Boston, 1990, Little, Brown.

Rozovsky FA: *Consent to treatment: a practical guide,* ed 2, cumm suppl, Gaithersburg, MD, 1998, Aspen.

White BC: *Competency to consent,* Washington, DC, 1994, Georgetown University Press.

Suggested Reading

American Bar Association, Division of Media Relations and Public Affairs: Facts about children and the law: Table 1, state laws allowing a minor to consent to medical treatment, 1998. www.abanet.org/media/factbooks/cht1.html. [Accessed 7/21/98].

American College of Emergency Physicians: Evaluation and treatment of minors, *Ann Emerg Med* 28:383, 1996.

Premack P: Obtaining legal medical consent without court intervention, *San Antonio Express-News,* Feb 22, 1996. www.premack.com/columns/960222.htm. [Accessed 4/26/99].

Roach WH Jr, The Aspen Health Law Center: *Medical records and the law,* ed 2, Gaithersburg, MD, 1994, Aspen.

Scott RL: Informed consent on behalf of children, 1998. www.law.uh.edu/healthlawper-spectives/Food/990125Informed.html. [Accessed 4/24/99].

Stavis PF: Sexual activity and the law of consent. NYS Commission on Quality of Care, 1999. www.cqc.state.ny.us/cc50.htm. [Accessed 5/5/99].

Thewes J, FitzGerald D, Sulmasy DP: Informed consent in emergency medicine: ethics under fire, *Emerg Med Clin North Am* 14:245, 1996.

Tomes JP: *Healthcare records: a practical legal guide,* Dubuque, IA, 1990, Kendall/Hunt.

6

Refusal to Consent or Withdrawal of Consent

CHAPTER OUTLINE

The patient's legal right to consent has a corresponding right to refuse or withdraw consent for medical treatment in most cases. A patient can consent or withdraw consent at any time. Suppose a patient signs a general consent upon entry to the emergency department (ED) but refuses an operation. If the patient has the requisite *capacity,* the patient's right to refuse consent to an operation or withdraw consent is paramount. Two situations in which the right to refuse treatment may be denied are public health emergencies and prison (Cohen, 1998; Dubler, 1998). The risks to the public may require quarantine, mandated treatment, mass vaccination, or immunization in public health emergencies. The state's interest in maintaining orderly prison administration and reducing risks of prison chaos are given for denying the right to prisoners to refuse treatment (Cohen, 1998; Dubler, 1998). The other situations associated with the refusal to consent or withdrawal of consent are discussed in the following sections.

MINORS

Minors require special consideration. Minors typically do not have constitutional rights equal to those of adults (Lonowski, 1996). Where to draw the line is often unclear. Some states adopt the Rule of Sevens as the standard of proof. Under the Rule of Sevens, minors younger than 7 years of age cannot make decisions for themselves. Between 7 and 14 years of age, the child may be held to an adult standard if engaging in adult activities. Typically, a presumption exists that children older than 14 years of age have the reasoning ability to consent to medical treatment (Lonowski, 1996). Although a minor may have the legal right to consent to medical care at a very young age, the right to refuse or withdraw consent may rest with the parent or legal guardian. If the minor is emancipated, he or she is treated as an adult. If a state accepts the mature minor doctrine (see Chapter 5), rejection of medical treatment may be allowed. The U.S. Supreme Court has not determined the issue of a minor's refusal to accept life-saving treatment (Lonowski, 1996). However, as demonstrated by the cases that follow, chronologic age cannot offer an absolute test.

The Illinois Supreme Court considered the mature minor doctrine in the case of E.G., a 17-year-old young woman with leukemia (*In Re E.G.,* 549 N.E.2d 322 [Ill. 1989]). E.G. and her mother refused blood transfusions based on their religious beliefs as Jehovah's Witnesses. The state filed a petition in juvenile court alleging neglect. The juvenile court appointed a guardian for E.G. after entering a finding of neglect against the mother. The appellate court upheld the neglect finding against E.G.'s mother but further held that E.G. was a mature minor and therefore could refuse the blood transfusions. The case was appealed to the Illinois Supreme Court.

A review of the testimony given at trial indicated that two physicians, including a psychiatrist, found that E.G. was competent, sincere in her beliefs, and mature and understood the consequences of her refusal (*In Re E.G.,* 549 N.E.2d at 324.) The court stated,

> Although the age of majority in Illinois is 18, that age is not an impenetrable barrier that magically precludes a minor from possessing and exercising certain rights normally associated with adulthood. Numerous exceptions are found in this jurisdiction and others which treat minors as adults under specific circumstances (*In Re E.G.,* 549 N.E.2d at 325).

The court set forth legal precedent in Illinois requiring proof of maturity by clear and convincing evidence. The court also established direction for future cases to ensure a weighing of the state's **parens patriae** (role of state as guardian of those who cannot care for themselves) power and interests against evidence of maturity. The four state interests identified by the court were (1) preservation of life, (2) protecting the interests of third parties (parents, guardians, and adult siblings), (3) prevention of suicide, and (4) maintaining the integrity of the medical profession (*In Re E.G.,* 549 N.E.2d at 328).

In addition to upholding E.G.'s status as a mature minor, the court remanded the case back to the trial court. The court ordered the trial court to expunge the finding of neglect against E.G.'s mother.

A similar case in New York had a different outcome. In *Application of Long Island Jewish Medical Center* (557 N.Y.S.2d 239 [Sup. Ct. 1990]), a minor, weeks short of his 18th birthday, and his parents refused blood transfusions based on religious grounds. The minor was admitted from the ED with a hemoglobin level of 6.4 g/dl and hematocrit of 19.2%. The hospital petitioned the court for authority to administer blood transfusions over the objections of the minor and his parents. Hearings held over the course of several days revealed that the minor had disseminated malignant disease. The parents were unable to arrange alternative treatment without the use of blood. Physicians would not administer chemotherapy without authority to administer blood transfusions.

The court recognized the merit of the mature minor doctrine but found that given the facts of this particular case, the minor was not mature. The facts cited by the court included the minor's consideration of himself as a child, he had never dated or been away from home, and he consulted his parents for all decisions (*Application of Long Island Jewish Medical Center*, 557 N.Y.S.2d at 242). The judge granted the petition of the hospital and authorized the administration of blood transfusions when medically necessary.

Although neither of these cases occurred in the emergency area, they demonstrate the difficulty in imposing treatment decisions on minors who refuse, especially if the minor is "mature" and the state recognizes the doctrine of the mature minor. The emergency health care professional may face a dilemma when a minor refuses emergency care. Most states allow an emergency exception to informed consent (see Chapter 5) but do not address emergency refusal of care. Seeking input from the parents, hospital counsel, and administration is necessary. If the problem is life-threatening, an emergency court order may be sought but one should not delay the patient's treatment.

LEFT WITHOUT BEING SEEN

One way patients withdraw their consent is leaving without being seen (**LWBS**). The patient may or may not inform the emergency health care professional before LWBS. LWBS is different from leaving against medical advice (**AMA**). Although a request may be made for the patient to sign a refusal form, the patient's voluntary removal of himself or herself from the facility is an act of refusal. The reasons a patient may leave before treatment are as varied as patient complaints. Delays, transportation concerns, or a simple change of mind can be the basis for LWBS. Although evaluation of the reasons patients leave may identify system inefficiencies, from a consent point of view, it is a method used by patients to withdraw their consent for treatment. George and Quattrone (1992) raised the issue of liability if a delay in care after triage results in additional injury to the patient. If a patient is told to wait without further evaluation and instruction, the risk is greater (George & Quattrone, 1992).

AGAINST MEDICAL ADVICE

Patients who leave AMA require different evaluations because of the different implications. Once a patient sees a physician and treatment starts, the patient still retains the right to refuse or withdraw consent. From a legal perspective, placing a standardized AMA form in front of a patient for a signature is insufficient, by itself, to constitute a legally acceptable withdrawal of consent.

First, the patient's *capacity* must be evaluated. An impaired patient's capacity to refuse treatment may be a serious consideration. If the patient does not have the capacity to refuse treatment, obtaining a signature on a form does not excuse the facility and emergency health care personnel from potential liability. If the patient has the capacity, a thorough discussion of the benefits of treatment versus the risks to the patient of leaving AMA is required. Often, such a discussion never occurs. If subsequent litigation occurs, the process by which the patient's signature on the AMA form was obtained will be closely scrutinized. A prudent approach is to inform the treating physician any time a patient desires to leave AMA. The physician should fully discuss the risks of leaving and the benefits of treatment. A witness to the discussion is invaluable. Documentation should clearly specify the risks explained to the patient. If, after a thorough process of informing the patient, the patient with capacity still decides to leave AMA, the potential liability is greatly reduced.

How does one verify that the patient understands the potential risks for leaving AMA? One way is to have the patient explain his or her understanding of the risks associated with leaving AMA. If death is a real risk, the patient should be able to tell the nurse or physician that death could, in fact, result. Often, the patient will skirt the issue because he or she is in denial about the seriousness of the problem. Should that occur, it is imperative to investigate the reasons behind the patient's decision to leave AMA.

For example, suppose that a patient with a trimalleolar fracture requires hospitalization and surgery. The patient asserts his or her desire to leave AMA. An investigation into the reason the patient wants to refuse treatment reveals that the patient is unemployed, has no medical insurance, and believes that he or she could not afford the treatment. Once the reason is ascertained, addressing the patient's underlying reason for refusal could in fact change the patient's mind.

Whatever the basis for the patient's withdrawal of consent, documentation should concisely and clearly reflect any discussions with the patient. A specific description of the patient's behavior is invaluable should the patient's capacity be an issue. A Georgia case demonstrated that documentation can be an issue in refusal of care. In *Kirby* v. *Spivey,* 307 S.E.2d 538 (Ga. Ct. App. 1983), the next of kin sued a nursing home and physician after the death of their relative. The allegation in the professional negligence action was that the physician did not refer the patient for treatment of suspected prostate cancer. The physician, by affidavit, testified that the patient was lucid and refused diagnostic tests and treatment. Although the physician won the case on summary judgment, on other grounds, the expert physician witness for the relatives testified that, "Failure to make a notation of such an important event as refusal of necessary treatment casts doubt upon . . . contention that it did in fact occur" (*Kirby,* 307 S.E.2d at 539).

TREATMENT OPTIONS

A patient with the capacity to consent has the capacity to refuse specific treatments. Some treatment options commonly addressed are blood transfusions, surgery, and removal of life-sustaining treatment.

Blood Transfusions

A common treatment option for which refusal occurs is blood transfusion. It is not uncommon to require that patients sign a written consent to a blood transfusion. A patient who is a Jehovah's Witness may refuse blood transfusions because of religious beliefs. One of the foundations of a democracy is the individual's right to practice his or her religious beliefs without interference. A religious practice or belief that blood transfusions are not allowed has to be respected regardless of the emergency health care professional's own beliefs. It is prudent to have the patient refuse, in writing, in the event that the patient suffers consequences from the refusal. If the patient who needs blood is a minor and the parents refuse to allow a blood transfusion, a court order is needed before that patient can be given a transfusion.

In *M.N.* v. *Southern Baptist Hospital of Florida, Inc.* (648 So.2d 769 [Fla. Ct. App. 1994]), an 8-month-old infant was admitted with a diagnosis of acute monocytic leukemia, severe anemia, and a low platelet count. The patient needed chemotherapy and blood transfusions, but the parents refused blood transfusions based on religious objections. The hospital filed an emergency petition, and the court authorized treatment. The parents appealed. The appellate court indicated that it was appropriate for a court to override the parent-child relationship where the state's interest is compelling and the least intrusive interference method is used. The court remanded the case to the trial court to balance the competing interests of the state. The court identified the interests the trial court was to consider: (1) parental interest in the parental role of decision maker for the medical care of the minor, (2) the state's interest in preserving human life, (3) the child's own welfare and best interests, (4) the severity of the child's illness, (5) the probability or likelihood that treatment will be effective, (6) the survivability of the child with and without treatment, and (7) the invasiveness and nature of the treatment and effect on the child (*M.N.,* 648 So.2d at 771).

Surgical Procedures

Surgical procedures are invasive. Although it may be difficult to comprehend a competent patient's refusal to undergo necessary, even lifesaving, surgery, the competent patient retains the right to refuse. Consent for surgical procedures should include a thorough discussion of the risks, benefits, and alternatives of the procedure.

One must always keep in mind that the patient's capacity to consent or refuse is paramount. If the patient is a minor and the parent(s) refuse treatment on behalf of the child, the facility may have to seek a court order. Why would a court substitute its judgment in place of a child's parent(s)? The state has an interest in protecting children. If an adult neglects or injures a child, the state intervenes. In the case of medical treatment, the state's interest in protecting the child may outweigh the parents' right to decide treatment options.

Refusal of treatment for a child because of religious beliefs and practices of the parent(s) can create tremendous conflict. A court will weigh the state's interests in protecting the child against the parents' interest in exercising religious freedom. The Tennessee Court of Appeals considered a case of a 12-year-old girl with Ewing's sarcoma (*Matter of Hamilton,* 657 S.W.2d 425 [Tenn. Ct. App. 1983]). The father refused medical care for his daughter because of his religious beliefs. The Department of Human Services (DHS) brought the case, alleging that the minor was dependent and neglected. Testimony revealed that without treatment, the child would die, painfully, within 6 to 9 months. The court appointed the DHS director to act on the child's behalf for medical treatment consent. The court instructed the director to respect and accede to the wishes of the parents. The caveat was that the parents could not interfere with or impair physician recommended treatment. The court stated the following:

> Our Constitution guarantees Americans more personal freedom than enjoyed by any other civilized society, but there are times when the freedom of the individual must yield. Where a child is dying with cancer and experiencing pain which will surely become more excruciating as the disease progresses, as in Pamela's circumstance, we believe, is one of those times when humane considerations and life-saving attempts outweigh unlimited practices of religious beliefs (*Matter of Hamilton,* 657 S.W.2d at 429).

In the *Matter of Thomas B.* (574 N.Y.S.2d 659 [Fam. Ct. N.Y.C. 1991]), the mother of a 15-year-old minor petitioned the court to mandate diagnostic surgery. The minor had an anterior mediastinal tumor but refused a surgical biopsy because of his fear. The mother asked that physical restraint be used, if needed, to compel the surgery. The Department of Social Services and court-appointed guardian agreed that the procedure was immediately necessary.

The court said, "If a person under 18 years of age may not give effective consent, it follows logically that such a person may not effectively withhold consent, either" (*Matter of Thomas B.,* 574 N.Y.S.2d at 661). The court expressed its reluctance to disregard the protests of the 15-year-old but ordered the minor to cooperate. The court further authorized the hospital to treat the minor and ordered the sheriff's department to use physical restraint, if needed, to enforce the order (*Matter of Thomas B.,* 574 N.Y.S.2d [Fam. Ct. N.Y.C. 1991]).

Removal of Life-Sustaining Treatment

The decision to withhold, remove, or stop life-sustaining treatment is difficult at best. Cases such as those of Karen Quinlan and Nancy Cruzan pointed out the significant issues associated with unexpected end-of-life decisions. An Ohio case addressed the issue. The care of a minor who sustained a severe head injury and remained comatose was central to *In Re Guardianship of Myers* (610 N.E.2d 663 [Ohio Com. Pl. 1993]). The minor received artificial nutrition and hydration, but the natural parents disagreed whether to continue the treatment. Each parent independently applied to be the child's guardian. The court appointed a nurse attorney as the child's guardian. Three physicians testified that the child was in a persistent vegetative state (PVS), the prognosis was poor, and there was no chance of a meaningful recovery. The guardian supported removal of the nutrition and hydration.

The court identified the difficulty between two tests used by the courts in evaluating when to allow removal of life-sustaining treatment. The best interest test is objective—a neutral third party (a judge) evaluates the facts and circumstances and renders a decision based on what is in the best interest of the patient. The second test is that of substituted judgment. The substituted judgment test requires the neutral third party (a judge) to attempt to make the same decision the patient would make if he or she were competent. Obviously, the substituted judgment test is difficult to use when the judge does not know the individual patient, and the testimony may conflict about what the patient would likely want. The child's status as a minor makes the substituted judgment test even more difficult to use. The court applied the best interest test and decided the removal of the life-sustaining treatment was in the best interest of the minor (*In Re Guardianship of Myers,* 610 N.E.2d at 671).

New Mexico (1978) allows, by statute, an unemancipated minor (defined as 15 and younger) to refuse life-sustaining treatment if the minor's capacity is sufficient. The characteristics the minor must demonstrate are an understanding of the medical conditions, benefits, and risks of treatment, and the ultimate decision to refuse life-sustaining treatment.

DO NOT RESUSCITATE

Do-not-resuscitate (**DNR**) orders reflect a withdrawal or refusal of consent should a patient suffer a cardiopulmonary arrest. If the patient is not conscious or competent, a DNR order may be written by an attending physician after consultation with the patient's family.

The dilemma created in emergency care depends, to some extent, on the circumstances of each patient. The situation of a nursing home patient who is reported as DNR, without the corresponding documentation, could place emergency health care professionals in a precarious position. If the patient is not resuscitated, liability can occur. If the patient has a DNR order and is resuscitated, liability may also result. Such a situation is a common occurrence and can leave the ED staff confused about the proper approach.

Another dilemma is created when a terminally ill patient receiving hospice care comes to the ED. Although the hospice program personnel probably instructed the patient's family about what to do in acute situations, the family may panic and misunderstand the instructions, or when faced with the imminent death of a loved one, change the procedure. Emergency health care personnel face the need to rapidly assess the situation and decide the approach.

Oklahoma (1998) addressed the dilemma by statute. The law in Oklahoma provides a presumption of consent for cardiopulmonary resuscitation (CPR) unless the health care provider has actual knowledge that consent is denied or refused. The statute requires documentation in the medical record of the notice of refusal from the patient or legal guardian to the health care provider. Emergency health care professionals will not have "actual knowledge" unless the medical record or an advanced directive is immediately available. In most resuscitation efforts, the medical record is not immediately available and thus, the presumption is that the patient consented to CPR.

Family conflict can also create difficult situations. It is not uncommon for family members to disagree about DNR orders and situations or about what exactly should be done if resuscitation may be needed. If the patient does not have an advance directive, the situation is even more problematic.

A Georgia case demonstrated the difficulty when parents disagree about the treatment of their child. A 13-year-old girl with chronic medical problems required intubation (*In Re Doe,* 418 S.E.2d 3 [Ga. 1992]). Although her physicians testified she suffered from a degenerative neurologic disease, a definitive diagnosis eluded them. The child had recurrent infections and her mental status was decreasing. Before performing a tracheotomy and gastrostomy tube insertion, the physicians discussed a DNR order with the parents. The parents disagreed. One parent wanted the DNR order and a deescalation of medical treatment while the other parent supported aggressive treatment, including resuscitation. The hospital ethics committee supported the DNR and deescalation of medical treatment approach. The hospital asked the court to identify which parent had the authority to decide. The trial court issued an injunction preventing the hospital from enforcing a DNR order or deescalating treatment *unless both parents agreed.* The Georgia Supreme Court upheld the trial court's judgment (*In Re Doe,* 418 S.E.2d 3 [Ga. 1992]).

ADVANCE DIRECTIVES

Advance directives allow individuals to preplan decisions about health care. The case of Nancy Cruzan brought the issue of advance directives to the public in 1989. Nancy Cruzan was in a PVS after a motor vehicle crash (*Cruzan* v. *Director, Missouri Department of Health,* 497 U.S. 261, 1990). Cruzan did not have an advance directive—she was young and vibrant and probably never thought she would need it. Cruzan's parents wanted to end her suffering and requested that Cruzan's life-sustaining artificial nutrition and hydration be removed. The parents sought authorization from a state trial court after hospital employees refused to stop the treatment.

The trial court, after hearing testimony, granted the parents the authority to stop treatment or life-prolonging procedures. The State of Missouri appealed and the Missouri Supreme Court reversed the trial court. Missouri law required clear and convincing evidence that Cruzan would refuse the nutrition and hydration if she could. The court said the testimony of Cruzan's friend and sister did not provide clear and convincing evidence of what Cruzan would want for herself. Cruzan's parents appealed the decision to the U.S. Supreme Court (*Cruzan,* 497 U.S. 261). The U.S. Supreme Court held that Missouri could require an evidence standard of clear and convincing evidence. The clear and convincing burden of proof was legitimate because of the State's interests in preserving life (*Cruzan,* 497 U.S. at 284). In addition, because Cruzan was incompetent to decide for herself, the state's procedure was upheld (Cohen, 1998).

Advance directives include living wills, durable powers of attorney for health care, and appointment of health care surrogates. Each state's laws set out the parameters for each type of advance directive. The **living will,** in general, allows a competent patient to decide that should a terminal illness, injury, or PVS exist, treatment should or should not be rendered. Because of recent cases involving removal of nutrition and water, some states allow an individual to decide under what circumstances, if any, nutrition and water should be withheld or given.

The **durable power of attorney** for health care differs in that the competent individual appoints another individual, known as a proxy or surrogate, as the health care decision maker should the patient be unable to decide. The substitute decision maker may be a family member or close friend. The individual usually selects someone who is trusted to make the decisions wanted by the patient. Sabatino (1999) identified surrogates as decision makers not legally authorized because they are not appointed by the patient or the courts. Some states recognize, by statute, the order of priority of surrogate decision makers. Although surrogates are not usually given unfettered discretion for any decision, laws identifying surrogates are one way to address medical decision making if the patient has not done so (Sabatino, 1999).

In some states, the living will and durable power of attorney for health care are combined. The individual completing the advance directive can elect to have the living will control decisions should conflict occur between the living will and the proxy. Congress passed a federal law known as the *Patient Self-Determination Act of 1991*. One of the requirements is that hospital personnel are required to ask on admission if a patient has an advance directive. The patient's response to the question must be documented according to the regulations. If the patient does not have an advance directive, the facility provides literature to the patient explaining the process.

Individuals who want to write their own advance directive should seek legal consultation. Seventeen states require that the advance directive must be uniform.

Wrongful Life

An emerging legal issue relating to advance directives is the theory of **"wrongful life"** (Donahue, 1998). A recent Pennsylvania case used the wrongful life theory of liability when physicians allegedly refused to follow a patient's living will (Duffy, ¶ 1, 1999). Although the case was dismissed from federal court, a state court action is pending (Duffy, ¶ 7, 1999). Individuals who execute advance directives expect that health care providers will comply. Although each factual scenario is different, the emergency health care professional should be aware of the emerging issue of wrongful life. Rather than rejecting a patient's advance directive outright and refusing to follow the patient's instructions, a more prudent approach would be to inform the patient's family and assist them in transferring the patient to a health care provider who will comply with the directive. If transfer of the patient is not an option, seeking court approval to ignore or to refuse to follow the advance directive will minimize a facility's liability.

CONCLUSION

Refusal or withdrawal of consent can lead to difficult interactions between patients, family members, and emergency health care professionals. The emergency health care professional must remember that if a patient is determined to have the capacity to consent, then a corresponding right to refuse or withdraw consent exists. Minors require special consideration as they do not have the same legal status as adults. Courts may review surrounding circumstances when a patient refuses medical care and the documentation should reflect any discussion with the patient. Blood transfusions, diagnostic procedures, and invasive interventions are examples of specific areas where patients may refuse consent. Do-not-resuscitate issues are common occurrences in today's health care environment. Advance directives are important in providing emergency health care professionals with information about the patient's desires and wishes. Refusal to follow a patient's directive may lead to a "wrongful life" action as an emerging legal theory (Donahue, 1998). Prudent communication and documentation of any discussions will minimize the liability exposure for the emergency health care professional.

References

Application of Long Island Jewish Med. Cntr., 557 N.Y.S.2d 239 (Sup. Ct. 1990).

Cohen EN: Refusing and forgoing treatment. In Macdonald MG, Kaufman RM, Capron AM, Birnbaum IM, editors: *Treatise on health care law,* vol 4, chap 19, New York, 1998, Matthew Bender.

Cruzan v. Director, Missouri Dept. Health, 497 U.S. 261 (1990).

Donahue J: Comments: "Wrongful living": recovery for a physician's infringement on an individual's right to die, *J Contemp Health Law Policy* 14:391, 1998.

Dubler NN: The collision of confinement and care: end of life care in prisons and jails, *J Law Med Ethics* 26:149, 1998.

Duffy SP: The stuff of tragedy: federal judge dismisses suit claiming 'wrongful life,' *The Legal Intelligencer,* Aug 18, 1999. www.lawnewsnetwork.com/stories/A4616-1999Aug17.html. [Accessed 8/18/99].

George JE, Quattrone MS: Law and the emergency nurse: patients who leave without being seen, *J Emerg Nurs* 18:267, 1992.

In Re Doe, 418 S.E.2d 3 (Ga. 1992).

In Re E.G., 549 N.E.2d 322 (Ill. 1989).

In Re Guardianship of Myers, 610 N.E.2d 663 (Ohio Com. Pl. 1993).

Kirby v. Spivey, 307 S.E.2d 538 (Ga. Ct. App. 1983).

Lonowski SC: Recognizing the right of terminally ill mature minors to refuse life-sustaining medical treatment: the need for legislative guidelines to give full effect to minors' expanded rights, *J Fam Law* 34:421, 1996.

Matter of Hamilton, 657 S.W.2d 425 (Tenn. Ct. App. 1983).

Matter of Thomas B., 574 N.Y.S.2d 659 (Fam. Ct. N.Y.C. 1991).

M.N. v. Southern Baptist Hosp. of Fla., Inc., 648 So. 2d 769 (Fla. Ct. App. 1994).

Okla. Stat. Tit. 63 § 3131.4 (1998).

Patient Self-Determination Act of 1991, 42 U.S.C. § 1395i.

Sabatino CP: The legal and functional status of the medical proxy: suggestions for statutory reform, *J Law Med Ethics* 27:52, 1999.

Suggested Reading

Dixon JL: Blood: whose choice and whose conscience? *NY State J Med* 88:463, 1988.

DNR orders, living wills and advance directives: the emergency physician's perspective, *Emerg Physician Legal Bull* 2(3):1, 1991.

Larabee M: An Oregon case shines a light on the issue, *The Oregonian,* Sept 29, 1998. www.oregonlive.com/todaysnews/9812/st120108.html.

Meisel A: *The right to die,* ed 2, cumm suppl, New York, 1995, 1998, Wiley.

Southard P: Cruzan v. Director, Missouri Department of Health: the recent Supreme Court decision and implications for emergency nursing, *J Emerg Nurs* 16:391, 1990.

Sulmasy DP: Killing and allowing to die: another look, *J Law Med Ethics* 26:55, 1998.

The Hemlock Society USA: Pivotal events in the right-to-die movement, 1995. www.hemlock.org.

Suggested Websites

watchtower.org/	Jehovah's Witnesses official website with articles related to blood transfusions
www.religioustolerance.org/medical.htm	Website of Religious Tolerance; essay that discusses religious groups and medical care
www.nwjustice.org/docs/5934.html	Health care rights for minors under 18 in the State of Washington
www.lawnewsnetwork.com/	Current legal news, including cases

7

Managed Care and Consent

Chapter Outline

The dramatic impact of managed care on the health care delivery system is present in emergency care. Confusion, increased workload, and conflict with statutory requirements for emergency care continue (Lenehan, 1999). In addition to private managed care plans, government health care programs implemented managed care plans. The high cost of health care, both in the private and public sector, was a key reason that managed care plans spread across the United States (Mariner, 1998). In addition to the differences in plans and benefits, the language used by managed care organizations (MCOs) is different from that of the traditional health care delivery system. Administrators speak about consumers rather than patients and contract benefits versus patient choice or physician recommendation, and price is a driving force (Mariner, 1998).

MANAGED CARE AND THE EMERGENCY DEPARTMENT

Managed care plans attempt to reduce the use of the emergency department (ED) by patients with nonurgent problems (Herr, 1998). One method used by managed care plans is the requirement that prior authorization be obtained by the ED or payment will not be forthcoming (Johnson & Derlet, 1996). Confusion occurs because of conflict with the hospital's obligations under the Emergency Medical Treatment and Active Labor Act (EMTALA) (see Chapter 12). Under EMTALA, all persons who come to a facility seeking emergency care must have a medical screening examination to determine whether an emergency medical condition exists. Yet, managed care plans often will not pay for medical screening examinations for patients with nonurgent complaints. The nonparticipating, or out-of-network, ED is placed in a dilemma—federal law requiring medical screening examinations, using all the resources available, and managed care plans requiring authorization for payment.

Because of the dilemma, the issue of consent for treatment often gets obscured. The emergency health care professional must keep consent for treatment and authorization for payment as separate and distinct issues. The patient retains the right to consent to treatment and the corresponding right to refuse. The managed care plan may control the decision regarding payment for services but has no right to consent to or refuse treatment on behalf of a patient enrolled in the managed care plan.

Patients may not know their particular plan's benefits. One dilemma faced in the ED is at what point patients are advised that payment for an ED visit may be their responsibility. If the patient contacts the managed care plan himself or herself, the payment issue may be addressed at that time. Otherwise, the ED personnel may be in the position to contact the MCO, seeking authorization for payment. However, the MCO should not be contacted until after the medical screening examination. Discussing what the plan will cover before completion of the medical screening examination, unless initiated by the patient, may lead to allegations of coercion or other violations of EMTALA.

Managed care personnel have a role in educating patients covered by the plan. If patients covered by a managed care plan go to the ED, have a medical screening examination performed, and receive advice for treatment, the prudent ED policy would ensure that the patient talk to managed care personnel—especially if the plan refuses to authorize payment. The patient will probably be responsible for payment in a nonparticipating ED for nonemergencies if the managed care plan refuses to pay.

Congress considered the problems with MCO plans and offered differing solutions. One proposed bill, "The Patients Bill of Rights Plus Act," addressed the issue of patient access to emergency medical care (S.B. 1344 § 721, 1999). Under the proposed legislation, if the MCO plan provides coverage for emergency care, preauthorization is not required for emergency medical screening examinations or emergency ambulance services. The proposed bill specifies that the standard used to evaluate such claims is that of the "prudent layperson." The prudent layperson is one who has "average knowledge of health and medicine" (S.B. 1344, § 721[a][1][a]).

There is difficulty in establishing the criteria for what constitutes a prudent layperson (Young, 1997). Is it prudent for a 23-year-old adult to go to the ED for diagnosis and treatment of chest pain? Although there is a strong likelihood that a young person will not have cardiac chest pain, is the 23-year-old "prudent" for seeking an evaluation to ensure that he or she is not having a myocardial infarction? If there is no family history of coronary artery disease, yet the patient uses cocaine, will those factors be considered by the MCO? Herr (1998) provided specific case scenarios and suggested responses for the dilemmas created by MCO plans when patients come to the ED for evaluation.

CONCLUSION

Managed care has distinct impacts on the ED. The prudent emergency health care professional will draw a distinction between the MCO's authorization for payment and the patient's retained right to consent or refuse emergency care.

References

Herr RD: Managed care and the emergency department: nursing issues, *J Emerg Nurs* 24:406, 1998.

Johnson LA, Derlet RW: Conflicts between managed care organizations and emergency departments in California, *West J Med* 164:137, 1996.

Lenehan GP: Patients' bill of rights offers welcomed protection of patients, nurses, and emergency departments, *J Emerg Nurs* 25:3, 1999.

Mariner WK: Standards of care and standard form contracts: distinguishing patient rights and consumer rights in managed care, *J Contemp Health Law Policy* 15(1):1, 1998. www.cua.edu/students/org/jchlp/mariner.html. [Accessed 4/24/99].

The Patients' Bill of Rights Plus Act. S.B. 1344 § 721 (1999).

Young CJ: Emergency! Says who?: analysis of the legal issues concerning managed care and emergency medical services, *J Contemp Health Law Policy* 13:553, 1997.

Suggested Reading

Derlet RW, Hamilton B: The impact of health maintenance organization care authorization policy on an emergency department before California's new managed care law, *Acad Emerg Med* 3:338, 1996.

8

Confidentiality and Privacy Issues

CHAPTER OUTLINE

Privacy is the right to be free from invasion and to be left alone (Badzek & Gross, 1999). The right to privacy is inherent in interactions between patients and health care providers. A patient's right to privacy may or may not be codified in state law. Federal statutes provide a right to privacy in limited circumstances. Patients expect that personal health information is private and confidential. **Confidentiality** refers to the management or nondisclosure of the private information provided by the patient or the patient's family. Yet, how many patients realize that information is routinely disclosed to insurers, managed care organizations, public health departments, employers, marketing firms, or law enforcement agencies (Carroll, 1999)? This chapter addresses some of the key issues associated with privacy and confidentiality in the health care setting.

FEDERAL AND STATE LAW

Laws affecting privacy and confidentiality of health information can be evaluated by the type of information and whether the information is held privately or by the government (Gostin et al., 1996). State and federal laws protect to, some degree, personal information held by government agencies.

Congress enacted the Privacy Act of 1974 (5 U.S.C. § 552a [1993]). The law applies only to personal information held by federal agencies. The law also does not address the release of information, without the individual's consent, if needed by federal agencies to meet the agency's statutory mandates. The law does not apply to state or private agencies or facilities. The Health Insurance Portability and Accountability Act of 1996 (HIPAA) required the Department of Health and Human Services (DHHS) to issue regulations governing privacy of health records if Congress did not pass statutory protections by August 1999 (Goldman, 1998). Congress' self-imposed deadline was not met, although bills were introduced in the House and Senate in 1999. DHHS' deadline to implement final regulations, pursuant to HIPAA, is February 2000 (Hamburg, 1999). DHHS recommended that Congress enact health information privacy legislation based on five key principles: boundaries, security, consumer control, accountability, and public responsibility (Hamburg, ¶ 14, 1999). DHHS will probably follow the same principles in development and implementation of final regulations.

The Health Care Financing Administration (HCFA) issued revised "Conditions of Participation" requirements for hospital participation in the Medicare program in 1999. One standard specifically addressed confidentiality. The published standard is that "The patient has the right to the confidentiality of his or her clinical records" (42 C.F.R. § 482.13[d][1] [1999]). The standards also specified that patients have a right to personal privacy (42 C.F.R. § 482.13[c][1] [1999]).

State laws vary in the degree of privacy and confidentiality afforded personal health information. Even with specific statutes, regulations, or case laws that provide for privacy and confidentiality of personal health information, exceptions exist. For example, virtually all states require mandatory reporting of communicable diseases. Public health considerations outweigh the individual's expectation and right to privacy when public health is threatened. Even though reporting may be necessary, many states mandate that personal identifiable information cannot be disclosed outside the public health network. Civil or criminal penalties may be imposed for inappropriate disclosure (Gostin et al., 1996).

Regardless of federal or state law, ethical standards for health care professionals incorporate privacy and confidentiality as basic foundational principles. If private information is disclosed inappropriately, confidentiality is breached, and the patient may have a legal cause of action.

PHYSICAL ENVIRONMENT

The physical environment may have an impact on the emergency health care professional's ability to maintain privacy and confidentiality. In the prehospital setting, emergency medical service (EMS) providers rapidly obtain a history and perform a physical examination in surroundings that are often difficult. Family members, neighbors, law enforcement officials, or other individuals may be present during the assessment and treatment by EMS. The underlying cause of the patient's condition may not be revealed because the patient is reluctant to discuss private matters in the presence of others.

Once the patient reaches the emergency department (ED), the physical layout and design of the facility may impair the ability of the emergency health care professionals to maintain privacy. Mlinek and Pierce (1997) studied how an ED's physical layout and design affected privacy and confidentiality. Breaches of privacy and confidentiality occurred in triage for more than 53% of patients during the study (Mlinek & Pierce, 1997). Other areas included the hallways, nurses or central station, and waiting room. The frequency of the breaches depended upon room location and design (Mlinek & Pierce, 1997). Although ED patient status boards can be controversial, Mlinek and Pierce (1997) found that only 2 of 100 patients noticed the status board.

Physicians, nurses, administrators, and clerical personnel should work with architects and designers before planning ED renovation or construction to ensure consideration of the impact on patient privacy. Principles of privacy can coexist with principles of staffing and observation of patients or other ED patient care delivery factors.

MEDICAL RECORDS

Tomes (1990) identified three key areas of security for health information systems: personnel, physical, and system. *Personnel* issues include requiring individual access identification, and the health care worker's duty not to disclose information. The *physical* issues relate to storage of data and access. For example, fireproof or fire-resistant storage facilities, and climate-controlled environments may be necessary (Tomes, 1990). *System* issues include controlling access and disclosure of patient information, user system security, transfer and reproduction of information, and maintenance of information. Correction of errors in information is also a system security issue.

The information documented in the patient's medical record belongs to the patient although the record itself is generally owned by the health care facility. Documentation of patient information, signs and symptoms, treatment, outcomes, and education is vital to communicate to other health care providers and to reflect the care provided to an individual patient. Minimum requirements for elements to be documented in a patient's record may be codified in state law.

Because of the patient's expectation that medical information is private and confidential, the prudent approach is to require a written release of information—reflecting the patient's consent to make the information available to a third party. If the patient received treatment for a psychiatric illness or substance abuse, a standard release of information may be insufficient.

The patient, if insured, usually signs a release for disclosure of the medical information to the insurer. Patients may elect not to sign the release, particularly if the nature of the illness or injury is sensitive. The patient may opt "private pay" rather than release information to the insurer. Emergency health care personnel who obtain signatures for release of information should inform patients the purpose of the release and to whom the disclosure will occur. Specific state law may provide a blanket release or consent to release information. For example, Alabama allows the release of Medicaid recipients' information to any health care provider (Ala. Code § 22-11B-3 [1975]). The act of receiving Medicaid assistance is implicit consent, made explicit by statute, to release the information.

Ongoing medical record issues relate to the release of medical records for medical research, law enforcement access, the use of registries (e.g., trauma registries, burn registries), and inconsistent legal standards from one state to another. As health care organizations merge and restructure, state barriers are crossed. The inconsistency of legal standards from one state to the next can be burdensome for large organizations.

IMPACT OF TECHNOLOGY

Computers

Changes in technology raise many issues concerning patient confidentiality (Sujansky, 1998). As discussed previously, confidentiality is the management of the private information disclosed by the patient. How a facility manages the information will often relate to the technology available. A "paperless" system of documentation of patient medical information may be a goal in highly automated facilities. Even without reaching the paperless pinnacle, many health care facilities document a wealth of patient information on computers. Whether the patient information is dictated via voice-activated technology or keyboard input, the number of people with access to the information far exceeds traditional means of documentation.

Computer technology, including storage capacity, retrieval of archival information, and access, creates potential pitfalls to maintaining patient confidentiality. Security of clinical information systems is a concern to the public and health care professionals (Bowen et al., 1997; Fiesta, 1996; Styffe, 1997). The explosion of Internet and intranet use affects confidentiality of medical information.

Ohio (1997) provided specific standards to use electronic signatures in health records. The facility must have a policy that addresses user compliance with confidentiality and security, as well as a description of penalties for misuse of the electronic system. The statute requires training to address the issues identified in the statute.

Computers allow for storage of vast quantities of data. A move toward electronic data banks of health care information will centralize information about patients (Gostin, 1997). Proponents of centralized health care data describe benefits of "cradle to grave" individual health data, electronic data cards, personal identifiers that allow sharing of information between various organizations, research on disease, and financial costs of health care (Agency for Health Care Policy and Research, 1996; Gostin, 1997). Access to an extensive database, whether by authorized or fraudulent users, is of great concern to proponents of individual privacy protections (Williams, 1999). A vast electronic network of health data raises questions about the right of the individual to maintain privacy and confidentiality versus the collective societal benefit of health information (Gostin, 1997). The debate involves complex issues without easy solutions.

Telecommunications Devices

Facsimile transmission (fax) of patient records, treatment information, and sometimes refusal of treatment is a common occurrence in the ED. ED personnel must ensure that a patient consents to the release of medical information. Fax cover pages should include a disclaimer that the information contained within the fax is privileged and confidential. Anyone receiving the fax in error should be directed to call the sending facility immediately. Persons sending or receiving faxes should verify phone numbers to prevent unintentional transmission to an unauthorized recipient (Dodek & Dodek, 1997).

Cellular telephones, cordless telephones, and paging devices are used by health care professionals in every type of facility. Conversations held over cellular or cordless telephones may not be private (Dodek & Dodek, 1997). The risks associated with discussing a patient's medical information from a cellular or cordless phone should be considered. Paging devices are generally private for the user. However, central paging via switchboard operators or operator-assisted communications may involve a third party who has no need to know patient information.

TELEMEDICINE

Telemedicine involves assessment, treatment, and evaluation via communication lines. A physician in a rural setting may consult with a tertiary care physician via telephone, facsimile, or computer. The advent of telemedicine has led a few states to pass specific legislation governing the practice. Arizona (1994) defined telemedicine as "the practice of health care delivery, diagnosis, consultation, treatment and transfer of medical data through interactive audio, video or data communications that occurs in the physical presence of the patient" (Ariz. Rev. Stat. Ann. § 36-3601[2] [1994]).

The use of technology over the last decade enhanced the ability of physicians in remote or rural areas to consult with physicians in tertiary care or specialty centers. Telemedicine has an advantage of increasing patient access to services that might not otherwise be readily available. The National Library of Medicine funded research to evaluate the use of telemedicine in underserved areas (Larkin, 1997). The use of technology in patient care at a distance raises several legal issues. The Cleveland Clinic Foundation, Mayo Foundation, the Midwest Rural Telemedicine Consortium, and Texas Children's Hospital founded the Center for Telemedicine Law (CTL) to address current legal issues in telemedicine (CTL, 1999). CTL monitors legislation in each state. As of July 13, 1999, 35 states had legislation introduced, pending, or enacted related to telemedicine, telehealth, or related licensure (CTL, 1999). Some of the legal issues associated with telemedicine are disclosure, informed consent, confidentiality, licensure, reimbursement, and liability jurisdiction.

Disclosure

Physician referrals require disclosure to the patient. If an emergency physician stabilizes a radial fracture and refers the patient to an orthopedist, the information about the referral is disclosed to the patient and the information about the patient is disclosed to the orthopedist. If the physician consults with another physician via telemedicine, disclosures about the process, risks and benefits, and security measures to protect confidentiality are the foundation of informed consent.

Informed Consent

States that implemented telemedicine statutes require some form of informed consent. Documentation of the consent should be included in the patient's record. Statutes may carve out emergency exceptions to informed consent. In addition to emergency exceptions, Arizona (1994) required that a parent give consent for a minor and legal guardians for incompetent patients.

Confidentiality

The security of the telemedicine system is vital to ensure confidentiality and privacy of patient information. Passwords, encryption, or other security measures may be used. Security measures should be sophisticated enough to protect patient information but user-friendly. Measures used to protect confidentiality should be disclosed to the patient. Any breaches in security should be immediately addressed and corrected.

Licensure

The current system of physician and nurse licensure is state based. Technology shrinks the distance between patients and health care providers. States generally do not allow the practice of medicine within a state without a license (Darer, 1998). States that enacted specific telemedicine laws usually address licensure. Arizona (1994) specified that the law applies to "telemedicine within the state of Arizona." The law does not change the existing licensure requirement.

The legal issue of licensure raises other questions. Does telemedicine bring the physician to the patient or does it bring the patient to the physician? Should there be a national licensure or a special telemedicine license (Eliasson & Poropatich, 1998)? Should physicians who provide telemedicine be required to obtain licenses in each state? The costs associated with multiple licenses may be prohibitive. Alternative approaches may include limited licensure or exceptions for consulting (Joint Western Governors Taskforce, 1997).

Reimbursement

Although telemedicine may reduce health care costs by providing a cost-effective method for greater access to patients, how does the physician obtain reimbursement for the services provided? As states contend with reimbursement, a key issue will be whether patient-to-physician contact is needed for reimbursement.

Liability Jurisdiction

If telemedicine occurs within a state, the issue of liability jurisdiction is minimized. However, if telemedicine crosses state boundaries, jurisdictional issues arise. Multiple providers in multiple jurisdictions can cause confusion. Who shares in liability? Which state's law governs? What is the standard of care in telemedicine jurisdictions and how is the standard of care determined (Darer, 1998)?

SPECIAL SITUATIONS

Acquired Immunodeficiency Syndrome

There are exceptions to the patient's general expectation of privacy of medical information. In the early days of the acquired immunodeficiency syndrome (AIDS) crisis, patients often suffered prejudice—sometimes by health care professionals—when there was a disclosure about the patient's human immunodeficiency virus (HIV) status. As a result of the difficulties encountered by patients with HIV infection or AIDS, many state legislatures passed laws protecting the privacy of HIV status or AIDS information. Anonymous testing, hospital admissions under an alias name, and privacy of treatment options often conflicted with public health demands for tracing contacts, identifying the numbers of people infected, and approaches to containing epidemics. Fear of consequences often led patients to withhold disclosure of their HIV status in emergency situations.

The consequences of disclosure were evident in *Estate of Behringer* v. *Medical Center of Princeton* (592 A.2d 1251 [N.J. Super. 1991]). Breach of patient confidentiality was a major legal theory in the case. The patient was an otolaryngologist and plastic surgeon with a successful surgical practice. After a brief period of flulike symptoms that progressed to dyspnea, the patient was admitted through the ED. *Pneumocystis carinii* pneumonia (PCP), an opportunistic infection commonly seen in patients with AIDS, was the preliminary diagnosis.

After a bronchoscopy the next day, the patient received a diagnosis of PCP and AIDS. Evidence at trial revealed that the patient—who was a staff physician at the hospital—was very concerned about the confidentiality of his diagnosis. He was discharged home when a transfer to another facility could not be arranged. Although he needed additional inpatient care, he went home to reduce the possibility that the AIDS diagnosis would become public knowledge.

Upon arriving home, the patient received phone calls from other physicians at the medical center who knew his diagnosis. He also received calls from nonmedical friends who knew about his diagnosis. Upon returning to his office a few weeks later and in the months following, doctors and patients called who indicated they knew about the diagnosis. Cancellations of appointments, office employee resignations, and repeated phone calls inquiring about the physician's diagnosis continued. The physician never operated again and saw his booming practice dwindle to almost nothing. He died and his estate sued the medical center.

The court extensively reviewed the hospital's policies and procedures related to HIV testing, pretest counseling, and confidentiality of records. The court stated the following:

> The confidentiality breached in the present case is simply grist for a gossip mill with little concern for the impact of disclosure on the patient. While one can legitimately question the good judgment of a practicing physician choosing to undergo HIV testing

or a bronchoscopy procedure at the same hospital where he practices, this apparent error in judgment does not relieve the medical center of its underlying obligation to protect its patients against the dissemination of confidential information (*Behringer,* 592 A.2d at 1273).

The court held that the medical center and laboratory director breached their duty and obligation to keep the information about the patient's diagnosis confidential (*Behringer,* 592 A.2d at 1274).

A Connecticut case also addressed disclosure of a patient's HIV status (*Doe* v. *Marselle,* 675 A.2d 835 [Conn. 1996]). Jane Doe disclosed her HIV status to her surgeon. The surgeon's assistant discussed her intention to disclose the information about Jane Doe with the surgeon. The surgeon gave approval so long as his assistant did not identify Jane Doe by name. When Jane Doe learned that the surgical assistant disclosed her HIV status to at least three people in the community, she sued the surgeon and his assistant (*Doe,* 675 A.2d at 836).

Connecticut statutes related to confidentiality and disclosure of HIV status were interpreted by the appellate court after the trial court granted defendants' motion to dismiss. The trial court said the plaintiff's complaint was insufficient because she did not allege "willful behavior" by the surgeon or his assistant. The Connecticut Supreme Court interpreted the statute and focused on the requirement of willfulness. The court defined "willful to mean a knowing disclosure of confidential HIV-related information" (*Doe,* 675 A.2d at 842). The appellate court reversed the trial court and remanded the case back to the trial court.

As these two cases demonstrate, confidentiality of HIV or AIDS status is a primary concern for patients. Discrimination continues to occur, and the emergency health care professional should ensure nondisclosure except when the information is needed to provide care to the patient, if the law mandates disclosure, or if the patient consents.

Reportable Diseases or Injuries

Another exception to the privacy expectations of patients involves laws that require reporting of certain diseases or injuries. For example, law enforcement authorities are notified if a patient arrives with a gunshot wound, stab wound, or extensive burn. Public health considerations require reporting of certain diseases. Tuberculosis is a reportable condition. Contagious diseases generally require reporting because of public health risks associated with unchecked contagion.

Hospital licensing state law may also require the reporting of certain events. In Rhode Island, for example, hospitals are required to report fires or internal disasters that harm patients or personnel or disrupt patient care, elopements of psychiatric inpatients, infection outbreaks, surgery on the wrong patient, and any incident reported to the hospital's insurance (Rhode Island, 1956). Facilities accredited by the Joint Commission on Accreditation of Healthcare Organizations (JCAHO) may voluntarily report "sentinel events" (JCAHO, 1999). For example, a deleterious impact on patient outcome unrelated to the patient's illness or underlying disease, such as surgery on the wrong extremity, is an example of a reportable sentinel event. Confidentiality of patient information, obtaining of consent before release of patient-identifiable information, and the JCAHO accreditation guidelines should be taken into consideration before voluntary release of the information. Gaps in confidentiality protection exist (JCAHO, 1999).

Minors

The state has a special interest in protecting minors. All states mandate that physicians and other health care professionals report suspected child abuse or neglect to the appropriate authorities. Most states established a central registry of information on child abuse. Issues of patient confidentiality may arise when the media seeks information about a particular case.

Not all states address minors' consent for HIV testing and treatment (Adams, 1994). Even if tested, health care providers may be allowed to disclose minors' test results to parents, thus defeating the goal of confidentiality. Maine (1995), by statute, gives minors the same rights of confidentiality as adults. The statute allows an exception and provides that a health care provider may notify the minor's parent or guardian "if in the judgment of the practitioner or provider, failure to inform would seriously jeopardize the health of the minor or seriously limit ability to provide treatment" (Maine, 1995).

Sexually Transmitted Diseases

The presence of sexually transmitted diseases (STDs) is another exception to patient privacy. Syphilis, gonorrhea, and chlamydia are reported to public health authorities for tracing of contacts, evaluation of treatment, and follow-up. Most state laws contain confidentiality provisions requiring that the information be confidential and not released once reported to public health authorities.

Psychiatric Patients

The social stigma of mental illness still exists. Patients with mental illness receive state and federal law protection against disclosure of confidential information. An important exception to psychiatric confidentiality is the duty to warn third parties. The landmark case of *Tarasoff* v. *Regents of the University of California* (1976) established a duty for psychotherapists to warn third parties if a patient made threats toward a specific individual. *Tarasoff* opened the door to imposing liability on psychotherapists for violent behavior of psychiatric patients in limited circumstances. Litigation and statutory remedies ensued.

In general, courts may require that a patient identify a specific victim with identifiable threats before the duty to warn arises (Allmason, 1997). Statutes generally require an actual or serious threat to identified or identifiable victims (Allmason, 1997).

An emerging legal issue, and often a concern for emergency health care professionals, is the attempt to extend a duty to warn beyond the patient-psychotherapist setting. In *Flynn* v. *Houston Emergicare, Inc.* (1993), the victim of a car accident sued an emergency physician and hospital for failing to warn a patient not to drive. The patient entered the ED with a complaint of chest pain after using cocaine. The patient was treated with a β-blocker to reduce his heart rate and blood pressure. The patient was discharged from the ED after diagnostic studies and administration of medication.

Approximately 1 hour later, the patient had a seizure and rear-ended the plaintiff's car, causing her to sustain injuries. The plaintiff asked the court to extend the emergency physician's duty beyond the patient to the general public. A failure to warn the patient not to drive was only one legal theory. The court granted defendants' motion for summary judgment, and the plaintiff appealed. The appellate court held that the defendants did not owe a duty to the plaintiff to warn the patient not to drive (*Flynn,* 1993, 869 S.W. 2d 403).

Alcohol/Drug Abuse

The Comprehensive Alcohol Abuse and Alcoholism Prevention, Treatment, and Rehabilitation Act of 1970 and the Drug Abuse Office and Treatment Act of 1972 provided specific confidential protection for patients admitted to a facility for alcohol or drug treatment. Any facility that receives federal funds is subject to the requirement of maintaining confidentiality of records and other patient information. Although these two federal laws apply to alcohol and drug abuse inpatient and outpatient centers, the concern by Congress that the information be confidential provides some federal direction to the emergency health care professional. The stigma associated with alcohol and drug abuse can be significant. Before releasing any information about patients treated for alcohol or drug abuse, the patient should provide specific consent for release of that information (Tilton, 1996).

Genetic Test Results

An emerging legal issue is the confidentiality of genetic test results (Badzek & Gross, 1999). When an illness or disease has a significant genetic component and probabilities of occurrence in certain populations, genetic testing may occur. However, the patient undergoing genetic testing must consider questions about possible discrimination in employment, ability to obtain health and life insurance, and the degree of disclosure (Hamburg, 1999).

CONCLUSION

Patients who perceive that confidentiality and privacy will not be maintained may respond by withholding information, paying for health care services out of pocket to prevent disclosure to an insurer, seeing multiple different doctors, or in the extreme, avoiding care altogether (Badzek & Gross, 1999). Illegal immigrants may avoid care for fear that the health care provider will report their immigration status to the Immigration and Naturalization Service. Regardless of one's opinion on immigration, there can be significant public health concerns if immigrants avoid health care (Badzek & Gross, 1999).

Balancing the individual's right to privacy and confidentiality with public benefit from health data will require thought, discussion, and societal decisions about what is important in protecting health data. The remarkable advances in technology must be included in the debate about the issues of privacy and confidentiality. As the old saying goes, "Just because you can, doesn't mean you should."

References

Adams W: "But do you have to tell my parents?" The dilemma for minors seeking HIV-testing and treatment, *John Marshall Law Rev* 27:493, 1994.

Agency for Health Care Policy and Research: Research in action: using computers to advance health care, 1996. www.ahcpr.gov/research/computer.htm. [Accessed 5/26/99].

Ala. Code § 22-11B-3 (1975).

Allmason AL: Comments: personal liability implication of the duty to warn are hard pills to swallow: from *Tarasoff* to *Hutchinson v. Patel* and beyond, *J Contemp Health Law Policy* 13:471, 1997.

Ariz. Rev. Stat. Ann. § 36.3601(2) (1994).

Badzek L, Gross L: Confidentiality and privacy: at forefront for nurses, *Am J Nurs* 6(99):52, 1999.

Bowen JW, Klimczak JC, Ruiz M, Barnes M: Design of access control methods for protecting the confidentiality of patient information in networked systems. *Proceedings of the AMIA Annual Fall Symposium,* pp. 46-50, 1997.

Carroll L: Medical records not so private, *MSNBC,* 1999. www.msnbc.com/news/78327.asp?cp1=1. [Accessed 9/18/99].

Center for Telemedicine Law, 1999. www.ctl.org. [Accessed 5/26/99].

Comprehensive Alcohol Abuse and Alcoholism Prevention, Treatment, and Rehabilitation Act of 1970. 42 U.S.C. § 4551 (1998).

Darer B: Telemedicine: a state-based answer to health care in America, *Va J Law Technol* 3:4, 1998.

Dodek DY, Dodek A: From Hippocrates to facsimile: protecting patient confidentiality is more difficult and more important than ever before, *CMAJ* 156:847, 1997.

Doe v. Marselle, 675 A.2d 835 (Conn. 1996).

Drug Abuse Office and Treatment Act of 1972. 21 U.S.C. § 1101 (1998).

Eliasson AH, Poropatich RK: Performance improvement in telemedicine: the essential elements, *Mil Med* 163:530, 1998.

Estate of Behringer v. Medical Center of Princeton, 592 A.2d 1251 (N.J. Super. 1991).

Fiesta J: Legal issues in the information age—part 2, *Nurs Manage* 27(9):12, 1996.

Flynn v. Houston Emergicare, Inc., 869 S.W.2d 403 (Tex. Ct. App. 1993).

Goldman J: Protecting privacy to improve health care, *Health Aff* 17(6):47, 1998.

Gostin L: Health care information and the protection of personal privacy: ethical and legal considerations, *Ann Intern Med* 127:683, 1997.

Gostin LO, Lazzarini Z, Flaherty KM: *Legislative survey of state confidentiality laws,* Atlanta, GA, 1996, Centers for Disease Control and Prevention.

Hamburg MA: Statement before the Subcommittee on Health, Committee on Ways and Means U.S. House of Representatives, Washington, DC, Department of Health and Human Services, July 20, 1999. www.hhs.gov/progorg/as1/testify/t990720a.html. [Accessed 9/9/99].

Health Care Financing Administration: Condition of participation: patients' rights, 42 C.F.R. § 482.13 (1999).

Joint Commission on Accreditation of Healthcare Organizations: Accreditation committee approves examples of voluntarily reportable sentinel events, *Sentinel Event Alert* 4, 1999.

Joint Commission on Accreditation of Healthcare Organizations: Protecting personal health information: executive summary, 1999. www.jcaho.org/pphi/3execsum.html. [Accessed 5/26/99].

Joint Western Governors Taskforce: Telemedicine report to Congress: legal issues— licensure and telemedicine, 1997. www.ntia.doc.gov/reports/telemed/legal.htm.

Larkin M: Telemedicine gets a chance to prove itself, *Ann Intern Med* Dec 15, 1997. www.acponline.org/journals/annals/15dec97/currtele.htm. [Accessed 9/18/99].

Maine Rev. Stat. Ann. § 1505 (1995).

Mlinek EJ, Pierce J: Confidentiality and privacy breaches in a university hospital emergency department, *Acad Emerg Med* 4:1142, 1997.

Ohio Rev. Code § 3701.75 (Anderson, 1997).

Privacy Act of 1974. 5 U.S.C. § 552a (1993).

R.I. Rev. Stat. § 23-17-40 (1956).

Styffe EJ: Privacy, confidentiality, and security in clinical information systems: dilemmas and opportunities for the nurse executive, *Nurs Adm Q* 21(3):21, 1997.

Sujanksy WV: The benefits and challenges of an electronic medical record: much more than a "word-processed" patient chart, *West J Med* 169:176, 1998.

Tarasoff v. Regents of University of California, 529 P.2d 553 (Cal. 1974), *modified* 551 P.2d 334 (Cal. 1976).

Tilton SH: Right to privacy and confidentiality of medical records, *Occup Med* 11:17, 1996.

Tomes JP: *Healthcare records: a practical legal guide,* Dubuque, IA, 1990, Kendall/ Hunt.

Williams BJ: Medical records privacy: a hot issue for action in 1999, 1999. www. law.uh.edu/healthlawperspectives/Privacy/990412Medical.html. [Accessed 4/24/99].

Suggested Reading

American Civil Liberties Union Freedom Network: Protect your medical privacy! www.aclu.org.

Brooks E, Delliquadri T, Meyer D, et al: Confidentiality and right to privacy issues in mental health managed care, *Whittier Law Rev* 19:39, 1997.

Brown LC, Stanton WC, Paye W: Facing the limits on uses of medical and peer review information: are high technology and confidentiality on a collision course? *Whittier Law Rev* 19:97, 1997.

Citizens' Council on Health Care: Protecting your medical records: top 10 strategies to protect patient confidentiality, 1999. www.cchc-mn.org/privstratsht.html.

Daar JF, Koerner S: Telemedicine: legal and practical implications, *Whittier Law Rev* 19:3, 1997.

Davis L, Domm JA, Konikoff MR, Miller RA: Attitudes of first-year medical students toward the confidentiality of computerized patient records, *J Am Med Inform Assoc* 6:53, 1999.

de Meyer F, Lundgren PA, de Moor G, Fiers T: Determination of user requirements for the secure communication of electronic medical record information, *Int J Med Inf* 49:125, 1998.

Ewy GA: Patient datasheets and generic evaluation sheets: tools for improving patient care, patient satisfaction, and chart documentation while decreasing physician frustration, *Clin Cardiol* 20:273, 1997.

Garrett MK: Telemedicine in Florida, *J Fla Med Assoc* 84:81, 1997.

Harris RE: The need to know versus the right to know: privacy of patient medical data in an information-based society, *Suff Univ Law Rev* 30:1183, 1997.

Jayawardena H: AIDS and professional secrecy in the United States, *Med Sci Law* 36:37, 1996.

Lowe HJ: Multimedia electronic medical record system, *Acad Med* 74:146, 1999.

Lowrance WW: Privacy and health research: 6. The U.S. legal context, 1997. http://aspe.hhs.gov/datacncl/PHR6.htm.

Privacy Rights Clearinghouse: Fact sheet #8: how private is my medical information? 1997. www.privacyrights.org/FS/fs8-med.htm.

Rosenblum J: Medical liability in cyberspace, *Health Lawyer* 8(3):10, 1995.

Scott RL: Privacy of pharmacy records, 1999. www.law.uh.edu/healthlawperspectives/ Healthpolicy/990331Pharmacy.html.

Yawn BP, Yawn RA, Geier GR, et al: The impact of requiring patient authorization for use of data in medical records research, *J Fam Pract* 47:361, 1998.

III

Unique Circumstances in Emergency Care

9

Forensics
in Emergency Care

Chapter Outline

Forensics is the study of evidence used in legal cases. **Medical forensics** relates to the collection, analysis, and interpretation of medical evidence presented in legal cases. Several patient care situations occur when emergency health care professionals collect evidence from patients for potential use in legal cases. Although medical evidence may be necessary in civil cases, the most common collection of evidence occurs in possible criminal cases. The most common types of forensic situations are discussed in the following sections. Consideration of the legal evidentiary issues associated with collection of medical evidence for forensic purposes is incorporated into the discussion.

PRINCIPLES REGARDING CHAIN OF CUSTODY

Chain of custody is a foundational principle in emergency care forensics. The main purpose of chain of custody is "to establish to a reasonable probability that there has been no tampering with evidence" (*Suttle* v. *State*, 565 So.2d 1197, 1198 [Ala. Ct. App. 1990]). The integrity of the evidence submitted in court is necessary before the evidence is admitted for consideration by a jury. Chain of custody integrity requires that the evidence is identified, and possession between taking the evidence and its analysis can be shown. Labeling any evidence with the name of the patient and any other identifying information is the first step in the chain of custody. The emergency health care professional should consider the way laboratory specimens and other items are routinely labeled. Rather than change the system, the usual label is generally sufficient along with the date, time, and initials of the individual who collected the evidence. Documentation of how the evidence was collected is also important. Once the evidence is handed to someone else, such as a law enforcement officer, sufficient information to identify the individual receiving the information should be recorded. The date and time specimens were handed to someone else is important to track the possession and location of evidence.

Documentation on the specimen may not be sufficient in and of itself. The clinician should record in the medical record, or on special forms designed for evidence collection, what time the evidence was collected, by whom and how, and what was done with the specimens. For example, an easily used phrase is, "specimen remained in my control, care, and custody until personally delivered to Officer _____, Badge No. _____, of the _____ (name of law enforcement agency)." Prepackaged kits, such as rape kits, blood alcohol kits, and urine drug screen kits may contain sufficient documentation for demonstrating chain of custody.

Often, the emergency health care professional may be asked to identify the chain of custody for specimens obtained not as evidence but through the regular course of emergency care. Civil lawyers will often want the information in personal injury or wrongful death cases. The emergency health care professional can take the opportunity to inform the lawyer about medical procedures and that chain of custody is not maintained unless, before collection, the emergency health care professional knows the specimen is collected for forensic purposes.

CRIME SCENE INTEGRITY IN PREHOSPITAL CARE

Prehospital care providers may respond to requests for emergency medical services for either crime victims or perpetrators. Regardless of the patient's status to the criminal justice system, it is important that the prehospital care provider's skills of observation are operating acutely when responding to a potential crime scene. Providing emergency care for the patient is the top priority. However, it is also important that the crime scene remain as undisturbed as possible without placing the patient's well-being in jeopardy.

If it is necessary to cut any of the patient's clothing to access areas of the body for physical assessment, observation of the condition of the clothing is important. No cuts should be made through holes in the clothing, whether the holes were made by knives or bullets. Information about the mechanism of injury can be obtained through evaluating the clothing. The condition and appearance of the skin is important to crime scene investigations. For example, the wounds of a victim of a gunshot wound at close range may demonstrate stippling or powder burns. Law enforcement investigators may be able to closely approximate the distance of the shooter from the victim by skin and wound appearance. Documentation of the wound appearance is especially important if alcohol or other cleansing agents are used in proximity to the wound. Any statements made by the patient should also be documented, particularly if the victim identifies the perpetrator. Although such statements will be scrutinized under the rules of evidence before admission in a trial, any statements made can assist investigators. If the patient dies at the scene, all rescue devices should be left in place so that investigators can distinguish between rescue attempts and possible inflicted injuries (Lee, 1994). In addition, control of the scene is important to prevent possible destruction of evidence (Lee, 1994).

The priority is the emergency care of the patient, but attention should also be focused on the responsibilities to preserve and protect as much evidence as possible. Documentation of the patient's behavior, statements, and appearance and a thorough description of the surrounding scene are important to the criminal investigation and patient care.

SEXUAL ASSAULT EVIDENCE COLLECTION

Collection of specimens from victims of sexual assault, and sometimes from alleged perpetrators, are common occurrences in emergency departments (EDs). Each state has laws, regulations, and customs that address what needs to be collected and how. As with other situations, minors and adults are treated differently under the law. For example, Arkansas (1997) law requires that facilities report incidents of sexual assault for all minors and directs that evidence shall be collected. Adults must provide permission before collection of evidence and are allowed to decide whether the alleged assault will be reported (Arkansas, 1997).

The collection of evidence in a sexual assault case is secondary to the care of the patient. For example, if the patient suffered injuries in addition to the sexual assault, the emergency health care professional must provide the same level of care as to other injured patients. For critically injured patients, evidence collection may occur simultaneously as much as possible. The patient's care cannot be compromised to ensure evidence collection.

Over the past decade, a growing trend is the implementation of sexual assault nurse examiner **(SANE)** programs (Hohenhaus, 1998b). In EDs without a SANE program, problems can occur because of various individuals collecting evidence for the "rape kit." Emergency physicians and nurses who rarely perform sexual assault examinations and evidence collection can inadvertently overlook pertinent evidence. Examinations and evidence collection by the same personnel can enhance the quality of the evidence.

Testifying in court is an important role for the emergency health care professional. The physical and behavioral characteristics of the patient are likely to be explored by both the prosecution and defense. SANE participants may qualify as expert witnesses in discussing the findings and possible causes of injury (Hohenhaus, 1998a).

Documentation is important but can be a two-edged sword. The current trend is a move away from documenting every single detail of the alleged assault in the medical record. Specific details are needed to guide the examination and collection of evidence, but the emergency health care professional should remember that the victim is required to repeat the details of the incident to law enforcement officers. Discrepancies in the details, however minor, can be difficult to address at trial. The documentation should reflect the patient's statements about the incident, but it is not the role of emergency health care professionals to probe into details that are unnecessary for the patient's examination, treatment, and collection of evidence.

Chain of custody of the evidence is vital. Sexual assault or rape kits generally contain evidence collection materials, including chain of custody documentation. The integrity of the rape kit is critical in the prosecution of sexual assault. Documentation about the identification and possession of the evidence from time of collection until delivery to a law enforcement official is a vital step in maintaining chain of custody.

SUSPECTS IN CUSTODY OF LAW ENFORCEMENT AUTHORITIES OR PRISONERS

The collection of evidence from suspects in the custody of law enforcement authorities can be challenging to emergency health care professionals. Emergency health care professionals should ensure that they are not placed in the position of an agent of law enforcement. Hospital policies and procedures should address the issues associated with collecting evidence from suspects or prisoners. As discussed in Chapter 5, suspects and prisoners retain their rights to consent to medical care. Principles of consent should be used by emergency health care professionals in collecting evidence as well. If the patient refuses to allow collection of evidence, law enforcement officials may seek a search warrant or court order to obtain the evidence. The use of physical force to collect evidence from a suspect may subject the emergency health care professional to civil liability for battery. The laws of each state govern how far and to what extent the emergency health care professional can go to obtain evidence for various alleged crimes.

In *Carroll* v. *State* (1996), a man was arrested and charged with disorderly conduct. The officers believed the suspect swallowed illegal drugs. An altercation ensued that resulted in the suspect sustaining a gunshot wound. Upon arrival in the ED, the suspect had a nasogastric tube inserted with evacuation of stomach contents. The officers arrived and requested the stomach contents. A later analysis revealed cocaine in the suspect's stomach contents. At trial, the defense lawyer filed a motion to suppress the evidence of narcotics and argued that the seizure of stomach contents was illegal. The court allowed the admission of the evidence. The emergency physician ordered the placement of the nasogastric tube and evacuation of the stomach contents in preparation for surgery and before any discussion with police officers. The court found that the stomach contents were obtained solely for medical purposes and that the analysis of the contents was admissible at trial (*Carroll*, 1996). Had the physician evacuated the gastric contents at the direction of a law enforcement officer, the outcome might have been different.

In a 1952 California case, the emergency physician forcibly administered an emetic down a nasogastric tube of a suspect at the direction of a law enforcement officer (*Rochin* v. *Calif.*, 342 U.S. 165 [1952]). Three officers forcibly entered the suspect's bedroom and observed the suspect swallow two capsules. The police took the suspect to a hospital and directed an emergency physician to retrieve the capsules. After forcibly inserting a nasogastric tube and administering an emetic, the physician retrieved the stomach contents. A later analysis revealed morphine in the stomach contents. The suspect was later convicted of illegal possession of morphine.

The case was eventually heard by the U.S. Supreme Court. The Supreme Court reversed the conviction. The Court stated, "This is conduct that shocks the conscience" (*Rochin,* ¶ 13, 1952). The Court held that the defendant was denied constitutional rights of due process.

The type of evidence, procedures used to collect the evidence, and risks to the suspect or prisoner will be considered by a court if a court order is sought to obtain evidence over the patient's objections. Such were the facts of *Winston* v. *Lee,* 470 U.S. 753 (1985). A shopkeeper received a gunshot wound during the course of an attempted robbery. The shopkeeper shot at the perpetrator. Eight blocks from the scene of the crime, an individual was discovered with a gunshot wound to the chest. The individual went to the ED. In the ED, the shopkeeper identified the individual as the attempted robber who shot him. The police charged the man with attempted robbery, malicious wounding, and use of a firearm in commission of a felony.

The suspect had an object, thought to be a bullet, lodged under his left collarbone. The State requested a court order to compel surgery on the defendant. The goal of the surgery, according to the State, was to remove the object and determine the guilt or innocence of the defendant. After hearing conflicting evidence about the mechanics of the proposed procedure, the trial court ordered the defendant to undergo surgery. The defendant appealed to the state supreme court without success. A case filed in federal district court was unsuccessful initially.

Just before scheduled surgery, radiographs showed that the object was lodged deep in the defendant's chest muscles and would require a general anesthetic for removal. The case ultimately was reviewed by the U.S. Supreme Court. The Court considered the proposed surgery under the requirements of the Fourth Amendment protections against unwarranted intrusions by the State. The personal privacy and dignity of the individual is of concern in cases where the State is demanding an intrusive search.

The initial threshold was probable cause. Other factors included an analysis of the "magnitude of the intrusion," including the threat to the safety or health of the individual. The individual's interests are weighed against the community's interest in "determining guilt or innocence" (*Winston,* ¶ 16, 1985). The Court weighed the factors and found the proposed surgery would be an unreasonable search and seizure under the Fourth Amendment.

When collecting specimens from suspects or prisoners, the emergency health care professional must ensure that he or she does not become an agent of the law enforcement agency requesting the evidence. The suspect retains the right to consent to and refuse treatment. If the law enforcement agency believes the evidence is vital to the investigation, a court order or search warrant can be obtained before the collection of the evidence.

BLOOD SPECIMENS FOR ALCOHOL OR DRUG TESTING

Criminal Cases

Runge et al. (1996) studied drivers injured in motor vehicle crashes with blood alcohol levels of 100 mg/dl or higher. The results were that the more severely injured the driver, the less likely he or she would be charged with driving under the influence (Runge et al., 1996). Individual motorists who drink or use drugs and drive are a possible threat to all other drivers on the road. All states have laws prohibiting the operation of a motor vehicle if under the influence of alcohol or drugs. However, emergency health care professionals see the results of noncompliance with these laws on a daily or weekly basis.

Most states have implied consent statutes for chemical testing of breath, blood, saliva, or urine for alcohol or drugs. For example, the Missouri statute provides that consent is implied, and the process may be videotaped and used as evidence at trial (Missouri, 1998). Many implied consent statutes address refusal as well. The Alabama statute implies consent, but if the patient refuses to allow the collection of specimens, the refusal is evidence that is admissible at trial (Ala. Code § 32-5A-194 [1975]). The difficulty for emergency health care professionals arises when the patient refuses collection of the specimens and a law enforcement officer demands the collection. Hospital policy should address the issue. Most facilities do not allow collection, absent a search warrant or court order, if the patient refuses. Implied consent statutes generally address unconscious suspects or individuals incapable of consenting. Because consent is implied, additional consent is generally not needed if the patient is unconscious or incapable of consenting.

Chain of custody is critical in obtaining blood or urine specimens for analysis by law enforcement officials. In *Suttle* v. *State* (1990), a vehicular homicide conviction was reversed by the Alabama Court of Criminal Appeals because the prosecution could not properly establish chain of custody of the defendant's blood sample. When urine samples are obtained for drug testing, direct observation of the collection of the sample, while maintaining patient privacy, should occur. The record should reflect direct observation to eliminate questions about the proper identity of the individual providing the specimen.

As with other types of evidence collection, documentation is critical. Special forms may be used to document the entire process, from the request by the law enforcement agency to the chain of custody of the specimen. Figure 9-1 is an example of a form that addresses many of the issues associated with chain of custody in collection of blood samples for forensic purposes.

The method by which the blood is drawn will be closely scrutinized by defense lawyers. Although no scientific studies show that preparing the skin with isopropyl alcohol increases serum blood alcohol levels, defense lawyers may attempt, in their zealous representation of their clients, to confuse the jury with the issue. The most prudent approach for the emergency health care professional is to prepare the skin with a non–alcohol-based solution. If a non–alcohol-based solution is used and use is documented, the issue of how the skin was prepared before the blood draw is avoided.

Employment-Related Requests

The ED often is used by employers to collect blood or urine specimens from employees. Employee work-related injuries, unusual behavior in the workplace, or the employee's position are only examples of factors considered by employers in testing. Before collecting blood or urine specimens from an employee, the ED staff should recognize that consent and chain of custody principles apply.

The employer should furnish the ED with the employer's drug or alcohol testing policy. If the employee/patient does not consent to testing, the collection of specimens should not proceed. If the employee/patient consents to the collection of specimens, the usual procedure for forensic collection should be followed. Identification and labeling of the specimens, once collected, are necessary to maintain chain of custody. The employer, laboratory, or courier service selected by the employer generally provides the form for documentation of chain of custody. Without a special form, the ED staff should remember the chain of custody principles discussed above and record the chain of custody in the patient's medical record.

BLOOD TEST REQUEST BY PEACE OFFICER
AT THE

The undersigned, a duly authorized peace officer of _____ (name of law enforcement body), hereby requests that a physician, registered nurse, registered clinical laboratory technologist or clinical laboratory technician obtain a blood sample from _____ (name of patient)

This is to certify that said person from whom the blood sample is to be obtained has been lawfully arrested for an offense allegedly committed by said person while driving a motor vehicle under the influence of intoxicating liquor and the undersigned peace officer has reasonable cause to believe that such person was driving a motor vehicle upon the highway while under the influence of intoxicating liquor.

DATE: _____
TIME: _____
_____
(Signature and badge no. of peace officer)

CONSENT TO BLOOD TEST

I, the undersigned, do hereby consent to the withdrawal of a blood sample from my body for police purposes. The undersigned specifically authorizes _____, its agents and employees, to cooperate, permit, and assist in the taking of the blood sample, and agrees that the Hospital, its agents and employees, will incur no liability whatsoever arising out of the taking of the blood sample. I further certify that I am not a person who is afflicted with hemophilia or with a heart condition which requires the use of an anticoagulant by the direction of a physician.

DATE: _____
TIME: _____   _____
WITNESS: (Signature of patient)

STATEMENT OF PHYSICIAN, REGISTERED NURSE, REGISTERED CLINICAL LABORATORY TECHNOLOGIST, OR CLINICAL LABORATORY TECHNICIAN

Upon the written request of _____, badge number _____,
(Name of peace officer requesting test)

Figure 9-1 Request, consent, and documentation of chain of custody for collection of blood specimens for forensic purposes.

Illustration continued on following page

109

I have drawn a blood sample from the above-named patient on _____ at _____ .

(Date)   (Time)

The site was prepped with _____ , a non-alcohol based solution. The blood sample was taken from the _____ (list site) after confirming the patient was not taking anticoagulants or afflicted with hemophilia. The blood sample was labeled by me and remained in my control and custody until hand-delivered, by me, to _____ .(name of peace officer receiving specimen)

_____
(Signature of physician, registered nurse, registered clinical laboratory technologist, or clinical laboratory technician)

_____
(Print name and title)

A blood sample was NOT obtained by me from the above-named patient because of the following reason(s):

☐ The patient refused to voluntarily consent to the procedure.
☐ Physical force, threats, or restraints would have been required to make the patient submit to the procedure.
☐ The patient stated, or evidence showed, that he (she) was a hemophiliac or using an anticoagulant.
☐ Other (specify): _____

Date: _____ Time: _____

_____
Signature of Person Authorized to Draw the Blood Sample

_____
Title/Position

Figure 9-1 *Continued*

110

If an adverse employment action is taken against the employee/patient based on the employee's test results, the staff who collected the specimens may receive a subpoena to testify either in a deposition or at trial. Hospital policies and procedures should address collection of specimens when requested by an employer.

CORONER/MEDICAL EXAMINER CASES

Each state has laws that identify which cases must be reported to the coroner or medical examiner. Some common examples are persons who died without being treated by a physician; unexpected, unexplained deaths; sudden, traumatic deaths; deaths caused by fire; and deaths that occur outside the hospital. If there is any uncertainty about referring a case to the coroner/medical examiner, the appropriate official in the county or parish where the individual died should be contacted. The coroner/medical examiner, once the circumstances are explained, can either accept or reject the case.

Jurisdictional issues may arise if the patient's injuries occurred in one county or parish, but the patient was transferred to a different county or parish. However, notifying the coroner/medical examiner in the county or parish where the individual died should be sufficient. If the coroner/medical examiner declines jurisdiction, he or she should identify if another county or parish has jurisdiction over the case.

Coroners or medical examiners are usually available for education of emergency health care professionals. Procedures identified by the coroner/medical examiner for packaging a deceased patient should be followed. For example, the coroner/medical examiner may want all the resuscitation devices left in place to ensure a complete picture of injuries versus medical interventions. If the individual died as a result of an alleged criminal act, the coroner/medical examiner may be called upon not only to determine cause of death, but also may be required to testify as to physical findings. Working closely with the coroner/medical examiner provides consistent procedures for collection of evidence for subsequent legal proceedings.

OTHER TYPES OF FORENSIC CASES

Child Abuse/Neglect

All states mandate reporting of suspected child abuse or neglect. Discrepancy between the "story" given by the caregiver and a child's injuries may alert the emergency health care professional to problems. The child's behavior and demeanor are important assessment parameters (Monk, 1998). Any injuries should be thoroughly documented and possibly photographed. The child should be separated from the caregiver if there is any suspicion or question about the child's condition. State law governs to whom a report is made—law enforcement officials or the department of human, family, or child services. State law also provides immunity from civil or criminal liability for good faith reporting.

Visible injuries should be clearly described in the medical record. Many emergency departments retain a camera for the purpose of photographic evidence. If the possible child abuse or neglect case is reported to law enforcement authorities, photographic evidence may be obtained.

As with refusal of treatment, religious practices may play a role in the care of a minor. In *Commonwealth* v. *Nixon,* 718 A.2d 311 (Pa. Sup. Ct. 1998), a teenager died from complications of new-onset diabetes. The parents were convicted of involuntary manslaughter and endangering the welfare of a child. The court sentenced the parents to a prison term of 2½ to 5 years and a $1000 fine. The parents appealed the conviction and sentence (*Commonwealth,* 718 A.2d at 312).

The Nixon family were members of Faith Tabernacle Church and practiced spiritual treatment rather than seeking medical care. When Shannon Nixon became ill, her parents took her to church and prayed for her. Initially, Shannon improved but became ill again, entered a coma, and died only hours later. The autopsy revealed the new onset of diabetes with complications (*Commonwealth,* 718 A.2d at 312). The appellate court upheld the conviction based on the parents' duty to seek medical treatment for Shannon's life-threatening condition.

During the sentencing phase of the trial, the trial court considered a prior death in the Nixon family. In 1991, the Nixons' 9-year-old child died from complications of an ear infection. The parents were sentenced to 2 years' probation. The appellate court ruled that considering the prior death was proper. The sentence and conviction were upheld (*Commonwealth,* 718 A.2d at 315).

Some states allow, by law, exceptions for religious practice and beliefs. In Ohio, for example, if the "failure to provide treatment is based 'solely in practice of religious beliefs,'" parents are not subject to criminal liability (Ohio, 1997). Courts can mandate treatment but not if death occurs before the court is aware that treatment is needed. The American Academy of Pediatrics (AAP) issued a position statement stating that child neglect occurs when parents or caregivers fail to seek medical care for children, regardless of the motivation (American Academy of Pediatrics, 1997). The AAP argued that justice requires the state to protect all children equally. The AAP opposed any "exemptions from child abuse and neglect laws" when children did not receive medical care (American Academy of Pediatrics, 1997).

Elder Abuse/Neglect

All states mandate reporting of suspected elder abuse or neglect. In one study of homicide in older adults, only 3 of 150 cases were attributed to abuse (Falzon & Davis, 1998). As with other types of homicide in older adults, the most common perpetrators were relatives or acquaintances of the victims (Falzon & Davis, 1998). If an older adult patient seen in the ED is severely dehydrated, is the underlying problem abuse or neglect or a medical problem? Differentiating medical problems from social problems can be difficult. As with children, if the history given by the patient and/or family does not match the patient's physical or mental condition, a thorough investigation should occur before the patient is discharged home.

In addition to a medical history, a social history is invaluable. According to Kleinschmidt (1997), endangered, neglected, or abused older adults typically are from situations where the *caregivers* are dependent on the victim emotionally and/or financially. Asking about living arrangements, financial arrangements, and support from other family or community members may provide significant information. Separating the caregiver from the older adult patient may be necessary to ensure open communication.

Behavior and physical findings should be described in the patient's medical record. Photographs are useful if injuries are obvious. Evidence of malnutrition, dehydration, decubitus ulcers, altered mental status, or unexplained injury requires a thorough investigation. State law dictates which agency should receive a report of elder abuse or neglect.

Domestic Violence

Domestic violence has received increased attention over the past few years. The emergency health care professional is in a pivotal role to identify, counsel, and treat victims of domestic violence. Although there is increased attention, one study indicated that mandatory reporting did not increase referrals to law enforcement authorities (Sachs et al., 1998). Federal and state law addresses domestic violence.

An example of a state law is the Minnesota Domestic Abuse Act (Minn. Stat. § 518B.01). The statute covers family or household members. The definition includes those currently or previously living together, and those involved in "significant romantic or sexual relationships" (Minn. Stat. § 518B.01). Alabama law includes those involved in a common law marriage, relatives, or those with a "child in common" (Ala. Code Ann. § 30-5-2 [1975]).

Photographs of injuries or accurate descriptions in the medical record can help with cases that are prosecuted (Pasqualone, 1996). Detection may be difficult if the patient is not willing to discuss the complete circumstances of the injury.

Nonjudgmental, objective evaluation of any injuries should occur with appropriate referrals to law enforcement agencies.

CONCLUSION

Emergency health care professionals collect evidence from patients, regardless of the patient's legal status, on a regular basis. Although the ED staff should not function as agents of law enforcement, it is important that forensic principles such as identification, chain of custody, and maintaining the integrity of the evidence are followed. Typical situations in which evidence may be required include child abuse, elder abuse, domestic violence, sexual assault, and drug or alcohol impairment. Coroner/medical examiner procedures should be reviewed to ensure that evidence is not destroyed while caring for the patient. Photography is a valuable tool that can aid in the documentation of injuries in any patient where abuse or neglect is suspected.

References

Ala. Code Ann. §§ 32-5A-2, 194 (1975).

American Academy of Pediatrics, Committee on Bioethics: Religious objections to medical care, *Pediatrics* 99:279, 1997.

Ark. Code Ann. § 20-9-303 (Michie 1997).

Carroll v. State, 1996 WL 549097 (Ala. Ct. App., Sept 27, 1996).

Commonwealth v. Nixon, 718 A.2d 311 (Pa. Sup. Ct. 1998).

Falzon AL, Davis GG: A 15 year retrospective review of homicide in the elderly, *J Forensic Sci* 43:371, 1998.

Hohenhaus S: Patterned injury and court testimony in a sexual assault, *J Emerg Nurs* 24:614, 1998a.

Hohenhaus S: Sexual assault: clinical issues. SANE legislation and lessons learned, *J Emerg Nurs* 24:463, 1998b.

Kleinschmidt KC: Elder abuse: a review, *Ann Emerg Med* 31:488, 1997.

Lee G: Death in the workplace, *Am Assoc Occup Health Nurs J* 42:590, 1994.

Mo. Rev. Stat. § 577.020 (Vernon's 1998).

Minnesota Domestic Abuse Act (Minn. Stat. § 518B.01).

Monk M: Interviewing suspected victims of child maltreatment in the emergency department, *J Emerg Nurs,* 24:31, 1998.

Ohio Rev. Code Ann. § 2151.03 (Anderson 1997).

Pasqualone GA: Forensic registered nurses as photographers: documentation in emergency department, *J Psychosoc Nurs Ment Health Serv* 34(10):47, 1996.

Rochin v. California, 342 U.S. 165 (1952).

Runge JW, Pulliam CL, Carter JM, Thomason MH: Enforcement of drunken driving laws in cases involving intoxicated drivers, *Ann Emerg Med* 27:66, 1996.

Sachs CJ, Peek C, Baraff LJ, Hasselblad V: Failure of the mandatory domestic violence reporting law to increase medical facility referral to police, *Ann Emerg Med* 31:488, 1998.

Suttle v. State, 565 So.2d 1197 (Ala. Ct. App. 1990).
Winston v. Lee, 470 U.S. 753 (1985).

Suggested Reading

Aiken M, Speck PM: Forensic considerations for the emergency department, *Tenn Nurse* 59:19, 1996.

Frampton DB: Sexual assault: the role of the advanced practice nurse in identifying and treating victims, *Clin Nurs Spec* 12:177, 1998.

Hoyt CA, Spangler KA: Forensic nursing implications and the forensic autopsy, *J Psychosoc Nurs Ment Health Serv* 34(10):24, 1996.

Ledray LE: SANE development and operation guide, *J Emerg Nurs* 24:197, 1998.

Pozzi CL: Forensic nursing: applications in the occupational setting, *Am Assoc Occup Health Nurs J* 44:550, 1996.

Smith K, Holmseth J, Macgregor M, Letourneau M: Sexual assault response team: overcoming obstacles to program development, *J Emerg Nurs* 24:365, 1998.

Winfrey M: Developing a graduate forensic nursing elective, *J Emerg Nurs* 22:54, 1996.

10

Psychiatric Emergency Care

CHAPTER OUTLINE

Psychiatric patients present special challenges to emergency health care professionals. Limited resources for psychiatric emergency care can lead to holding patients in the emergency department (ED), delays in services, concerns for safety of staff and the patient, and increased focus on liability issues. Patients may arrive with prehospital professionals, law enforcement officers, family members, or alone. The ED personnel must consider what can and should be done to manage a patient with a psychiatric emergency. Unless the patient has legal or medical incapacity, treatment decisions remain the patient's. A diagnosis of mental illness does not mean the patient cannot make decisions (MacArthur Research Network, 1998).

Wyatt v. *Stickney* (1971) was a landmark case related to the rights of the mentally ill. Patients in an Alabama state psychiatric hospital sued the state, alleging violation of their constitutional rights. The court established minimum constitutional standards for the care and treatment of mentally ill patients. The *Wyatt* standards had a dramatic impact on care of the mentally ill throughout the United States. The minimum standards included individual privacy and dignity, least restrictive treatment conditions, visitation and telephone communications, freedom from unnecessary medications, freedom from physical restraint and isolation, and the right to wear and keep personal clothing and possessions that were not dangerous to treatment regimens (*Wyatt,* 325 F. Supp. 781, Appendix A). Although the *Wyatt* standards related specifically to inpatient psychiatric care, the principles apply in the ED. Some states expanded the *Wyatt* standards to require that mentally ill patients receive written notice of their specific rights and notice when rights were denied.

MEDICAL CLEARANCE

Patients who are seen in the ED with a mental illness complaint require a medical clearance examination before psychiatric evaluation. The use of illicit drugs, medical illness, or injury can cause physiological, behavioral, or cognitive changes. It is imperative that behavioral or cognitive changes in patients with mental illness be evaluated to rule out physiological causes. In addition to a thorough history and physical examination, diagnostic tests such as serum blood alcohol levels, urine drug screen, and serum chemistry analysis are useful tools for the emergency physician in formulating a diagnosis.

Patients who ingest drugs in suicide attempts require stabilization and medical therapy before a psychiatric evaluation. Once the patient's condition stabilizes medically, the underlying issues related to the suicide attempt can be addressed. Patients who abuse alcohol and/or other substances often arrive at the ED in an intoxicated state. Liability for emergency health care professionals occurs when patient injuries or illnesses are not discovered. An intoxicated patient with an altered mental status requires close evaluation, observation, and monitoring to detect subtle changes that may relate to a closed-head injury rather than the intoxication. Professional negligence actions can result from improper management of psychiatric patients' medical illnesses and injuries.

INVOLUNTARY COMMITMENT OF PSYCHIATRIC PATIENTS

The process of **involuntary commitment** of psychiatric patients may begin in the ED, although involuntary commitment is a judicial process. In *Montgomery* v. *State* (1996), the police brought a woman to the ED for psychiatric evaluation. The police reported that the woman was running in the road, stopping traffic, and throwing rocks at cars. In the ED, the patient attacked police personnel and ED staff. The woman was admitted for psychiatric evaluation and had a probable cause hearing for involuntary detention. The patient informed the judge that a conspiracy existed between various federal law enforcement agencies to cause a stroke, by electronic means, and that the cars were inhabited by a white supremacist group trying to kill her. The psychiatrist testified that the patient suffered from paranoid psychosis and required inpatient treatment. She was involuntarily committed to the Department of Mental Health and the probate judge's decision was upheld by the appellate court.

Although state law commitment procedures vary, the constitutional minimal protection before involuntary commitment of psychiatric patients to inpatient treatment is **clear and convincing evidence.** Clear and convincing evidence is a higher burden of proof than the preponderance of the evidence standard used in civil cases and a lesser burden than beyond a reasonable doubt used in criminal cases. Clear and convincing evidence can be demonstrated by the following factors:

- The patient is given a diagnosis of mental illness (states may specifically include or exclude substance abuse and alcoholism).
- As a result of mental illness, the individual poses a real and present threat of substantial harm to himself or herself and/or others (there must be a recent overt act, attempt, or threat).
- The patient will, if not treated, continue to suffer mental distress and will continue to experience deterioration of ability to function independently.
- The patient is unable to make a rational and informed decision as to whether or not treatment for mental illness would be desirable.
- Involuntary commitment is the least restrictive alternative available (Ala. Code §§ 22-52-1.1-15 [1975]).

Many states provide for emergency detention of patients before involuntary commitment proceedings in the court. Laws designed for emergency evaluation and treatment of psychiatric patients are procedural protections and should be followed. The Lanterman-Petris-Short Act in California provides for a 72-hour or "5150" **emergency detention.** In California, if a patient is a danger to himself or herself or others or is gravely disabled resulting from mental illness, inebriation, or the use of narcotics, he or she qualifies for a 72-hour hold. A written application is necessary, and the patient must receive oral notice and reason(s) for the detention (Calif. Welfare & Inst. Code § 5157 [1994]). In states that provide for emergency detention, the time may vary from 24 to 72 hours. If a judicial involuntary commitment proceeding is not started within that time, the psychiatric patient must be released (Kentucky, 1988).

Law enforcement officers are often in a difficult position because most states do not allow for confinement in jail for mental illness. South Dakota (1991) specifically allows a peace officer who has probable cause to confine, in jail, for up to 24 hours, someone who is a danger to himself or herself or others as a result of severe mental illness.

Reeves et al. (1998) studied errors in the ED related to involuntary commitment. The medicolegal errors included incomplete documentation of the psychiatric patient's mental status examination, lack of documentation of the specific reason the patient met requirements for involuntary confinement, and the reasons given were not always appropriate for psychiatric patients. Emergency health care professionals should be familiar with the laws related to emergency detention and involuntary commitment to fully comply with the procedural protections granted to patients.

RESTRAINTS

The use of restraints in health care evolved from common use to today's enhanced regulation of restraint use (Rogers & Bocchino, 1999). Federal government regulation includes the Health Care Financing Administration (HCFA) revised Conditions of Participation for Health Care Facilities published in the *Federal Register* in 1999 (HCFA, 1999). The Conditions of Participation established guidelines for the use of restraints in acute-care and psychiatric facilities. The overall standard is that patients have the right to be free from restraint or seclusion and that staff coercion, convenience, retaliation, or discipline are inappropriate reasons for the use of restraints or seclusion. The Joint Commission on Accreditation of Healthcare Organizations' (JCAHO) revised restraint standards for nonpsychiatric patients became effective in January 1999. Restraints, according to JCAHO, should be used only to respond to emergent, dangerous behavior; as an adjunct to planned care; or as a component of an approved protocol (JCAHO, 1999). The use of restraints in the ED requires careful evaluation and monitoring because the patient's underlying problem may not be readily identified initially.

The JCAHO established a "sentinel event" tracking method to encourage health care organizations to voluntarily report critical issues. Over a 2-year period, JCAHO reviewed 20 cases of patients who died while restrained. Most deaths occurred in psychiatric facilities. Death occurred from asphyxiation in 40%(8) of the cases. The remaining patients died from strangulation, cardiac arrest, and fire. The contributing factors, according to JCAHO, were patients who smoke, patients who have physical deformities that make proper application of restraints difficult, patients lying supine or prone, and patients restrained in a room not under continuous observation (JCAHO, 1998b).

The improper use of restraints could lead to allegations of false imprisonment and battery in civil cases. For a discussion of false imprisonment and battery, see Chapter 16. The medical record should clearly reflect the clinical nature of the patient's behavior, the reason for the restraint, the choice of restraints, any notice to the patient, and the documented monitoring and evaluation of the patient while restrained. Some hospitals use flow charts to aid the staff in documenting the monitoring and evaluation of restrained patients (Figure 10-1).

RESTRAINTS FLOW SHEET

Time Placed in Restraints _____ Time MD Ordered Restraints _____ Limited to _____ hrs.

Time Placed in Restraints _____ Time MD Ordered Restraints _____ Limited to _____ hrs.

Time Restraints Wen D'od _____

CODES TO USE FOR DOCUMENTATOIN OF OBSERVATION

1. Shouting / Screening
2. Threatening (Verbal)
3. Resting / Quiet
4. Sleeping
5. Attempting to Leave
6. Confused
7. Self Injury
8. Combative
9. Co-operative
10. Other _____

CODES TO USE FOR DOCUMENTATION OF PT. CARE

A. Check For Adequate Peripheral Circulation q 30 Minutes.
B. Check For Intact Skin.
C. ROM / Reposition as Patient's Condition Requires (at least q 4 hrs)
D. Offer Fluids q 2 hrs (pt. In upright position)
E. Assist With Meals (pt. In upright position)
F. Daily Bath
G. Offer Bathroom Privileges q 2 hrs.
H. Physical Safety Needs (General Welfare)
I. No Intervention Necessary.

Patient Keyplate

Time	Obs	Pt Care	Initial
0715			
0730			
0745			
080			
0815			
0830			
0845			
0900			
0915			
0930			
0945			
1000			
1015			
1030			
1045			
1100			
1115			
1130			
1145			
1200			
1215			
1230			
1245			
1300			

Time	Obs	Pt Care	Initial
1315			
1330			
1345			
1400			
1415			
1430			
1445			
1500			
1515			
1530			
1545			
1600			
1615			
1630			
1645			
1700			
1715			
1730			
1745			
1800			
1815			
1830			
1845			
1900			

Time	Obs	Pt Care	Initial
1915			
1930			
1945			
2000			
2015			
2030			
2045			
2100			
2115			
2130			
2145			
2200			
2215			
2230			
2245			
2300			
2315			
2330			
2345			
2400			
0015			
0030			
0045			
0100			

Time	Obs	Pt Care	Initial
0115			
0130			
0145			
0200			
0215			
0230			
0245			
0300			
0315			
0330			
0345			
0400			
0415			
0430			
0445			
0500			
0515			
0530			
0545			
0600			
0615			
0630			
0645			
0700			

SIGNATURE

NAME	DATE	NAME	DATE
NAME	DATE	NAME	DATE

Figure 10–1 Restraint flow sheet. (Courtesy of Evergreen Medical Center, Evergreen, Alabama. Used with permission.)

Physical Restraints

ED staff are accustomed to the use of physical restraints for protection of patients as well as for control of behavior. Soft extremity restraints or leather four-point restraints may be used. The safety of the patient in physical restraints must take precedence over control of behavior. Proper placement of physical restraints is imperative because death can occur as a complication of improper placement. Before applying physical restraints, emergency health care professionals should evaluate whether the clinical situation justifies the application of restraints (Wigder & Matthews, 1998). If the situation requires restraint, documentation should reflect the appropriate monitoring of the patient.

Seclusion is a form of physical restraint because the patient is involuntarily confined and prevented from leaving an area. Seclusion rooms are rare in the ED unless a large volume of psychiatric patients are routinely evaluated and treated. Seclusion rooms allow the patient to move about freely while confined to a room rather than physical restraint to a gurney or stretcher. Before use of a seclusion room in the ED, a thorough environmental evaluation should be completed to ensure that the secluded patient will not have access to any objects that could be used as weapons against himself or herself or others. Close observation is required once a patient is placed in a seclusion room. As with other types of restraint, seclusion should never be used for punishment or staff convenience.

Chemical Restraints

With the development of pharmacological therapy, options to restrain ED patients with chemicals, rather than physical devices, increased. The same principles apply to chemical restraints as apply to physical restraints. Monitoring of the patient restrained by use of drugs is vital. North Carolina (1999) recognized the use of medication to restrain a patient and specified that medications used to restrain patients were not to be used for punishment, discipline, or staff convenience. Arizona (1994) recognized that pharmacological restraints, as well as seclusion and mechanical restraints, are emergency measures for safety.

Exceptions

Exceptions to restraint practices and policies exist. For example, patients involved in forensic situations who are restrained for security purposes, perhaps by corrections or law enforcement personnel, are usually exempted from a requirement for a physician's order. The documentation in the medical record should include a statement that the restraints are for nonmedical reasons. Other exceptions may be immobilizing devices (arm boards for intravenous catheter stabilization), protective devices (side rails), and orthopedic appliances (casts, splints, or external fixators) and patients dependent on mechanical ventilation. The emergency health care professional must recognize that immobilizing or protective devices could be considered restraints if the patient is limited in movement.

Monitoring

Monitoring of restrained patients is critical. Components of the monitoring combine physiological parameters as well as activities of daily living that the restrained patient cannot do for himself or herself. Peripheral circulation and mental status evaluation should occur at regular intervals. If the restrained patient is combative and resisting the restraints, peripheral circulation and mental status should be monitored more frequently. Meals or supplements, fluids, and elimination needs should be considered routinely. Restraints render patients immobile and therefore position change should occur as with other immobile patients. It is important to rotate restraints to reduce the possibility of injury to extremities. Chemical restraint requires monitoring of the patient's airway status and evaluation for possible drug interactions (Wigder & Matthews, 1998). Chemical restraint is contraindicated for patients who have overdosed because of unreliable patient history and the possibility of drug interactions.

A summary of the requirements related to the use of restraints, as established by HCFA, is provided in Box 10-1.

DUTY TO WARN THIRD PARTIES

Confidentiality is discussed in detail in Chapter 8. It is important to identify the limited circumstances of duty to warn third parties. The landmark case of *Tarasoff* v. *Regents* (1976) identified a duty for a psychotherapist to warn a specific third party of a threat made by a mentally ill patient during the course of treatment. Although attempts have been made to expand *Tarasoff* to other areas, many states limit the requirement to warn a third party only to a serious threat against a victim or victims who are clearly or reasonably identified. New Hampshire (1995) requires a "serious threat of physical violence against clearly identified or reasonably identified victim" and only requires a "reasonable effort" to tell the victim about the threat. The duty to warn third parties extends to those identified by the patient as a specific target. Mental health professionals recognize the difficulty in predicting future violence (Mason, 1998).

BOX 10-1   Standards for Use of Restraint and Seclusion

1. Patient is free from restraint and seclusion unless needed for patient safety.
2. Least restrictive alternative (medical record should reflect least restrictive measures considered) should be used.
3. Restraint is ordered by physician or licensed independent practitioner:
   a. Behavioral: face-to-face evaluation within 1 hour of application
   b. PRN (as-needed) orders not allowed
   c. Time-limited initial orders:
      1. Adults: 4 hours
      2. Adolescents 9 to 17 years of age: 2 hours
      3. Children younger than 9 years of age: 1 hour
   d. Original order can only be renewed up to 24 hours; subsequent orders require examination and evaluation by physician or licensed independent practitioner.
4. Consider patient safety and comfort when selecting restraint.
5. Physical restraint + seclusion are only allowed in combination when
   a. Patient receives one-to-one or continuous face-to-face monitoring, or
   b. Continuous monitoring by audio and video devices when staff are in close proximity to patient
6. Chemical restraint: control behavior or restrict patient's freedom of movement; excludes drugs used as standard treatment for patient's medical or psychiatric condition.
7. Ongoing assessment, intervention, evaluation, and reintervention are critical and should be reflected in the medical record.
8. Direct care staff must receive ongoing training and education.
9. Deaths that occur while patients are restrained or secluded are reported to HCFA; HCFA will track.
10. Hospitals and health care organizations that do not receive federal funds are excluded from HCFA's requirements.

From Health Care Financing Administration, U.S. Dept. of Health and Human Services: *Fed Register* 64:36070, July 2, 1999.

SUICIDE/ATTEMPTED SUICIDE

In *Keebler* v. *Winfield Carraway Hospital* (1988), the police responded to a motel for a man complaining of chest pain. Upon arrival in the ED, an examination revealed a patient suffering from alcohol abuse and possible benzodiazepine abuse. The patient was described in the medical record as being uncooperative and unruly and yelling at hospital staff. A gastric lavage was done as well as charcoal administration. An electrocardiogram was normal. The patient refused to stay in the treatment area, repeatedly talked on the telephone, and was generally belligerent. The staff called the police back to the ED. The patient was advised to cooperate or he would be taken to jail. He was taken to jail. Two hours later, the patient was found hanging from his jail cell door with his T-shirt around his neck. The cause of death was asphyxiation secondary to hanging.

The patient's wife sued the ED physician, nurse, and hospital, claiming negligence. The court said the issue was whether the defendants had a duty to the patient. In answering the question, the court studied the medical record. The focus of the court was the foreseeability that the patient would commit suicide. The court said, "When a physician has undertaken the treatment of a patient whose condition, known to the physician, is such that without continuous or frequent expert attention, he is likely to suffer injurious consequences, he must either render such attention himself or see that some other competent person does so." The court held that there was no duty to the patient because no facts led to foreseeability on the part of the physician or nurses to expect that the patient would commit suicide. The court reviewed the facts: there were no threats of suicide and no history of suicide attempts, and the patient did not come to the ED for a suicide attempt.

The JCAHO studied 65 cases of inpatient suicide over a 2-year period (JCAHO, 1998a). Seventy-five percent of deaths resulted from hanging and 20% from jumping from a roof or window. The use of sitters, one-on-one monitoring, and serious attention to suicide gestures are all recommended measures to prevent suicides in health care facilities. Many patients seek treatment in the ED for suicidal gestures. Although attention-seeking behavior does occur, taking suicidal ideation seriously and making patient safety a priority are some ways to prevent the death of suicidal patients once they reach the health care environment.

Georgia (1999) allows emergency medical service personnel to treat and transport victims of attempted suicide who are in imminent danger of death with or without consent.

ALCOHOL/SUBSTANCE ABUSE

Although the definition of mental illness may exclude alcohol and/or substance abuse, a common occurrence in the ED is the presentation of a patient with mental illness who concomitantly is intoxicated. Some states provide for emergency detention of these types of patients. Iowa (1997), for example, allows emergency detention for an intoxicated person who threatened to, attempted to, or inflicted injury on himself or herself or others. The law also requires a determination that the individual is "likely" to inflict physical harm unless detained or is incapacitated by chemicals. The law recognized that access to the courts should not prevent the treatment of a patient. The individual is entitled to legal counsel and a magistrate can order the individual's release or continued detention.

South Carolina (1998) also allows for emergency admission of chemically dependent adults. Alcohol and drug use are included in the definition of chemical dependency. A written affidavit alleging chemical dependency, substantial risk of harm, and the supporting facts and a statement that the individual "is incapable of exercising judgment concerning emergency care" is required. A licensed physician must certify that the situation requires an immediate response rather than the involuntary commitment process through the courts. New Mexico has a similar statute and sets forth a limit of 5 days (New Mexico, 1978). New York (1993) law prohibits the holding of an intoxicated person in need of emergency treatment longer than 48 hours.

RIGHTS OF PSYCHIATRIC PATIENTS

States codified the rights of the mentally ill. The rights of the mentally ill do not exceed those of other individuals, but societal discrimination led to specific rights being set out in the law. For example, Alabama (1975) set out specific constitutional rights (e.g., free exercise of religion, vote, marry) and added specific rights as a "consumer of mental health services." In addition to maintenance of confidentiality, the law specifies the right to be free from abuse and the right to access mental health services. Mississippi (1999) has similar rights set forth in its laws.

EMERGING ISSUES

An emerging issue in psychiatric emergency care is **psychiatric advance directives.** Wyoming (1999), for example, specifically provides for psychiatric advance directives. The psychiatric advance directive is valid only for 2 years unless reaffirmed. The advance directive can address medication, physical restraint, seclusion, crisis counseling, and administration or refusal of treatment for mental illness.

As patient medical record privacy continues to receive attention, privacy of psychiatric patients' medical records and treatment information will be an ongoing issue.

CONCLUSION

Psychiatric emergency care presents legal as well as medical challenges to the emergency health care provider. Patients who are a threat to themselves or others may require emergency detention, if state law allows, while the involuntary commitment process is started in the courts. Behavioral or cognitive changes or alcohol or substance abuse can lead to violent behavior requiring physical or chemical restraint of patients in the ED. Proper clinical justification, monitoring, and evaluation will lead to a reduction in complications from application of restraints. The mentally ill have specific rights outlined in state and federal laws. The right to individual privacy and dignity is a basic human right regardless of an individual's diagnosis of mental illness. Psychiatric advance directives and privacy of medical and treatment information are emerging issues.

References

Ala. Code §§ 22-52-1.1-15, 22-56-4 (1975).

Ariz. Rev. Stat. Ann. § 36-528 (1994).

Calif. Welf. & Inst. Code §§ 5000, et seq., 5150 (West 1994).

Ga. Code §31-9-8 (1999).

Health Care Financing Administration, U.S. Department of Health and Human Services: Hospitals' conditions of participation, *Fed Register* 64:36070, July 2, 1999.

Iowa Code § 125.91 (1997).

Joint Commission on Accreditation of Healthcare Organizations: Revised restraint standards for non-psychiatric patients, 1999. wwwa.jcaho.org/.

Joint Commission on Accreditation of Healthcare Organizations: Inpatient suicides: recommendations for prevention, *Sentinel Event Alert,* issue 7, Nov 6, 1998a.

Joint Commission of Accreditation of Healthcare Organizations: Preventing restraint deaths, *Sentinel Event Alert,* issue 8, Nov 18, 1998b.

Keebler v. Winfield Carraway Hosp., 531 So.2d 841 (Ala. 1988).

Ky. Rev. Stat. Ann. §202A.031 (Baldwin 1988).

MacArthur Research Network: Executive summary: the MacArthur treatment competence study, 1998. http://ness.sys.virginia.edu/macarthur/treatment98.html. [Accessed 5/5/99].

Mason T: *Tarasoff* liability: its impact for working with patients who threaten others. *Int J Nurs Stud* 35:109, 1998.

Miss. Code Ann. § 41-21-102 (1999).

Montgomery v. State, 685 So.2d 747 (Ala. Ct. App. 1996).

N.H. Rev. Stat. Ann. § 329:31 (1995).

N.M. Stat. Ann. § 43-2-8 (Michie 1978).

N.Y. Ment. Hygiene Law § 21.09 (McKinney, 1993).

N.C. Gen. Stat. §122C-3 (1999).

Reeves RR, Pinkofsky HB, Stevens L: Medicolegal errors in the emergency department related to involuntary confinement of psychiatric patients, *Am J Emerg Med* 16:631, 1998.

Rogers PD, Bocchino NL: Restraint-free care: is it possible? *Am J Nurs* 99(10):26, 1999.

S.C. Code Ann. §§ 44-52-10, 44-52-50 (West 1976).

S.D. Codified Laws Ann. §§ 27A-10-1, 27A-10-3 (1991).

Tarasoff v. Regents of Univ. of Calif., 17 Cal.3d 425, 551 P.2d 334, 131 Cal. Rptr. 14 (1976).

Wigder H, Matthews MS: Restraints, 1998. www.emedicine.com/emerg/topic776.htm.

Wyatt v. Stickney, 325 F. Supp. 781 (M.D. Ala. 1971).

Wyo. Stat. §§ 35-22-301-308 (1999).

Suggested Reading

Allmason AL: Comments: personal liability implications of the duty to warn are hard pills to swallow: from *Tarasoff* to *Hutchinson v. Patel* and beyond, *J Contemp Health Law Policy* 13:471, 1997.

George JE, Quattrone MS, Goldstone M: Suicidal patients: what is the nursing duty to prevent a patient's self-inflicted injuries? *J Emerg Nurs* 22:609, 1996.

MacArthur Research Network on Mental Health and the Law, 1998. http://ness.sys. virginia.edu/macarthur/. [Accessed 5/5/99].

Margolis MR: Do physicians of potentially dangerous patients owe a duty to third parties? June 15, 1998. www.law.uh.edu//healthlawperspectives/Tort/980615DoPhysicians.htm.

Stavis PF, Johnson PW: Informed medical consent for the mentally disabled: a problem in need of a solution. N.Y.S. Commission on Quality of Care, 1999. www.cqc.state.ny.us/ cc22.htm. [Accessed 5/15/99].

11

Laws and Regulations for Special Treatment Centers

CHAPTER OUTLINE

A hospital or other health care facility that holds itself out to the public as offering special services or treatment centers may be held to a higher legal standard of care (see Chapter 17 for a discussion of the standard of care). State law or regulations may or may not specify minimum standards for facilities with specialized services. Special treatment centers range from trauma centers to obstetric services. The Emergency Medical Treatment and Active Labor Act of 1993 requires special treatment centers or hospitals that offer special services to accept patients in transfer if resources are available (42 U.S.C. 1395dd).

State laws and regulations governing the licensing of hospitals, voluntary accreditation through the Joint Commission on Accreditation of Healthcare Organizations, and other mechanisms for ensuring care are not eliminated with special treatment centers. Additional laws and regulations may govern the specialized treatment centers.

TRAUMA CENTERS

The 1966 White Paper, *Accidental Death and Disability in America,* provided a disturbing view of trauma care in the United States (Diehl, 1999). Preventable deaths were high, and trauma care was not coordinated. Trauma centers were part of the effort to regionalize emergency medical services (EMS) in the late 1960s and early 1970s. Some states legislated trauma center requirements and standards.

Iowa (1995) identified a goal of coordinated trauma care with an expected result of a decrease in preventable deaths. A reduction in costs associated with preventable mortality and morbidity was identified in the statute. The Iowa legislature specified that injured persons should have access to "an integrated system of optimal and cost-effective care." Trauma center verification is valid in

Iowa for up to 3 years. The statute required a trauma registry to monitor the effectiveness of the trauma system. Confidentiality of records is provided for in the statute so that trauma registry data are reported in the aggregate and individual patient information is not disclosed.

Washington (1992) included trauma systems in EMS legislation. The trauma care system legislation addressed prevention, prehospital care, hospital care, and rehabilitation. The law also defined the different levels of trauma services for pediatrics, adults, and rehabilitation. Wyoming (1997) addressed trauma designation and the system of trauma care in the state. Prevention was incorporated into the Wyoming statute, requiring an identification of causes of trauma and proposed programs to prevent death and disability from trauma. New Hampshire (1995) established a trauma medical review committee to evaluate the trauma care system throughout the state.

North Dakota (1997) specified the trauma system components required in that state. The legislature identified a need for a system plan that addressed prehospital care, hospital standards, data collection in a trauma registry, and a trauma quality improvement plan (Box 11-1).

Nevada (1998) identified trauma system requirements and designated the State Board of Health as the appropriate body to designate trauma centers. Nevada specified in statute that the conditions for continuing designation as a trauma center were (1) admission of any injured person who required medical care, (2) qualified physicians to care for trauma patients, and (3) maintenance of hospital standards established by regulation.

Florida (1994) defined the levels of state-approved trauma centers. Maps to trauma centers, identification of the levels of trauma centers, and contact information is available on the website for the Florida chapter of the American College of Surgeons (Florida Chapter, ACS, 1997).

BOX 11-1 North Dakota Trauma System Components

1. System plan
2. Prehospital care
3. Hospitals: standards
   a. Designation
   b. Redesignation
   c. Dedesignation
   d. Quality improvement plans
   e. Qualification for personnel
4. Trauma registry
5. Trauma quality improvement plan

From N.D. Cent. Code §23-01.2-.01 (1997).

The American College of Surgeons (ACS) provides a voluntary trauma verification and consultation program (ACS, 1999b). ACS evaluates the training and capability of the facilities and personnel, as well as quality monitoring. Hospitals in states that do not have legislated trauma system criteria may voluntarily proceed with ACS verification to ensure that the standards for trauma centers are maintained. An ongoing self-assessment is required as part of the ACS verification process. Pennsylvania has a voluntary program of ACS verification for Level I and Level II trauma centers (Pennsylvania Trauma Systems Foundation, 1999).

BURN CENTERS

The American Burn Association (ABA) and ACS developed a burn verification and consultation program. As with trauma verification, the verification of a burn center is voluntary in those states that do not legislate burn center criteria or standards. The burn verification program evaluates the systems approach to burn care with evaluation of personnel and facilities, and the ongoing self-assessment of the program. The 1997 publication *Guidelines for the Operation of Burn Centers* established criteria by which a facility can measure itself against a national standard (ACS, 1999a).

PEDIATRIC CENTERS

The 1990s brought the care of children to the forefront. Tennessee (1998) addressed emergency care for children by legislating issues associated with facility personnel, equipment, and continuing education. In addition, an annual report to the legislature on the status of emergency care for children was required.

Traumatic injury in the pediatric population is generally addressed by statute in those states with trauma legislation. In states without trauma legislation, the care of children may not be addressed specifically except through licensure or accreditation processes.

HEART OR CHEST PAIN CENTERS

In the 1990s, some hospitals developed a new marketing strategy—advertising heart centers or chest pain centers. The use of thrombolytic agents and advances in interventional procedures in the patient with an acute myocardial infarction brought a different focus to the care of the cardiac patient. The concept of the Golden Hour of trauma care was transferred to the care of patients with chest pain. "Time is muscle" became the phrase for managing patients with chest pain. Attempts to educate the public about prompt evaluation of chest pain stimulated some facilities to market their cardiac services directly to the public.

Legislation did not occur to address chest pain or cardiac centers, and no mechanism of verification exists at the time of this writing. As a result, facilities that advertise themselves as heart centers or chest pain centers may not be governed by regulation other than licensure and accreditation processes. However, a facility that holds itself out as offering the special service of cardiac care and that advertises prompt evaluation by cardiology physicians and specially trained staff should consider an internal mechanism to identify standards of care. An internal evaluation of the program should also occur through a self-assessment process. Advertising a facility as a chest pain center without changing any procedures, using the same staff without additional training, and designating a room in the emergency department as a "chest pain center" without immediate and prompt access to specialty physicians could lead to legal difficulties. A patient who chooses one hospital over another because of advertising of special cardiac services has a higher expectation of what should occur. The risks of voluntarily assuming a community position that special services are available should be legally evaluated and not just evaluated based on market share.

OBSTETRICAL CARE

Obstetrical care is a specialized service not always available. The dearth of hospitals offering obstetrical care reached a nadir in the mid-1980s as a malpractice crisis loomed throughout the United States. Obstetrical care is a high-risk endeavor because of the significant ramifications of adverse outcomes to the pregnant woman and fetus. Wrongful death cases and professional negligence cases are common in obstetrics. Categorization of care of obstetrical patients and neonatal patients is common. Obstetrics and neonatal intensive care units for high-risk patients are generally identified on a regional basis. State licensing regulations should be consulted to identify the requirements of varying levels of obstetric care.

CONCLUSION

Specialized treatment centers may have specific laws and regulations governing designation, identification, and components of patient care. In situations of specialized services without laws, facilities may hold themselves out to the public as offering special services. Voluntary assumption of specialized services and advertising to the public should be legally evaluated. Specialized treatment centers and the regulation of such services are likely to continue into the 21st century.

References

American College of Surgeons: ABA and ACS burn verification and consultation. (online). 1999. www.facs.org/about_college/.

American College of Surgeons: ACS trauma verification and consultation. (online). 1999. www.facts.org/about_college/acsdept/trauma_dept/ntdbacst.html.

Diehl D: The emergency medical services program. In Issacs SL, Knickman JR, editors: *To improve health and health care 2000: The Robert Wood Johnson Foundation anthology.* San Francisco, 1999, Jossey-Bass.

Emergency Medical Treatment and Active Labor Act. 42 U.S.C. § 1395dd (1993).

Fla. Stat. Ann. ch. 395.401 (Harrison 1994).

Florida Chapter, ACS: Florida trauma centers (online). 1997. www.facts.org/chapters/florida/fcot/centers.htm.

Iowa Code Ann. § 147A-21 et seq. (West 1995).

Nev. Rev. Stat. Ann. § 450B.237 (Michie 1998).

N. H. Rev. Stat. Ann. § 151-B:7a (1995).

N. D. Cent. Code § 23-01.2-.01 (1997).

Pennsylvania Trauma Systems Foundation: Pennsylvania trauma systems (online). 1999. www.patraumasystemsfdn.com/html.

Tenn. Code Ann. § 68-11-251 (1998).

Wash. Rev. Code § 70.168.015 (30) (1992).

Wyo. Stat. § 35-1-801 through 805 (1997).

12

Emergency Medical Treatment and Active Labor Act (EMTALA)

CHAPTER OUTLINE

Congress originally enacted the Emergency Medical Treatment and Active Labor Act (EMTALA) in 1986 as part of the Consolidated Omnibus Budget Reconciliation Act (COBRA). Amendments to the law occurred on a regular basis. Initially known as COBRA, the current acronym for the federal patient antidumping law is EMTALA (42 U.S.C. §1395dd).

In the early 1980s, media reports of patients denied treatment or transfer of patients from emergency departments (EDs) because of "negative wallet biopsies" appeared. Hospitals were, in effect, accused of "dumping" patients in unstable conditions who were unfunded, uninsured, or poor (Wood, 1999). Public hospitals and citizen groups lobbied to prevent the transfer of patients solely on the basis of medical indigence or inability to pay. Patients in active labor were included in the initial media reporting as well as in the lobbying efforts.

The estimated total number of ED visits in the United States in 1997 was 97 million, with approximately 1.7 million patient transfers (Nourjah, 1999). ED patients and patients in labor and delivery evaluated for active labor come under the umbrella of EMTALA initially. EMTALA imposes a federal duty on hospitals that receive federal funds to initially screen ED and active labor patients. The Office of the Inspector General (OIG) and the Health Care Financing Administration (HCFA) increased their enforcement efforts over the past 2 to 3 years. The first EMTALA case decided by the U.S. Supreme Court occurred in early 1999 (*Roberts* v. *Galen of Va., Inc.,* 1999).

DEFINITIONS IN THE LAW

EMTALA established specific definitions to ensure consistency in enforcement. Yet, some of the most important situations are not clearly defined in the law, and courts are left to interpret meanings. EMTALA mandates that any individual who arrives at the ED seeking emergency care or is in active labor is entitled to receive a **medical screening examination** (MSE), within the hospital's capability, to determine whether an emergency medical condition exists. The meaning of the terms, identified either in the statutes, regulations, or case law follows. The process is displayed in Figure 12-1.

Any individual: The individual patient, parent or legal guardian of a minor, or guardian or custodian of an incompetent person. The emergency health care provider should note that the individual's status as a citizen, legal alien, or illegal alien is not addressed in the statutory language.

Who comes to the emergency department: Initial challenges to COBRA/EMTALA attempted to specify exactly when an individual "came to" the ED. For example, in an early case, *Johnson* v. *University of Chicago Hospitals* (1992), an infant was en route to the hospital in an ambulance. The hospital base station telemetry nurse diverted the patient to another hospital. The infant was transferred from the original receiving hospital and ultimately died of her medical illness. The infant's mother sued the base station hospital under EMTALA for diverting the infant. The appellate court ruled that the patient had not come to the ED for purposes of EMTALA because the patient never arrived on hospital property. The court stated that, "a hospital-owned telemetry system is distinct from that same hospital's ER" (*Johnson,* p. 232, 1992).

Case law and recent regulations make distinctions for prehospital patients based on ownership of the ambulance. The current law is that if a patient is in a hospital-owned ambulance, the patient has come to the ED for purposes of EMTALA analysis. If the hospital does not own the ambulance, helicopter, or airplane, the patient has not "come to the emergency department." Case law and regulations also specify that the individual is not required to enter the hospital through the ED in order for EMTALA to apply. The individual may enter through any door and into any part of the hospital, including property outside the walls of the hospital, for EMTALA to apply. The implication is that all hospital personnel should receive training and education regarding EMTALA to ensure that the hospital's responsibilities under the law are met.

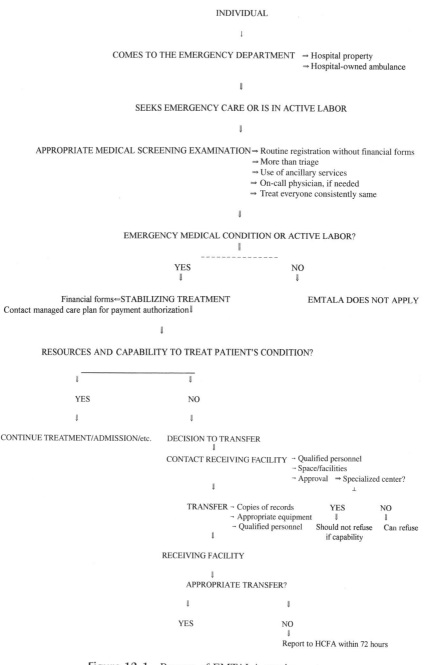

Figure 12-1 Process of EMTALA requirements.

And requests examination or treatment: EMTALA does not apply if the individual is not seeking emergency care. The emergency health care professional should be cautious not to force care on individuals. An individual does not have to use magic words to request emergency care. For example, an individual who is seen by the ED triage nurse and says, "I need to see a doctor" is obviously seeking care. In urban areas, where several hospitals may be in close proximity, individuals may present to an unintended ED. For example, if a parent thinks he or she brought his or her child to a pediatric ED but inadvertently comes to an adjoining or nearby adult ED, is the parent "seeking emergency care" from the adult ED? What is the adult ED's obligation to the patient? The prudent approach is to offer an MSE. If the patient or parent refuses the MSE, documentation of the refusal should occur.

Or is in active labor: EMTALA may or may not apply to the pregnant woman who comes to the ED requesting obstetrical care. EMTALA applies only to active labor situations. However, if the hospital's obstetrical area is not in the ED or is totally unavailable, the ED staff may or may not know if the patient is in active labor until evaluation by the obstetrical staff. The prudent approach is to treat all pregnant women who come to the hospital seeking care as if they are in active labor.

Hospital must provide an appropriate: EMTALA creates a hospital's duty to each individual who seeks care in an ED or a hospital-owned ambulance. In *Cleland* v. *Bronson Health Care Group, Inc.* (1990), the court referred to "appropriate" as "one of the most wonderful weasel words in the dictionary." Neither the law nor the regulations identify "appropriate." Cases brought under EMTALA related to "appropriate" are numerous. One measure of appropriateness, for EMTALA analysis, is that all patients with same or similar problems are treated equally. In *Cleland* (1990), the appellate court indicated that reasons other than indigence could lead to substandard attention: race, gender, ethnicity, disapproval of the individual's occupation, politics, or culture, and distaste for the patient's condition *(Cleland,* p. 272, 1990).

Some patients attempt to bring EMTALA claims after an adverse patient outcome. Cases are often brought alleging both an EMTALA violation and professional negligence. The federal law does not preempt or supersede professional negligence law. Neither is EMTALA a replacement for state professional negligence laws. An EMTALA violation could occur without injury to the patient unlike state professional negligence laws that require proof of injury or damages. If personal injury to the patient occurs, EMTALA damages are based on the individual state's personal injury damages.

Medical screening examination: The hospital is required to use available resources to conduct an MSE. The law does not specify who can or should perform the MSE. If someone other than a physician conducts the MSE (e.g., a physician assistant, nurse practitioner, or registered nurse), the governing body of the hospital and medical staff should incorporate language into documents (e.g., meeting minutes, bylaws) designating who has the responsibility for performing MSEs. Although the MSE will vary depending on the individual's presenting complaint and symptoms, consistency in the MSE is important should a challenge occur under EMTALA. Triage does not suffice as an MSE. **Triage** is the process of sorting patients based on complaint, assessment, and initial evaluation of acuity. The MSE, on the other hand, is a more comprehensive evaluation to determine if an emergency medical condition exists. The hospital is required, under EMTALA, to use available ancillary services and on-call physician consultation during the MSE, if needed, to determine the presence of an emergency medical condition.

A Louisiana EMTALA case, *Marshall* v. *East Carroll Parish* (1998), raised a question about the MSE. A 15-year-old minor arrived in the ED for evaluation of her failure to communicate. She was evaluated and discharged home. She was taken to a different ED later the same day, and the diagnosis was a cerebrovascular accident (CVA) caused by a left middle cerebral artery infarction. The EMTALA allegations were that the minor did not receive an appropriate MSE, and the hospital failed to stabilize her condition before discharge home. The plaintiff submitted an affidavit of a licensed practical nurse (LPN) to support the allegations that the ED physician did not perform an appropriate MSE. The Fifth Circuit reviewed case law and reiterated that an appropriate MSE is judged by whether it was applied equally to patients with similar symptoms, not whether an accurate diagnosis of the patient's illness occurred. The appellate court reviewed the LPN's affidavit although the court questioned whether the LPN was competent to compare Marshall's symptoms and treatment to those of other patients. The court found no genuine issue of material fact and upheld the summary judgment in favor of the hospital.

EMTALA specifies that an MSE should not be delayed to determine a patient's financial status (42 U.S.C. 1395dd[h]).

To determine whether an emergency medical condition exists: The law defines an **emergency medical condition** as acute symptoms of sufficient severity, including severe pain, such that the absence of immediate medical attention would reasonably result in serious jeopardy to the health of the individual, serious impairment of bodily functions, or serious dysfunction of any bodily organ or part. If the patient is pregnant and is having contractions, an emergency medical condition exists if a safe transfer cannot be effected before delivery or a transfer poses a threat to the health or safety of the woman or unborn child (42 U.S.C. 1395dd[e]). Thus the MSE should be sufficiently thorough to detect medical problems that can produce serious consequences to the patient. Severe pain, although identified in the law as a component of an emergency medical condition evaluation, is not quantified in the law. Confusion exists among emergency health care professionals and patients as to the meaning of severe pain. Using a rating scale, for example, if the pain is "rated" as a 5 on a scale of 1 to 10, with 10 being severe, the emergency health care professional may have an indication about how bad the patient perceives the pain, but does nothing to quantify the pain for purposes of classifying "severe pain" under EMTALA. If a patient complains of "severe pain" but has no discernible physiologic signs of a pain response, EMTALA may still apply.

Stabilization or transfer? If the patient has an emergency medical condition, the hospital must provide stabilization or transfer (42 U.S.C. § 1395dd[b]). **Stabilize** means the provision of medical treatment for the patient's condition to ensure "within reasonable medical probability" that the patient's condition will not materially deteriorate as a result from or during transfer (42 U.S.C. § 1395dd[e][3][A]-[B]). **Transfer** is the movement of an individual outside the hospital facilities. Transfer includes the discharge of the individual but excludes patients declared dead or who leave without permission of the hospital staff (42 U.S.C. § 1395dd[e][4]).

If the patient's condition is not stabilized, a transfer can occur under the following circumstances: (1) the patient or a family member on the patient's behalf requests the transfer; (2) the physician certifies that the benefits of transfer outweigh the risks; (3) if the physician is not physically available, a qualified medical person certifies, after consultation with the physician, that the benefits of transfer outweigh the risks; or (4) transfer is effected with appropriate equipment and qualified personnel. If the patient has an emergency medical condition and does not request a transfer and the hospital has the capacity to treat the emergency medical condition, stabilization and treatment should occur without a transfer.

HOSPITAL AND PHYSICIAN ROLES

Hospital

The hospital is required to post a notice to individuals outlining its responsibilities under EMTALA. The hospital is required to maintain a log of patient transfers for use by surveyors or investigators. The law requires that the hospital ascertain specific information before a transfer—availability of resources at the receiving hospital, acceptance by a receiving physician, and transport with the appropriate equipment and personnel. The hospital is also required to send the patient's medical records, including the result of the MSE and laboratory and x-ray results, to the receiving hospitals. Records of patient transfers must be kept for a period of at least 5 years. Figure 12-2 is an example of a transfer record.

The issue of medical records was present in *Dickey* v. *Baptist Hospital* (1998), a Mississippi EMTALA case. ED physicians discovered Dickey had a mass in his right lung during an evaluation for chest pain. Dickey requested a transfer to the Veterans' Administration (VA) Hospital for follow-up care. It was undisputed that the ED physician contacted the medical officer of the day at the VA in Memphis to request a transfer of Dickey. The radiology report was not sent to the VA, and a dispute existed about the actual radiographs (or copies) being sent. The ED record indicated a finding of a mass in Dickey's right lung. Radiographs repeated at the VA did not reveal the mass, and 15 months later, Dickey received a diagnosis of lung cancer. He died within 4 years of the initial questionable x-ray study. The EMTALA portion of the suit was dismissed as time-barred. Dickey's state law claim for professional negligence in failing to transfer the records was considered during an appeal of a summary judgment.

Expert witnesses testified that it was customary to send copies of radiographs and x-ray reports (if available) as well as a copy of the medical record to the receiving hospital once a patient was transferred. The appellate court overturned the summary judgment, finding a "genuine issue of material fact" in whether the hospital exercised ordinary and reasonable care. The case was sent back to the trial court. The dissenting opinion discussed the difference between communicating pertinent information and sending records.

Receiving hospitals that have specialized centers such as burn centers or trauma centers are required to accept transfers if the resources are available to care for the patient. Resources include available beds and personnel (42 U.S.C. § 1395dd[c][2]).

Hospitals are required to report inappropriate transfers to HCFA within 72 hours. Although an investigation may require more than 72 hours to determine the facts and circumstances surrounding a transfer, the report of a transfer that might be inappropriate cannot end without some form of investigation.

Transferring Physician

The transferring physician is required to certify that the benefits of transfer outweigh the risks. The physician is required to stabilize the patient's condition before transfer. Whether or not stabilization occurred before the transfer is also the basis for legal disputes. Contacting the physician at the receiving hospital is routinely done to ensure that the receiving physician is available and has the

NURSING DEPARTMENT
TRANSFER FORM

Address-O-Graph

Facility transferring to: _____

Name of physician accepting patient: _____

Name of physician referring patient: _____

Diagnosis: _____

Mode of Transport   ____ Ambulance   ____ Helicopter   ____ Private Vehicle

Level of Care   ____ EMT I - Basic (BLS)

                                     ____ EMT II - Intermediate (BLS, IV Fluids, Cardiac Monitor, Defibrillation)

____ Not Applicable   ____ EMT P - Paramedic, RN, or MD (ALS, Medications, Critical IV drips)

Criteria (Check all that Apply & Fill in Blanks)

___ Patient has been stabilized   ___ Patient has not been stabilized   ___ Patient is in labor   ___ Consent form signed

___ Copies of the medical record sent with patient ___ Copy of this form sent with patient

___ **Receiving facility has space, Verified with:**_____ **By:**_____ (House Supervisor)

Report called to _____ (Receiving Nurse) **Time:**_____ **By:**_____

PHYSICIAN TRANSFER CERTIFICATION

Summary of risks and benefits of transfer: _____

_____

Did any on-call physician refuse to attend the patient in a reasonable time? _____ If so, name, address, and phone
number of physician. _____

I certify that based upon the information available, the medical benefits reasonably expected from medical treatment at
another medical facility outweigh the risks of transfer of the patient (and in the case of pregnancy, to the unborn child).

_____   Date: _____
Signature of Physician (Physician must sign at time of transfer if available, otherwise countersign after transfer)

_____   Date: _____
Signature of Qualified Medical Person (Required only if Physician does not sign at the time of transfer)

White Copy - Medical Record / Pink - Patient / Yellow - Nursing Supervisor

Figure 12-2 Nursing department transfer form. (Courtesy Evergreen Medical Center, Evergreen, Alabama. Used with permission.)

resources to continue the patient's care. The transferring physician is usually responsible for determining the mode of transport for the patient. Transfer orders are given to the transporting personnel to provide guidance during the transport of the patient from one facility to another.

Receiving Physician

The receiving physician has no duty under EMTALA other than to accept patients if adequate resources are available and the hospital has specialized services. If a suspected inappropriate transfer occurs, the receiving hospital is obligated to notify HCFA. The receiving physician may choose to notify HCFA as well. Receiving physicians in tertiary care centers with burn centers, trauma centers, pediatric centers, or other specialized care should understand the potential violation of EMTALA if a transfer is refused.

TRANSPORT

Once a decision is reached that a patient should be transferred, the physician should determine the mode of transport and level of personnel needed to effectuate a safe transport (42 U.S.C. § 1395dd[c][2][D]).

Mode

Patients may be transferred by ground or air. Ground modes of transport include private automobile or ground ambulance. Aeromedical transport could involve helicopter or fixed-wing service. Factors such as transport time, the time the patient is out of a controlled environment, and rapid transport to definitive care are concerns when selecting a mode of transport (Boyko, 1994). For example, a helicopter may take longer to get to the patient, but the transport time may be less than that for ground transport. The weather conditions both at the helicopter base and the receiving hospital may have an impact on the mode of transport selected. A fixed-wing transport requires ambulance transport from the hospital to the airport and the reverse at the destination. EMTALA does not specify the mode of transport but requires that transfer should occur with "appropriate equipment." The mode of transport and the capability of the transfer equipment and personnel are vital to a safe transfer.

Personnel

The patient's condition should dictate the "qualified personnel" who accompany the patient during the transfer. A first assessment is whether the patient requires medical personnel at all during the transfer. Some patients could transfer from one facility to another by private automobile accompanied by family members. Other patients may require helicopter transport with a physician on board. Basic life support versus advanced life support is an issue. The scope of practice of emergency medical technicians, registered nurses, and physicians should be taken into consideration when the decision is made about who needs to accompany the patient during the transfer.

PENALTIES FOR VIOLATIONS

The penalties available to HCFA to sanction hospitals and physicians range from civil monetary penalties to administrative sanctions such as removal of the individual's or facilities' provider status with government programs such as Medicare and Medicaid.

Negligent violation results in civil monetary penalties of not more than $50,000 for hospitals with more than 100 beds and $25,000 for hospitals with fewer than 100 beds. The penalty is for *each* violation. If the physician, including the on-call physician, negligently violates EMTALA, the penalty is not more than $50,000 per violation. If the conduct is gross, flagrant, or repeated, the physician may be excluded from participation as a Medicare or Medicaid provider.

In *Cherukuri* v. *HHS* (1999), a general surgeon appealed a judgment of $100,000 imposed upon him by the Secretary of Health and Human Services for alleged violations of EMTALA. Dr. Cherukuri was the on-call general surgeon for a small rural hospital in Kentucky on the night that five motor vehicle crash patients arrived in the ED. Dr. Cherukuri responded to the ED and evaluated all five patients. Two of the five patients had brain injuries, and the hospital did not have the capability or resources to perform neurosurgery. The technical question before the Sixth Circuit Court of Appeals was whether Dr. Cherukuri violated EMTALA's stabilization provisions because he did not perform surgery to stop internal abdominal bleeding before the transfer of the two patients with brain injuries and did not receive express consent to transfer from the physicians at the receiving trauma center 1½ hours away (by ground transport). After an administrative enforcement action and a levied fine of $100,000, Dr. Cherukuri appealed.

The case involved testimony from medical experts that supported the transfer and Dr. Cherukuri's stabilization efforts while other medical experts supported the government's position that the patients were improperly stabilized and transferred. The relevant reported facts were that the anesthesiologist refused to anesthetize the patients because intracranial pressure monitoring was not available, the two patients' blood pressures were stabilized, Dr. Cherukuri contacted the trauma surgeon at the receiving hospital and was advised to operate on the patients before transfer, helicopter transport was not available because of weather conditions, and both patients were transferred without a deterioration in their medical conditions.

The receiving hospital and trauma surgeon contacted the government to report an inappropriate transfer. The receiving surgeon, after reviewing the facts presented, testified that Dr. Cherukuri had no choice but to transfer and did what was in the patients' best interests. The focus of the case was the interpretation of "stabilize" under EMTALA. The Sixth Circuit Court of Appeals indicated that "stabilize" under EMTALA required a "flexible standard of reasonableness that depends on the circumstances" (*Cherukuri,* ¶ 30). The Sixth Circuit cited *Bryant* v. *Rectors & Visitors of the University of Virginia* (1996), a Fourth Circuit Court of Appeals' decision that described stabilize as "a relative concept that depends on the situation." The Sixth Circuit court set aside the administrative findings and fine against Dr. Cherukuri.

A different result occurred in *Burditt* v. *U.S. Department of Health & Human Services* (1991). The physician transferred a severely hypotensive patient in active labor. A $20,000 fine was imposed on the physician and upheld by the Fifth Circuit Court of Appeals.

If the patient is injured as a result of an EMTALA violation, he or she may sue the hospital for damages. The amount of damages available to the injured party is governed by individual state personal injury law. There is no private cause of action, under EMTALA, against a physician.

STATE LAWS

EMTALA is a federal statute that preempts or supersedes state law when a direct conflict occurs between the two sets of law. Some states have laws governing the evaluation, stabilization, and transfer of patients. Florida (1994), for example, has a statute in place governing access to emergency care. The Florida statute, as that of other states, closely tracks EMTALA requirements. Any fines collected for violation of the state statute in Florida are deposited into a fund for public medical assistance.

New York law was the basis for action in *People* v. *Anyakora* (1993). A physician was charged with refusing to treat a patient in need of emergency medical treatment, falsifying a business record, and tampering with physical evidence. A patient in active labor was brought to the obstetrical area of a New York hospital. The physician refused to evaluate the patient, and emergency medical service providers assisted with the delivery of the neonate approximately 50 minutes after arrival. Hospital staff did not assist. There was evidence that the physician falsified records to "cover up" his refusal to treat the patient. The state statute allowed criminal sanctions against a provider who refused to treat patients in need of emergency medical care. The defendant's motion to dismiss was denied. EMTALA was also probably violated.

EMERGING ISSUES

A Special Advisory Bulletin issued jointly by OIG and HCFA on November 10, 1999, addressed EMTALA requirements for managed care enrollees (*Fed Register* 64:61353). Issues addressed in the Bulletin were dual staffing, prior authorization, financial concerns, voluntary withdrawal, and dealing with patient inquiries. Dual staffing raised concerns but was not a per se violation of EMTALA. (*Fed Register* 64:61354). Prior authorization requirements in hospital contracts with managed care plans may lead to violations of EMTALA. The OIG/HCFA stated that the managed care plan can be contacted for payment authorization once stabilizing treatment is underway (*Fed Register* 64:61354).

Financial forms, including advance beneficiary notices, should not be given to patients until stabilizing treatment is under way. General registration procedures can occur, but asking the patient to sign financial forms may, according to OIG/HCFA, deter the patient from staying for treatment or cause a delay in care. If the patient inquires about payment or financial obligations, only "qualified" individuals should answer such inquiries. The Bulletin provides no definition of what constitutes qualifications of individuals who answer financial questions raised by patients. Voluntary withdrawals or "left without being seen" are of concern to OIG/HCFA. The burden is on the hospital to show it took the appropriate steps to encourage the patient to stay for the MSE or treatment he or she was entitled to.

CONCLUSION

EMTALA is a federal statute that prohibits patient dumping. Individuals who come to the ED are entitled to an MSE to determine whether an emergency medical condition exists. If an emergency medical condition exists and is beyond the resources and capabilities of the hospital, a transfer may be necessary. Patient transfers, according to EMTALA, should be done only after stabilizing treatment has begun and after the receiving hospital accepts the patient in transfer. Records, logs, and other means of documenting the transfer records of patients should be maintained for at least 5 years. Delays in the MSE should not occur while financial inquiries are made.

References

Boyko SM: Interfacility transfer guidelines: an easy reference to help hospitals decide on appropriate vehicles and staffing for transfers, *J Emerg Nurs* 20:18, 1994.
Bryant v. Rectors & Visitors of the Univ. of Virginia, 95 F.3d 349, 352 (1996).
Burditt v. U.S. Dept. Health & Human Serv., 934 F.2d 1362 (5th Cir. 1991).
Cherukuri v. HHS, 1999 FED App. 0160P (6th Cir. 1999).
Cleland v. Bronson Health Care Grp., Inc., 917 F.2d 266, 271 (6th Cir. 1990).

Dickey v. Baptist Memorial, 1998 FED App. 60681 (5th Cir. 1998).

Examination and treatment for emergency medical conditions and women in labor. 42 U.S.C. § 1395dd (1998).

Fla. Stat. Ann. ch. 395.1041 (Harrison 1994).

Johnson v. Univ. of Chicago Hosp., 982 F.2d 230 (7th Cir. 1992).

Marshall v. East Carroll Parish, 1998 FED App. 30592 (5th Cir. 1998).

Nourjah P: National hospital ambulatory medical care survey: 1997 emergency department summary. *Advance Data: Centers for Disease Control and Prevention/ National Center for Health Statistics,* No. 304, 1999.

Office of Inspector General and Health Care Financing Administration: OIG/HCFA special advisory bulletin on the patient anti-dumping statute, *Fed Register* 64:61353, Nov 10, 1999.

People v. Anyakora, 616 N.Y.S.2d 149 (Sup. Ct. 1993).

Roberts v. Galen of Va., Inc., 525 U.S. 249 (1999).

Wood J: COBRA laws, 1999. http://emedicine.com/emerg/topic737.htm.

13

Advanced Health Care Professionals in Emergency Care

James T. Noland, CRNP, MSN, CEN

CHAPTER OUTLINE

The delivery of services within the health care industry is continually changing. Before the health care system can adjust to one major change, another one occurs. Managed care is a major driving force behind the change taking place in today's health care system. Streamlining, downsizing, and restructuring of services are flattening organizational charts. Managed care is forcing hospital administrators, nurse executives, and physicians to seek alternative methods for delivering cost-efficient high-quality health care. Among the newest health care professions are nurse practitioners (NP), certified nurse midwives (CNM), certified registered nurse anesthetists (CRNA), clinical nurse specialists (CNS), case managers (CM), and physician assistants (PA). This chapter does not address certified nurse midwives or certified registered nurse anesthetists.

NURSE PRACTITIONER
Practice Settings

The **nurse practitioner** (NP) is a masters prepared advanced-practice nurse with a broad scope of practice involving nursing and medical management (Betancourt et al., 1996). Dr. Henry Silver and nurse Loretta Ford developed the first NP program at the University of Colorado in the 1960s. Silver and Ford empowered nurses with advanced skills, knowledge, and training so that children in underserved and impoverished areas of Colorado would have access to health care (Edmunds & Havens, 1994). Since the mid-1960s, the autonomy, independence, and practice setting of NPs have continually evolved. NPs practice in every health care setting from the armed forces to inpatient tertiary care centers; managing acute and chronic health problems with appropriate referral for complex illnesses. Inpatient areas of practice include hospital-based clinics, such as trauma clinics, and surgery clinics, rehabilitation units, intensive care units, transport teams, and emergency departments (EDs). NPs are certified in areas such as adult health, family, pediatrics, gerontology, women's health, and neonatal. NPs may also be certified in areas of primary care and acute care (New Jersey State Nurses Association, 1998).

Practice Regulations

NPs must have legal authorization to practice. The state board of nursing grants the authorization to practice. Each state, under the state nurse practice act, establishes the requirements for NPs (National Council State Boards of Nurses, 1997). Most states require certification in the specialty area of practice. NPs obtain national certification through a nationally recognized professional organization. The American Nurses Credentialing Center (ANCC) is an example of such a professional organization. The ANCC outlines the minimum criteria an individual must meet before taking a certification examination.

Once the certification process is complete and the NP is credentialed, some jurisdictions require a collaborative practice agreement between a physician and the NP (Table 13-1). The collaborative practice agreement is a legally binding document that defines the specific parameters of NP functions, types of patients seen, procedures performed, when consultation is needed, and arrangements for emergency care. Under the collaborative practice model, the physician serves to direct and guide the NP's performance while allowing autonomy of practice. The state nurse practice acts that require collaborative practice agreements provide specific parameters that must be included (National Council State Boards of Nursing, 1997). For example, in Alabama, a physician is not required to be on site while an NP is working. However, there must be a mechanism in place for immediate consultation with the collaborating physician should the need arise. In addition, there must be a defined mechanism by which the collaborating physician conducts chart reviews of patients seen and treated by the NP (Alabama Board of Nursing, 1999).

Role Autonomy

Independent, self-directed, autonomous practice allows NPs to orchestrate multidisciplinary services for clients with a variety of health care needs. Since the inauguration of the NP role, numerous studies validated the effectiveness of NPs enhancing role autonomy. All 50 states have different laws focusing on traditional issues such as prescriptive authority, limited physician supervision, and other autonomy measures. Most states allow NPs to prescribe under a physician's supervision or through collaborative efforts. A number of states permit prescriptive authority without direct physician involvement. Table 13-1 summarizes all 50 states in terms of prescribing authority and the requirements for entry-level practice. A comprehensive study of state NP authority related to access, use, and distribution of drug samples was published in 1999 (Wiltz et al., 1999).

Reimbursement

A top agenda item for NPs is reimbursement. The federal government, under the Balanced Budget Act of 1997 (BBA), mandated reimbursement for NPs by Medicare. Under the BBA, NPs are eligible for Medicare reimbursement regardless of location or specialty practice. The physician is not required to be on

Text continued on page 168

State	Legal Authority Minimum Practice Requirements	Prescriptive Authority and Regulations	Practice Requirements	Reciprocity	Website
Alabama	State licensure Successful completion of NP program National certification Title: CRNP	Legend drugs only	Collaborative practice Written protocols	Yes	www.abn.state.al.us
Alaska	State licensure Successful completion of NP program National certification Title: ANP	Independent treatment authority Includes Schedules II-V drugs May dispense drugs under regulations by BON	Independent practice permitted	Yes	www.com.state.ak.us/dom/owa/comdata.occlic
Arizona	State license in good standing Successful completion of NP program National certification Title: RNP	Full treatment and dispensing authority Includes Schedules II-V drugs	Collaborative practice	Yes	www.nursing.state.az/us/
Arkansas	State license Education approved by BON Certified as NP by a nationally recognized certifying body Title: RNP/APN	Treatment authority granted Includes schedules III-V drugs Must have a collaborating MD for Rx authority	Consulting MD for CNMs only Collaborative practice for RNPs not nationally certified	Yes	www.state.ar.us

Table continued on following page

TABLE 13–1   Summary of State Statutory and Regulatory Requirements for Nurse Practitioners *Continued*

State	Legal Authority Minimum Practice Requirements	Prescriptive Authority and Regulations	Practice Requirements	Reciprocity	Website
California	State licensure Successful completion of NP program Board of registered nurses (BRN) issued certificate to NPs, CNM, CNs Function under "standardized procedures"	Treatment authority granted Schedules III-V controlled substances No DEA number BRN issues a "furnishing number"	Independent and collaborative practice	Yes	www.dca.ca.gov/
Colorado	State licensure Successful completion of NP program National certification Graduate degree required after June 30, 2008	Treatment authority granted Schedules II-V drugs with DEA number Have a treatment collaborative agreement with MD in specialty area May dispense or distribute medication samples pertaining to their standard operating procedure	Independent practice permitted	Yes	www.dora.state. co.us/nursing/

State	Requirements	Treatment Authority	Practice		Website
Connecticut	State licensure Successful completion of NP	Treatment authority granted including controlled substances	Independent practice permitted	Yes	No website
District of Columbia	State licensure Successful completion of NP program National certification	Full treatment authority CA abolished Includes Schedules II-V drugs DEA number	Independent practice permitted without collaborative agreement or protocols	Yes	No website
Delaware	State licensure National certification One year of postbasic education Masters prepared if no certifying examination is available	Treatment authority granted including Schedules II-V controlled substances May dispense professional samples	Both independent and collaborative practice permitted		No website
Florida	State licensure Successful completion of NP program of at least one academic year leading to a master's degree Certification by appropriate specialty board	Treatment privileges granted includes Schedules II-V drugs	Collaborative practice with Florida MD	Yes	www.doh.state.fl.us/

Table continued on following page

TABLE 13-1 Summary of State Statutory and Regulatory Requirements for Nurse Practitioners *Continued*

State	Legal Authority Minimum Practice Requirements	Prescriptive Authority and Regulations	Practice Requirements	Reciprocity	Website
Georgia	State licensure Successful completion of an NP program in specialty area Jan 1, 1999, must have MSN Passed national certification examination	Delegated authority to order and dispense medications including controlled substances Must comply with protocols	Collaborative practice with Georgia MD	Yes	www.sos.state.ga.us/
Hawaii	State licensure Successful completion of NP program National certification	NPs can prescribe, excluding controlled substances	Collaborative practice agreement	Yes	No website
Idaho	State licensure Completion of an approved APPN program National certification	Treatment authority granted, including Schedules II-V controlled substances DEA number with independent prescribing authority	Collaborative practice	Yes	www2.state.id.us/ibn/ibnhome.htm
Illinois	State licensure Successful completion of NP program National certification	Treatment authority for legend and Schedules III-V drugs	Collaborative practice	Yes	www.state.il.us/

State	Requirements	Treatment authority	Practice	Prescriptive	Website
	By 2001 must have graduate degree				
Indiana	State licensure Successful completion of NP program National certification	Treatment authority granted for legend and controlled drugs Must have a DEA number	Collaborative practice	Yes	www.ai.org/hpb/
Iowa	State licensure Successful completion of NP program National certification Title: ARNP	Independent treatment authority DEA number for controlled substances ARNPs use own prescriptive pads	Collaborative practice	Yes	www.state.ia.us/government/nursing/
Kansas	State licensure Successful completion of NP program National certification	Treatment authority granted, including controlled substances under protocol with MD	Collaborative practice	Yes	www.ink.org/public/ksbn/
Kentucky	State licensure Successful completion of NP program National certification	Treatment authority granted, excluding controlled substances	Collaborative practice	Yes	www.kbn.state.ky.us/
Louisiana	State licensure Successful completion of NP program National certification Masters degree after Jan 1, 1996	Treatment authority granted No information available regarding the scope of authority	Collaborative practice	Yes	www.rnboard.lsbn.stat.la.us/

Table continued on following page

TABLE 13-1 Summary of State Statutory and Regulatory Requirements for Nurse Practitioners *Continued*

State	Legal Authority Minimum Practice Requirements	Prescriptive Authority and Regulations	Practice Requirements	Reciprocity	Website
Maine	State licensure Successful completion of NP program National certification	Prescriptive authority Treatment authority granted, including Schedules III-V controlled drugs	Independent practice after 2 yr of physician-supervised clinical experience	Yes	www.state.me.us/ sos/cec/rcn/apa/ 02/chaps02.htm
Maryland	State licensure Successful completion of NP program National certification	Treatment authority granted, including controlled substances Federal and state DEA numbers May dispense including samples	Collaborative practice agreement with Maryland MD	Yes	http://dhmh.state. md.us/mbn/
Massachusetts	Current RN licensure Successful completion of NP program Current certification by accrediting body in specific area	Treatment authority granted Includes Schedules II-VI drugs State and federal DEA number	Collaborative practice	Yes	www.state.ma.us/ reg/boards/rn/
Michigan	State licensure Successful completion of NP program National certification	Treatment authority granted, excluding controlled substances	Independent practice when designated as having a "specialty certification"	Yes	www.cis.state. mi.us/

State	Requirements	Treatment authority	Collaboration		Website
Minnesota	State licensure Successful completion of NP program National certification	Treatment authority granted to include controlled substances under a written agreement with a collaborating MD	Collaborative practice	Yes	www.nursingboard.state.mn.us/
Missouri	State licensure Successful completion of NP program National certification	Treatment authority granted, excluding controlled substances	Collaborative practice agreement is needed if NP is performing physician-delegated medical acts	Yes	www.ecodev.state.mo.us/pr/nursing/
Mississippi	State licensure Successful completion of NP program National certification Dec 31, 1998, must have graduate degree	Treatment authority granted, excluding controlled substances	Collaborative practice Written protocols	Yes	No website
Montana	Holds a current license Submits application for advanced practice National certification After June 30, 1995, MSN Before June 30, 1995, may be recognized in Montana	Treatment authority granted, including Schedules II-V controlled substances after approval by the Prescriptive Authority Committee	Collaborative	Yes	www.com.state.mt.us/

Table continued on following page

State	Legal Authority Minimum Practice Requirements	Prescriptive Authority and Regulations	Practice Requirements	Reciprocity	Website
Nebraska	State licensure Completion of NP program Licensed as ARNPs by BON July 1996 must have graduate degree Title: ARNP	Treatment authority granted, including Schedule II drugs May dispense samples incident to practice	Integrated practice agreement (IPA) with a collaborating MD Within certain circumstances, IPA may be waived	Yes	http://hhs.state. ne.us/
Nevada	State licensure Masters degree in nursing or health-related field on or after June 1, 2005	Treatment authority granted after documented MD-supervised clinical practice of 1000 hr Must also apply to board of practice to Rx Must have dispensing certificate to dispense	Collaborative practice agreement required with written protocols	Yes	www.state. nsbnreno@ govmail.state. nv.us/
New Hampshire	State licensure Graduate of a program acceptable to the board Passing a national certification examination	Plenary authority to prescribe controlled and noncontrolled drugs Must have dispensing authority	No requirement for physician collaboration or supervision	Yes	http://state. nh.us/

State	Requirements	Prescribe/order	Collaborative/Supervision	Prescriptive Authority	Website
New Jersey	State licensure Oct 29, 1994, masters in nursing Completion program of studies	Prescribe/order medications based on medication/device protocol No controlled substances as of January 1999	Collaborative protocols are not required unless prescribing medications and devices	Yes	www.state.nj.us/lps/ca/home.htm
New Mexico	State license with designation as CNP Must complete graduate program as of 1997 amendment Must have masters after Jan 2001 Title: CNP	Treatment authority to prescribe and dispense independently, including Schedules II-V controlled substances DEA number granted Formulary required	Can practice independently without MD agreement or supervision	Yes	No website
New York	State licensure Certified by the State Education Department as NP	Authorized to prescribe drugs, including Schedule II-V without restrictions	Collaborative agreement with written protocols	Yes	www.nysed.gov/prof/
North Carolina	State licensure Completion of approved program of studies and certification by BON approved certifying body	May prescribe drugs and devices, including controlled substances, identified in written protocols Must have DEA number	Collaborative practice Written protocols	Yes	www.ncbon.com/
North Dakota	State licensure Advanced education and certification After Jan 2001 must have masters degree with a nursing focus	Treatment authority for controlled and noncontrolled substances passed in 1991	Collaborative agreement	Yes	www.ndbon.org/

Table continued on following page

TABLE 13-1   Summary of State Statutory and Regulatory Requirements for Nurse Practitioners *Continued*

State	Legal Authority Minimum Practice Requirements	Prescriptive Authority and Regulations	Practice Requirements	Reciprocity	Website
Ohio	State licensure As of Jan. 2001 must have masters degree in nursing or related field and hold applicable certification from a national certifying organization	Legislation pending in the Ohio legislature attempting to achieve prescriptive authority	Collaborative agreement	Yes	www.state.oh. us/nur/
Oklahoma	State licensure Successful completion of NP program National certification	Optional treatment authority for NPs Physician supervision required only for the treatment authority portion of advanced practice	Independent	Yes	No website
Oregon	State licensure Successful completion of NP program National certification Masters required for entry into practice	Treatment authority granted, including Schedule III-V drugs		Yes	www.osbn.state. or.us/

State	Licensure/Certification	Prescriptive Authority	Practice Requirement		Website
Pennsylvania	State licensure Successful completion of NP program National certification	BON and BOM proposed regulations, granting CRNPs treatment writing privileges No final decisions as of Jan 1999	Collaborative practice agreement required	Yes	www.dos.state.pa.us/bpoa/nurbd.htm
Rhode Island	State licensure Successful completion of NP program National certification	Treatment privileges include legend and Schedule II-V controlled drugs	No requirements for MD collaboration	Yes	www.doc.board.org/ri/main.htm
South Carolina	State licensure Successful completion of NP program National certification	Treatment authority, including noncontrolled and only controlled drugs in Schedule V	Collaborative practice with written protocol	Yes	www.llr.state.sc.us/
South Dakota	State licensure Successful completion of NP program National certification	As of 1997, can prescribe both controlled and noncontrolled substances as outlined in practice agreement	Practice agreement required with on-site MD supervision one half day/week	Yes	www.state.sd.us/dcr/nursing/
Tennessee	State licensure NP role is not specifically defined except by BON administrative rules	Must qualify for a "certificate of fitness" to prescribe Then may prescribe Schedule II-V controlled and noncontrolled substances	Written medical protocols required	Yes	www.170.142.76.180/bmf-bin/BmFproflist.p1

Table continued on following page

TABLE 13–1 Summary of State Statutory and Regulatory Requirements for Nurse Practitioners *Continued*

State	Legal Authority Minimum Practice Requirements	Prescriptive Authority and Regulations	Practice Requirements	Reciprocity	Website
Texas	State licensure Certification as APN Successful completion of advanced program of studies	Treatment authority is based on a collaborative practice model using protocols, practice guidelines, and standing medication orders	Collaborative practice	Yes	www.bne.state. tx.us
Utah	State licensure Successful completion of NP program National certification	Treatment authority granted, including controlled substances	Collaborative practice only for those ARNPs prescribing Schedule II-III controlled substances	Yes	www.commerce. state.ut.us
Vermont	State licensure Successful completion of NP program National certification	Treatment authority granted, including controlled substances	Performs medical acts independently with a collaborative practice with a MD under practice guidelines	Yes	www.sec.state. vt.us
Virginia	State licensure Completion of NP program National certification	Treatment authority granted, including Schedule VI drugs with exceptions as stipulated by the BON and BOM	Must practice under medical direction and supervision of a MD with written protocols	Yes	www.dhp.state. va.us/

Washington	State licensure Successful completion of NP program National certification	Independent treatment authority for Schedule V and legend drugs Legislation to include Schedule II-IV drugs is pending		Yes	www.doh.wa.gov/hsqa/hpgad/nursing
West Virginia	State licensure BON-recognized national certification Beginning Jan 1999 must have an MSN	Treatment authority, including controlled substances became effective July 1992 Exclusionary Schedule drugs include I and II	No collaboration required unless prescribing	Yes	www.state.wv.us/nurses/rn/
Wisconsin	State licensure Completion of NP program	May prescribe including controlled substances May dispense samples and prepackaged doses	Currently practice within a broad scope that specifies follow protocols jointly determined by RN and MD	Yes	www.state.wi.us/
Wyoming	State licensure Completion of NP Program National certification	May independently prescribe legend and controlled substances (Schedules III-V)	Collaborative	Yes	nursing.state.wy.us

DEA, Drug Enforcement Agency.

site at the time of service. The reimbursement rate is 80% of the lesser charges or 85% of the fee schedule amount for physicians (Sharp, 1996).

To receive reimbursement, the NP must have a Medicare provider number. Medicare provider numbers are obtained through third-party administrators (e.g., Blue Cross and Blue Shield). Hospital business offices should have the names, addresses, and phone numbers of third-party administrators. NPs can own rural health clinics where reimbursement is covered under the Medicare program with payment made to the clinic, not directly to the NP. Extending reimbursement to NPs encourages practice in remote areas, thus providing health care to those who might have otherwise been unable to obtain any type of health-related services (Sharp, 1996).

Title XIX of the Social Security Act authorizes the Medicaid program. Pediatric nurse practitioners (PNPs) and family nurse practitioners (FNPs) are eligible for Medicaid reimbursement. PNPs and FNPs may bill directly to Medicaid and apply for a state provider number. Under the Budget Reconciliation Act of 1989, states are required to cover services provided by certified PNPs and FNPs. This act became effective July 1, 1990, and requires states to provide reimbursement whether or not the NP is practicing under direct supervision of, or associated with, another physician or provider. Like Medicare reimbursement, Medicaid reimbursement is made directly to the clinic, not to the NP.

Legal Implications

As mentioned previously, state boards of nursing (BONs) and state boards of medicine (BOMs) are key decision makers in regulating the practice of NPs. Therefore BON and BOM determine the extent to which a NP may function. Some NPs work independently of a physician; however, most NPs work under protocols. For NPs working under the direction of a physician, protocols must be in place as stipulated by the state BON and BOM. Protocols must be evaluated and updated periodically. There must be a formal quality-assurance program in place for evaluating the NP's practice.

In terms of institutional billing practices, some facilities bill under the physician number. Also, insurance and managed care programs may not list NPs as providers in clinics or other agencies where a physician is also available. Billing is also under the physician's provider number, not the NP's. Issues associated with fraud and abuse must be addressed by any billing policies.

Employment contracts are another source for legal consideration. Employment contracts protect both the employee and employer. In the absence of an employment contract, in many states, employment is "at will," meaning that either party, the employee or employer, may terminate the employment at any point without specific reason. Unreasonable hardship on both parties can be avoided with an employment agreement. There are several issues the NP should consider when negotiating a contract. First, is the NP an employee or independent contractor? If the NP is an employee, the employer must withhold payroll taxes. The employer must also provide workers compensation, provide for liability insurance, and offer health insurance. If the NP is working as an independent contractor, the employer provides none of the above, and it is the sole responsibility of the NP to ensure that taxes are paid and malpractice and health insurance is obtained (Buppert, 1996).

The NP should apply for medical staff privileges if his or her practice is in a hospital setting. Medical staff bylaws outline the type of membership the NP can assume and delineates the scope of practice of an NP in that particular setting. Although the NP has a license and is credentialed, additional credentialing requirements may be necessary to obtain privileges from a facility's medical staff.

The Nurse Practitioner in the Emergency Department

The American College of Emergency Physicians (ACEP) supports NPs working in the emergency care arena. ACEP drafted and published guidelines for NPs working in the ED. Under these guidelines, ACEP supports written protocols for NPs with clearly defined responsibilities. The NP's scope of practice should be clearly defined with a description of the types of patients and conditions the NP is credentialed to treat. In addition, a list of specific procedures the NP is allowed to perform should be kept on file. These procedures should be included in the NP's protocol (American Health Care Consultants, 1996).

NPs continue to play instrumental roles in every aspect of health care. Mechanisms that enhance the scope of practice, gain NPs prescriptive authority, and allow reimbursement for services provided improve NPs' ability to provide health care services to many needy individuals. As the federal government continues to restructure health care services, NPs will become more visible. Many physicians support the use of NPs in the form of intensive mentoring through training and education. Empowerment yields the provision of high-quality health care in terms of NPs who are highly skilled and knowledgeable in their specific arena of practice.

PHYSICIAN ASSISTANTS

Practice Settings

Physician assistants (PAs) are graduates of accredited PA educational programs who are licensed by a state or credentialed by the federal government to practice medicine as delegated by, and with the supervision of, physicians. PAs work in virtually all areas of health care, from primary care to surgical subspecialties, and every kind of setting, including the White House (Hughes, 1999). PAs practice with the supervision of physicians and are governed by the state Board of Medicine or PA licensing authority. Physicians in all practice areas, from surgery to medicine, geriatrics to pediatrics, and in specialty areas, employ or supervise PAs as "physician extenders" (American Academy of Physician Assistants, 1999). The American Academy of Physician Assistants (AAPA) lists PA specialty organizations as diverse as nephrology, allergy and pulmonary medicine, occupational medicine, family practice, obstetrics, pediatrics, and psychiatry (AAPA, 1999).

The first PA education program was started by the chairman of the Department of Medicine at the Duke University Medical Center in North Carolina in 1965 (Hughes, 1999). The first students were former military corpsmen. Today, students in PA education programs come from a variety of professional backgrounds, including nurses, physical therapists, and emergency medical technicians. PA education is modeled on physician education, and the first curriculum was based in part on the chairman's experience with the fast-track training of physicians during World War II (Hughes, 1999).

Practice Regulations

As with NPs, each state regulates the practice of PAs. For a summary of state statutory and regulatory requirements, see Table 13-2. A detailed list of each state's requirements for PA regulations can be found on the World Wide Web site of the AAPA (www.aapa.org). All states that authorize PAs require that PAs successfully complete the national initial certification examination developed jointly by the National Commission on Certification of Physician Assistants (NCCPA) and the National Board of Medical Examiners before licensure. To maintain certification, PAs must log 100 hours of continuing medical education every 2 years, reregister with the NCCPA every 2 years, and pass the NCCPA national recertification examination every 6 years.

Role Autonomy

The PA practices medicine with the supervision of a physician. Clinical protocols generally are not required; protocols are useful to PAs to the same extent they are useful to physicians (AAPA, 1999). Several studies examined the quality of health care provided by PAs. Sox reviewed data from more than a dozen studies on the clinical performance of PAs and concluded that they provide quality care (Health Resources and Services Administration, 1994).

TABLE 13–2 State Summary of Statutory and Regulatory Requirements for Physician Assistants

State	Graduation from PA Program	Passage of NCCPA Examination	Temporary Authorization	Renewal Requirements	Prescribing Privileges
Alabama	X	X	X		X
Alaska	X	X	X	NCCPA	X
Arizona	X	X	X	CME	X
Arkansas	X	X	X		—*
California	X	X	X		Written prescription transmittal authority
Osteopathic	X	X			
Colorado	X	X	—†		X
Connecticut	X	X	X	NCCPA	X
Delaware	X	X	X		X
District of Columbia	X	X		CME	X
Florida	X	X	X	CME	X
Osteopathic	X	X	X	CME	X
Georgia	X	X	X	CME	X
Hawaii	X	X	X	NCCPA	X
Idaho	X	X	X	CME	X
Illinois		X	X	NCCPA	—*
Indiana	X	X	X	NCCPA	
Iowa	X	X	X	CME	X
Kansas	X	X	X	CME	X
Kentucky	X	X	X	NCCPA	X
Louisiana	X	X	X	NCCPA	X

Table continued on following page

TABLE 13–2 State Summary of Statutory and Regulatory Requirements for Physician Assistants *Continued*

State	Graduation from PA Program	Passage of NCCPA Examination	Temporary Authorization	Renewal Requirements	Prescribing Privileges
Maine	X and/or	X	X	CME	X
Osteopathic	X and/or	X	X	CME	X
Maryland	X	X	X	CME	X
Massachusetts	X	X	X	CME	X
Michigan	X	X	X		X
Osteopathic	X	X	X		X
Minnesota		X	X	CME (NCCPA for treatment)	X
Mississippi	X	X			X
Missouri	—†	X	X	NCCPA	X
Montana	X	X	X	NCCPA	X
Nebraska	X	X	X		X
Nevada	X	X	X	NCCPA	X
Osteopathic		X	X	X	X
New Hampshire	X	X	X	NCCPA	X
New Jersey	X	X	X	CME	X
New Mexico	X	X	X	NCCPA	X
Osteopathic	X	X		NCCPA	X
New York	X	X	X		X
North Carolina	X	X	X	CME	X
North Dakota		X		NCCPA	X
Ohio		X	X	NCCPA	X

State			Requirements	
Oklahoma	X	X	CME	X
Oregon	X			X
Pennsylvania	X	X	NCCPA	X
Osteopathic	X			
Rhode Island	X	X	CME	X
South Carolina	X	X	NCCPA	X
South Dakota	X	X	CME	X
Tennessee	X	X	CME	X
Texas	X	X	CME	X
Utah	X	X		X
Vermont	X	X	CME	X
Virginia	X	X	NCCPA	X
Washington	X	X	CME	X
Osteopathic	X	X	CME (NCCPA for treatment)	X
West Virginia	X	X	CME (NCCPA for treatment)	X
Osteopathic	X	X	CME (NCCPA for treatment)	X
Wisconsin	X	X		X
Wyoming	X	X	NCCPA	X

From American Academy of Physician Assistants, September 1999. Used with permission.

CME, Continuing medical education.

*Regulations to implement prescribing authority not yet in effect.

†New graduates may practice under supervising physician's delegatory authority with direct supervision.

‡Program requirement waived for those employed as PAs before 1986.

An article in the *Journal of the American Medical Association* examined indirect indicators of quality, such as physician acceptance and patient satisfaction; these parameters also reflected PAs in a favorable manner (Jones & Cawley, 1995). The U.S. Department of Health and Human Services' *Physician Assistants in the Health Workforce Report of 1994* cited a high level of patient acceptance and satisfaction with the care they received from PAs.

Nearly all states (48 as of June 2000) provide the practicing PA with prescriptive authority, meaning the physician is not required to cosign a prescription written by a PA (Hughes, 1999).

Reimbursement

Private insurers generally cover medical services provided by PAs. Under Medicare, the Balanced Budget Act of 1997 increased PA reimbursement to a uniform 85% of the physician's fee schedule in all settings. This includes hospitals (inpatient, outpatient, and EDs), nursing facilities, offices and clinics, and first assisting at surgery. According to the Balanced Budget Act, PAs may be either W-2 employees or independent contractors. All PAs who treat Medicare patients must have a provider identification number (PIN).

As of September 1999, 48 states cover medical services provided by PAs under their Medicaid program. The rate of reimbursement, which is paid to the employing practice and not directly to the PA, is either the same as or slightly lower than that paid to physicians.

Legal Implications

The PA role was established as a dependent provider in the health care system. Physician supervision is integral to the PA role. Although the PA makes autonomous decisions in a practice setting, legally the PA is dependent to the supervising physician. State law governs the degree of supervision by the physician (e.g., chart review, frequency of face-to-face meetings). All states allow PAs to see patients when the supervising physician is not on site and require a mechanism for immediate consultation if the PA determines that the physician's services are required.

PAs either carry their own malpractice insurance, or it is provided by the practice. They may practice as employees or independent contractors. The PA practicing in the hospital setting should seek medical staff privileges delineating the functions allowed in that setting. Many hospitals use virtually the same criteria and forms to credential PAs as they use to credential physicians.

The Physician Assistant in the Emergency Department

According to the AAPA (1998), approximately 3200 PAs practiced in emergency medicine in 1998. The areas of practice included prehospital patient care, triage, ED patient care, and selective administrative functions. They also provided emergency care for patients in various settings, including, but not limited to, critical care units and ground or air transport of patients (AAPA, 1998). The Society of Emergency Medicine Physician Assistants incorporated in 1992. PAs and NPs often work together in EDs to assist physicians with often heavy patient care responsibilities.

The ACEP supports the use of PAs in EDs. In September 1996, the ACEP revised its "Guidelines on the Role of Physician Assistants in Emergency Departments." The revised guidelines reflect that PAs "provide services in ED's varying from departments that are staffed 24 hours a day by emergency physicians to departments in rural areas, where the coverage is provided by the PA, with off-site physician supervision as allowed by state law." They further state that "PAs work clinically with the supervision of an emergency physician who is present in the ED or available for consultation" (ACEP, 1996).

CASE MANAGERS

Practice Settings

Case management is a recent advanced practice role. **Case managers** practice in all settings and cover a continuum of care (Williams & Swartz, 1998). The case manager role may be assumed by social workers, registered nurses, advanced practice nurses, PAs, or physicians. The case manager has two primary roles: facilitator and gatekeeper (NJSNA, 1993). The fragmentation in delivery of health care services, both in inpatient and outpatient settings, may be addressed by case management (Cook, 1998).

Case managers may handle complex cases or those involving long-term medical care (Blue Cross Blue Shield of Massachusetts, 1995). Workers compensation cases lend themselves to case management because of the complexity, expense, and potential to reduce worker productivity. There are reports of cost savings if case management is used with chronic diseases (Kretz & Pantos, 1996).

Practice Regulations

Very few states specify case managers as separate entities from other health care professionals for purposes of regulations. The case manager must comply with the laws and regulations governing his or her profession. Arizona (1994) statutes addressed the requirements for case managers practicing in that state.

Role Autonomy

The degree of autonomy held by the case manager depends on the practice setting. The governing body, whether a hospital, outpatient clinic, third-party payer, or government agency, has considerable freedom in determining the parameters of the case management role. If an organization does not have a case management program, the case manager may be able to establish the role with a great deal of flexibility.

Reimbursement

Case managers are not directly reimbursed by health plans. Cost savings is a primary focus for case managers. An insurer may employ case managers to reduce the costs of workers compensation cases or to manage patients with chronic complex diseases or catastrophic illnesses or injuries. The parameters used to assess the effectiveness of case managers may include cost savings, average length of time patients cannot work, easier access to services, and reduction in inappropriate use of the ED.

Legal Implications

Case management as a role has not entered the sights of regulatory bodies in most states. A case manager must know the requirements established by the employer or employing agency. Because the case manager focuses on quality as well as cost containment, he or she should also be knowledgeable of state law and regulations governing quality of patient care, reimbursement regulations, and patient rights. Arizona (1994) established a case management certifying board.

The Case Manager in the Emergency Department

Minimal information exists about ED case management. As the case management role evolves, EDs will likely explore the potential use of case managers in that setting. Case management programs that focus on chronic disease include EDs as a health care delivery location. Reducing inappropriate use of EDs by patients with chronic disease may be a focus of the case management program (Woolbright, 1997).

CLINICAL NURSE SPECIALISTS
Practice Settings

Clinical nurse specialists (CNSs) practice in all areas of health care. The growth of NP programs in recent years has had an impact on the role of the CNS. The CNS may practice in inpatient or outpatient facilities, physician practices, skilled nursing facilities, rehabilitation facilities, and any other area where health care occurs. With the advent of case management, the CNS has often assumed the role of case manager.

Practice Regulations

Each state regulates and determines whether the CNS is an advanced practice nurse. In some states, the CNS has additional educational preparation but does not have any special regulatory oversight. In other states, the CNS has prescriptive authority and has a case load (Baltimore & Gillett, 1998). Preparation at the masters degree level is usually required for a CNS.

Role Autonomy

The CNS practices under the state nurse practice act. The five traditional roles of the CNS are clinician, teacher, consultant, researcher, and manager. In traditional programs, the CNS's focus is on specific patient populations. Each role may be implemented in varying degrees of specificity, depending on the CNS's job requirements and expectations of employers. Because the focus of the CNS is nursing (as it relates to patient care), there is less overlap with physician practice.

Reimbursement

In most states, the CNS is not directly reimbursed. In states where the CNS assumes a role similar to an NP, reimbursement may be available.

Legal Implications

Each state board of nursing regulates and determines the scope of practice of the CNS. If the CNS functions similar to an NP, obtaining medical staff privileges should be considered. In the traditional CNS role, the hospital policies and procedures will outline what activities the CNS can engage in daily.

The Clinical Nurse Specialist in the Emergency Department

The role the CNS assumes in the ED will be determined by the facility's demands and needs as well as the interest of the CNS. The CNS is probably an expert in emergency nursing care and may fulfill that obligation in one of five traditional roles as mentioned above.

CONCLUSION

The changes in the health care delivery system resulted in additional health care team members. Advances in technology, increased ED visits, the push for decreasing patient delays in the ED, and the saturation of managed care in some markets led to the enhanced need for "physician extenders." Whether the physician extender is an NP, PA, case manager, or CNS, the patients in EDs throughout the United States benefit from experienced, educated, and dedicated professionals who practice in EDs daily.

Regardless of the practice setting, the health professional and the employing agency should clearly define the parameters of practice, within regulatory guidelines. Reimbursement is an issue that must be addressed if advance practice nurses or PAs are used in the ED. Each practitioner has different educational requirements and role autonomy and the legal implications of using each are different also. The delivery of quality care in a cost-effective manner is a goal of facilities and health care professionals.

References

Alabama Board of Nursing: *Alabama Board of Nursing administrative code* § 610-X-9-.15, 1999.

American Academy of Physician Assistants: Summary of state regulation of physician assistant practice, 1999. www.aapa.org/gandp/statelaw.html. [Accessed 7/31/99].

American Academy of Physician Assistants: Physician assistants and emergency medicine, 1998. www.aapa.org/gandp/emerg.html. [Accessed 7/31/99].

American College of Emergency Physicians: Guidelines on the role of physician assistants in emergency departments, 1996. www.acep.org.

American Health Care Consultants: ED management: the monthly update on emergency department management, *ED Management* 8(1):5, 1996.

Ariz. Rev. Stat. § 32-3261 (1994).

Baltimore JJ, Gillett P: Clinical nurse specialist prescriptive authority and the legislative process, *Adv Pract Nurs Q* 4(2):78, 1998.

Betancourt J, Valmocina M, Grossman D: Physicians' and patients' knowledge and perceptions of the roles and functions of nurse practitioners, *Nurs Pract* 21(8): 13, 1996.

Blue Cross Blue Shield of Massachusetts: Case management at Blue Cross Blue Shield of Massachusetts, 1995. http://bcbsma.com. [Accessed 7/31/99].

Buppert C: Nurse practitioner private practice: three legal pitfalls to avoid, *Nurse Pract* 21(4):32, 1996.

Cook TH: The effectiveness of inpatient case management: fact or fiction? *J Nurs Adm* 49(4):36, 1998.

Edmunds MW, Havens HD: Trends, professional issues, health policy. In Millonig VL, editor: *Pediatric nurse practitioner certification and review,* ed 2, Potomac, MD, 1994, Health Leadership Associates.

Gelman E: Be prepared—with a masters degree, *Patient Care Nurse Pract* 2(1):5, 1999.

Health Resources and Services Administration, Bureau of Health Professions: *Physician assistants in the health workforce 1994,* Washington, DC, 1994, US Department of Health and Human Services, pp. 38-55.

Hughes N: Personal communication, American Academy of Physician Assistants, Sept 17, 1999.

Jones PE, Cawley JF: Physician assistants and health system reform, *JAMA* 271: 1266, 1995.

Kretz SE, Pantos BS: Cost savings and clinical improvement through disease management, *J Case Manag* 5(4):173, 1996.

National Council State Boards of Nursing: Using nurse practitioner certification for state nursing regulation: An update. *Issues* 18, 1997. www.ncsbn.org/files/publications/issues/vol181/usingnpc181.asp.

New Jersey State Nurses Association: Expanding the prescriptive authority of nurse practitioners/clinical nurse specialist to include controlled substances in New Jersey. www.nurse.org/nj/njsna/pages/whtpapr.html.

New Jersey State Nurses Association: Position statement on case management. www.njsna.org/Position_Statements/Case%20Management.DOC. [Accessed 7/31/99].

Sharp N: Nurse practitioner reimbursement: history and politics, *Nurse Pract* 21(5): 134, 1996.

Society of Emergency Medicine Physician Assistants: SEMPA history. www.sempa.org/history.htm. [Accessed 7/31/99].

Wiltz P, Zimmer PA, Scarcliff KJ: Nurse practitioner authority to request, receive and/or dispense drug samples: a state-by-state study, *NP World News* 4(1):3, 1999.

Williams J, Swartz M: Treatment boundaries in the case management relationship: a clinical case and discussion, *Community Ment Health J* 34:299, 1998.

Woolbright D: Pediatric case management in the emergency department, *Nurse Manage* 49(10):39, 1997.

Suggested Reading

Armstrong P: The role of the clinical nurse specialist, *Nurs Stand* 11(16):40, 1999.

Blackburn KM: Roles of advanced practice nurses in oncology, *Oncology* 12:591, 1998.

Blunt E: Role and productivity of nurse practitioners in one urban emergency department, *J Emerg Nurs* 24:234, 1998.

Bousfield C: A phenomenological investigation into the role of the clinical nurse specialist, *J Adv Nurs* 25:245, 1997.

Briody ME: The future of the CNS in the USA, *Int Nurs Rev* 43:17, 1996.

Buchanan L, Powers RD: Establishing a NP-staffed minor emergency area, *Nurs Manage* 27(2):25, 1996.

Cairo MJ: Emergency physician attitudes toward the emergency nurse practitioner role: validation versus rejection, *J Am Acad Nurse Pract* 8:411, 1996.

Chuk PK: Clinical nurse specialist and quality patient care, *J Adv Nurs* 11:501, 1997.

Ellis GL, Brandt TE: Use of physician extenders and fast tracts in United States emergency departments, *Am J Emerg Med* 15:229, 1997.

Fox-Grage WF: States study scope of practice and reimbursement. *Issues* 17(2), 1996. www.ncsbn.org/files/publications/issues/vol1172/statesstudy172.asp. [Accessed 8/18/99].

Hales A, Karshmer J, Montes-Sandoval FA: Preparing for prescriptive privileges: a CNS-physician collaborative model. Expanding the role of the psychiatric-mental health CNS, *Clin Nurse Spec* 12(2):73, 1998.

Holmes SB: Advanced practice nursing role: clinical nurse specialist, *Orthop Nurs* 17(6):61, 1998.

Hooker RS, McCaig L: The emergency nurse practitioner: an educational model, *J Emerg Nurs* 24:234, 1997.

Hooker RS, McCaig L: Emergency department uses of physician assistants and nurse practitioners: a national survey, *Am J Emerg Med* 14(3):245, 1996.

Karshmer JF, Hales A: Role of the psychiatric clinical nurse specialist in the emergency department, *Clin Nurse Spec* 11:264, 1997.

Lindeke LL, Canedy BH, Kay MM: A comparison of practice domains of clinical nurse specialists and nurse practitioners, *J Prof Nurs* 13(5):281, 1997.

National Council of State Boards of Nursing: National Council position paper: regulation of advanced nursing practice. www.ncsbn.org/files/publications/positions/apreg.asp. [Accessed 8/18/99].

Pinelli JM: The clinical nurse specialist/nurse practitioner: oxymoron or match made in heaven? *Can J Nurs Adm* 10:85, 1997.

Sechrist KR, Berlin LE: Role of the CNS: an integrative review of the literature, *AACN Clin Issues* 12:306, 1998.

Shea SS, Selfridge-Thomas J: The emergency department nurse practitioner: pearls and pitfalls of role transition and development, *J Emerg Nurs* 23:235, 1997.

Sparacino PS: CNS versatility is a key to opportunity, *Clin Nurse Spec* 11(3):111, 1998.

Wells N, Erickson S, Spinella J: Role transition: from CNS to CNS/case manager, *J Nurs Adm* 26(11):23, 1996.

Wright KB: Advanced practice nursing: merging the CNS and NP roles, *Gastroenterol Nurs* 12(2):57, 1997.

14

Prehospital Care: Emergency Medical Services (EMS)

CHAPTER OUTLINE

Prehospital care before the late 1960s was provided by funeral home personnel, law enforcement officials, and members of the public. A publication describing a prehospital cardiac care program in Belfast, Northern Ireland, changed the direction of prehospital care in the United States. The Belfast program provided a physician-nurse team that went to patients in a mobile coronary care unit (Eisenberg et al., 1996). In 1966, the National Academy of Sciences published a White Paper titled *Accidental Death and Disability in America* (Diehl, 1999). Emergency medical services (EMS) personnel were identified as the weak link in care of the injured. Also in 1966, the National Highway Traffic Safety Act provided federal funding for equipment, training, and communications in prehospital care (Sayah, 1998). The Emergency Medical Services (EMS) Systems Act of 1973 identified 15 components of a prehospital EMS system (Box 14-1). Regionalization was a prerequisite for funding (Diehl, 1999). The Robert Wood Johnson Foundation also funded 44 sites that catalyzed the development of and changes in regional systems. Development of a communications system for the public to request emergency assistance led to the development of 911 services. In addition, the military lessons of the Vietnam experience led to advances in the care of the critically injured (Diehl, 1999). Dramatic changes

Nurses in Prehospital Care

In some states, nurses provide on-line medical control using protocols. Mobile intensive care nurses are governed by county and state laws in those states that specify the role of nurses in prehospital care. Some states require that the prehospital provider speak directly with a physician for on-line medical control. The role of nurses in prehospital care became an issue in the 1980s. The Emergency Nurses Association and National Flight Nurses Association developed a joint position statement related to nurses in prehospital care. Some states legislated the nurse's role in prehospital care. Hawaii (1993) required that registered nurses working in prehospital care attend a prehospital training course and receive certification. Iowa (1997) exempted registered nurses from regulation by the health agency governing prehospital care if the registered nurse could document equivalent education and additional skills training related to prehospital care. New Hampshire (1995) did not restrict registered nurses from participating in prehospital care as long as the nurse received education and training appropriate to EMS. New Hampshire specifically prohibited restrictions on registered nurses engaged in interfacility transport.

Contagious or Infectious Diseases

Federal law required notification of EMS providers if the receiving hospital determined that a patient transported by EMS had an airborne infectious disease (42 U.S.C.A. §300ff-82). All states have laws that require notification, not only of airborne infectious diseases but also blood-borne contagious diseases and other types of infectious diseases. Each state established the mechanism of reporting to the EMS provider when it was discovered that an infectious or contagious disease existed. Before the law establishing reporting, EMS providers could be exposed to patients with tuberculosis or other communicable diseases and never receive notice. In addition, an EMS provider with substantial exposure (e.g., a needle stick) might never be able to determine the patient's communicable disease status.

DOCUMENTATION

Computerized prehospital medical records are an evolutionary trend in prehospital documentation (Mattera, 1999). The documentation of care at the scene and during transport is vital to the care of the patient. In addition to the use of documentation for patient care, the EMS provider's documentation may be used in professional negligence actions (see Chapter 17). Some states have a standardized tool for recording the medical care received by the patient in a prehospital setting. Whatever tools are used, the principles of good documentation apply to prehospital providers. Legible, accurate, and specific documentation related to the care the patient received and responses to prehospital treatment are important.

DATA COLLECTION

Many states have standardized run reports that are used in data collection. As with registries and other types of data collection tools, the run report may be used for data collection and reported in aggregate numbers. Information about dispatch times, response times, length of time on scene, transport time to the hospital, and length of time a unit is out of service can be obtained from the run report. The raw data may be of interest when an individual case is audited or reviewed but should be analyzed when the EMS system is evaluated. Prehospital providers should provide meticulous recording of events on run reports to capture good data. Data analysis may be tied to funding and to an overall evaluation of the system's functioning. Vermont (1987) required data collection to evaluate the care patients received in the prehospital setting.

PATIENT CARE LEGAL ISSUES

Consent

A recent trend allows EMS treatment without the consent of the patient. A few states specifically provide that treatment can occur even if the patient does not consent (McCrary, 1999). Florida (1994) does not allow recovery of damages against a prehospital provider for failing to obtain consent if the patient is intoxicated, under the influence of drugs, or "otherwise incapable of informed consent." EMS providers are prohibited from using "unreasonable force" in treating patients who fall under the jurisdiction of the statute. New Hampshire (1995) provided protection to EMS providers who fail to obtain consent if the provider has no "knowledge of facts negating consent." Iowa (1997) exempted liability if the patient is unable to give consent for any reason and no other person who is legally authorized to give consent is available.

The recent trend recognizes the difficulty of determining a patient's capacity to consent in the prehospital setting (McCrary, 1999). Some of the reasons used to override a patient's refusal include saving lives, the benefit of saving lives outweighs the risks of civil liability, there are fewer complications than from patient refusal, and patients who are temporarily incapacitated because of serious injury or illness may accept treatment were the incapacity removed (McCrary, 1999).

Iowa Code Ann. §§ 147a-10, 12 (West 1997).

Lavonas E: Medical control, 2000. www.emedicine.com/emerg/topic716.htm.

Mattera CJ: Computerization of prehospital medical records: a planning primer from one EMS system, *J Emerg Nurs* 25:127, 1999.

McCrary SV: Patient consent for emergency care: recent state initiatives, 1999. www.law.uh.edu/healthlawperspectives/HealthPolicy/990331Emergency.html.

Nev. Rev. Stat. §450b.140(2) (1993).

N.H. Rev. Stat. Ann. §§ 151-b:14, 16 (1995).

N.M. Stat. Ann. § 24-10-3 (Michie 1978).

Sayah AJ: EMS systems, 1998. www.emedicine.com/emerg/topic709.htm.

Tex. Health Code Ann. § 197-2-(5) (West 1999).

Vt. Stat. Ann. tit. 17, § 906 (1987).

Wydro GC, Cone DC, Davidson SJ: Legislative and regulatory description of EMS medical direction: a survey of states, *Prehosp Emerg Care* 5:233, 1997.

Suggested Reading

George JE, Quattrone MS, Goldstone M: Emergency nurses as "good Samaritans," *J Emerg Nurs* 24:431, 1998.

Suggested Websites

http://health.hss.state.ak.us/dph/ems/ems_home.htm	Alaska EMS Program
www.aaainfonet.com/emsrules.htm	Arkansas Ambulance Association
www.aams.org	Association of Air Medical Services
www.emsa.cahwnet.gov/	California EMS Authority
www.state.co.us/gov_dir/cdphe_dir/em/emhom.html	Colorado EMS
www.nhtsa.dot.gov/people/injury/ems	Department of Transportation, EMS Homepage
www.gaemt.org	Georgia Association EMTs
www.hgea.org/E911	Honolulu Emergency Services
http://hultgren.org/	Kentucky EMS
janus.state.me.us/dps/ems/homepage.htm	Maine EMS
www.home.ici.net/~jdemtd/home.html	Massachusetts EMS
http://156.98.156.25/	Minnesota EMS Regulatory Board
www.state.nj.us/health/ems/hlthems.htm	New Jersey Office of EMS
www.ncems.org/	North Carolina Office of EMS
www.voicenet.com/~medic345/paems.html	Pennsylvania EMS
www.scems.com/	South Carolina EMS Educators Association
www.9-11.com/EmergServ/EMS%20Organizations/Index.html	State Organizations

www.tdh.state.tx.us/HCQS/EMS/EMSHome.htm	Texas Department of Health, EMS
www.hlunix.hl.state.ut.us/ems/homepage.html	Utah Department of Health, EMS Bureau
www.vdh.state.va.us/oems/index.htm	Virginia EMS
www.wisconsinems.com	Wisconsin EMS

15

Aeromedical Transport

James T. Noland, CRNP, MSN, CEN

CHAPTER OUTLINE

HISTORY

The first recorded air ambulance transport took place in 1866 via a hot air balloon named the Albatross. During the Parisian war in 1870, balloon airships proved to be vital in transporting injured soldiers from battlefields. These balloon airships were the first means of aeromedical transport (Manning, 1999). In the United States, the development of the helicopter in the late 1930s led to rapid growth in aeromedical services. The United States Army is credited with the development, testing, and use of the first helicopters. The first helicopter test flight occurred in 1942. The helicopter was used to transport personnel and medical supplies. During World War II and the Korean and Vietnam wars, the use of Army helicopters and pilots for transport of injured soldiers to front-line treatment stations increased (Manning, 1999). The use of helicopters and fixed-wing aircraft for the transport of ill and injured individuals continues today.

GOVERNING LAWS

In the early days of air travel, no laws existed to govern the use of aircraft, and as the demand for air travel increased, midair collisions occurred. The federal government became involved and began regulating the licensure of pilots, certification of aircraft, and air travel regulations. With the advent of federal regulation of airlines, a group of pilots saw a need to control and manage the flow of air traffic. The first group of air traffic controllers consisted of pilots from various federally regulated airlines (Eichenberger, 1999).

The Department of Transportation (DOT), an executive agency of the federal government, was created in 1966. DOT's purpose is to promote and develop rapid, safe, efficient, and convenient transportation. A division of DOT is the Federal Aviation Administration (FAA). The FAA's primary mission is aviation safety. Activities of the FAA include regulation, certification, registration, education, and investigation. The FAA issues various certificates to certify pilots, aircraft dispatchers, aviation maintenance technicians, and repair specialists. Pilots are required to obtain annual medical certificates. The FAA maintains a centralized registry for each aircraft issued an N-number. The N-number indicates the aircraft is registered in the United States. The centralized registry contains a comprehensive history of the aircraft, including ownership, liens, and encumbrances. The FAA, under the authority of the National Transportation Safety Board (NTSB), investigates aircraft accidents. The NTSB determines the likely or probable cause of aircraft accidents (Hamilton, 1996).

The FAA issues Federal Aviation Regulations (FAR) that address virtually every aspect of air travel safety (Hamilton, 1996). The section of the FAR governing aircraft with medical crews is Part 135. Part 135 addresses pilot duty time, rest period limitations, storage of equipment, maintenance, training of crew members, and emergency egress procedures (Krauss, 1996). The FAA issues Visual Flight Rules (VFR) and Instrument Flight Rules (IFR) that dictate weather minimums and conditions for visual or instrument flying. Pilots must have additional training for IFR conditions. The helicopter or fixed-wing aircraft is rated by the FAA as a VFR or IFR aircraft.

Another executive agency in the federal government that regulates a portion of aeromedical transport is the Federal Communications Commission (FCC). The FCC regulates the use of radio frequencies throughout the country. Aeromedical dispatchers and pilots register as FCC radio operators and are expected to comply with the federal regulations that govern the use of radio frequencies.

Individual states may, by statute or regulation, govern air ambulance services. Although the regulation of the air ambulance by states is an emerging issue, it is important to recognize that a state law governing air ambulances is subordinate to federal regulations issued by the FAA and FCC. Careful review of federal law is important to ensure that state and federal laws do not conflict. If any conflict exists between federal and state laws, the federal law preempts state law. One should also recognize that aeromedical safety and radio communications are regulated by the federal government. Aeromedical pilots are required to comply with the federal requirements and should not be pressured or coerced to do anything that might jeopardize the individual's license.

PERSONNEL

Aeromedical programs employ a variety of personnel—the most valuable aspect of any aeromedical program. Pilots, aircraft mechanics, communication specialists, physicians, registered nurses, emergency medical technician (EMT)-paramedics, and respiratory therapists have different, but equally important, roles in aeromedical patient care. Flight crews and program personnel interact with law enforcement agencies, fire departments, local ambulance services, hospitals and other health care organizations, and the news media.

The flight crew is composed of the pilot(s) and the medical team. Crew configuration for the medical team varies, and there is no "ideal" configuration. The individual program mission, scope of service, and intended market determine to a great extent the medical crew configuration. The majority of programs operate using the registered nurse–paramedic medical crew configuration (Manning, 1999). In some programs, emergency or pediatric physicians are used in select cases. Physician–registered nurse medical teams may be an ideal marketing configuration but are costly to maintain. Specialized teams may receive training and serve as the medical flight crew when patient needs dictate. For example, aeromedical transport of neonatal patients is often accomplished by specialized neonatal transport teams. Each program must evaluate the types of patients using the service and whether there are special circumstances that should be considered in arranging flexible crew configurations.

The scope of practice of the individual medical crew members is vital. Although flight nurses and paramedics are skilled, trained, and experienced in the aeromedical environment, is the configuration of flight nurse–paramedic appropriate for all types of patients? State regulatory agencies, such as boards of nursing and emergency medical services regulators, establish the scope of practice. Approval for advanced procedures may be necessary from the regulating agencies. Some advanced procedures may be more appropriately delineated as physician-only procedures. The scope of practice is important not only to patient care but also to reduce the potential liability exposure of the program. Professional negligence actions against medical flight crews are possible, even likely, if an adverse outcome occurs because the medical flight crew did not recognize the limitations of scope of practice.

COMMUNICATION

Effective communication is essential to the safe operation of any aeromedical program. Communication is enhanced when crew members are familiar with aeromedical communication etiquette. Clarity, brevity, and organized thoughts are keys to effective communication. The phonetic alphabet used by pilots is useful and facilitates the communication between the pilot(s) and medical crew members.

aeromedical transport before obtaining consent for the mode of transport. If the patient's condition prohibits a discussion of risks and benefits, discussion with a family member is preferable. Interfacility transfers may allow time for such a discussion, but scene flights usually are time-critical. Brief discussion with and explanation to the patient at the scene may be all that time allows. Documentation of the discussion should occur in the event the issue of consent is raised at a future time.

Refusal

Patients with the capacity to consent have the corresponding right to refuse treatment or transfer via helicopter or fixed-wing aircraft. Rapid assessment of the patient's capacity, medical condition, and reasons for refusal should occur. If the patient has the capacity to consent and refuses to consent to aeromedical transport, a signed refusal is important should a future adverse outcome occur.

Documentation

In addition to the documentation of patient care delivered in the aeromedical environment, a flight record related to patient safety, protection, and response to the aeromedical environment should be maintained. The impact of altitude on physiology should be considered and addressed in the flight record should the patient be affected by the altitude. Pilot documentation required by the FAA for each trip should be thorough and complete but is separate from the medical flight record.

CONCLUSION

Federal law governs aircraft safety including aeromedical transport. Oxygen use in aircraft is governed by the FAA as well as pilot requirements and aircraft safety regulations. The medical care of patients, including the scope of practice of flight crew members, is governed by state law. Consent and refusal are also governed by state law. A comprehensive understanding of federal and state law applicable to aeromedical transport is necessary to safely offer services to patients.

References

Air & Surface Transport Nurses Association: Organizational philosophy, 1999. www.astna.org/NFNA-FACT.html.

Eichenberger JA: *Your pilot's license,* ed 6, New York, 1999, McGraw-Hill.

Emergency Nurses Association and National Flight Nurses Association: Joint position statement: role of the registered nurse in the prehospital environment, 1999. www.astna.org/position-papers/prehospital.html.

Hamilton JS: *Practical aviation law,* ed 2, Ames, IA, 1996, Iowa State University Press.

Holleran RS: *Flight nursing: principles and practice,* ed 2, St Louis, 1996, Mosby.

Krause SS: *Aircraft safety: accident investigations analyses and applications,* New York, 1996, McGraw-Hill.

Manning T: The helicopter in air medical service: the history of the air ambulance, 1999. www.bellhelicopter.com/encyclopedia/applications.

Meade DM: Expanded scope of practice: EMS at the crossroads of care, *Emerg Med Serv* 27(5):39, 1998.

Millonig VL: *Pediatric nurse practitioner certification and review guide,* ed 3, Potomac, MD, 1998, Health Leadership Associates, Inc.

National Association Air Communication Specialists, 1999. www.naacs.org.

National Highway Traffic Safety Administration: *NHTSA: leading the way,* Washington, DC, 1995.

Suggested Readings

Arfken CL, Shapiro MJ, Bessey PQ, Littenberg B: Effectiveness of helicopter versus ground ambulance services for interfacility transport, *J Trauma* 164:785, 1998.

Cunningham P, Rutledge R, Baker CC, Clancy TV: A comparison of the association of helicopter and ground ambulance transport with the outcome of injuries in trauma patients transported from the scene, *J Trauma* 43:940, 1997.

Nathan D, Ruell S: Communications. In Lee G, editor: *Flight nursing: principles and practice,* St Louis, 1991, Mosby.

Phillips RT, Conaway C, Mullarkey D, Owen JL: One year's trauma mortality experience at Brooke Army Medical Center: is aeromedical transportation of trauma patients necessary? *Mil Med* 164:361, 1999.

Sing RF, Rotondo MF, Zonies DH, et al: Criteria for aeromedical transport, *Int J Trauma Nurs* 164:92, 1996.

Sing RF, Rotondo MF, Zonies DH, et al: Rapid sequence induction for intubation by an aeromedical transportation team: a critical analysis, *Am J Emerg Med* 164:598, 1998.

Suggested Websites

www.acep.org/	American College of Emergency Physicians
www.aams.org/	Association of Air Medical Services
www.astna.org/	Air & Surface Transport Nurses Association
www.dot.gov/	Department of Transportation
www.ena.org/	Emergency Nurses Association
www.flightweb.com/	Legal Resources for Air Medical Services

IV

Torts: Injury to the Person

16

Intentional Torts

Chapter Outline

Tort law reflects cases that are based on injury to a person or property. **Intentional torts** differ from other types of torts. **Intent,** under the law, is an objective standard. The individual emergency health care provider may say, "I did not mean or was not trying to hurt the patient." Such a statement reflects a subjective standard—what was in the person's mind at the time. In civil and criminal litigation, a person may not subjectively intend to injure someone. However, the law imposes an objective standard—what was the conduct and did the emergency health care provider know or should have known that the conduct could likely cause injury to the patient. The intentional torts discussed below may have corresponding criminal liability.

ASSAULT AND BATTERY

Although *assault* and *battery* are terms often used together, the terms identify different conduct. **Assault** is the intentional immediate threat of harm to another with the ability to carry out the threat. **Battery** is offensive touching of another person, including clothing the person is wearing, in anger, rudeness, or a hostile manner (Alabama Pattern Jury Instructions, §5.00, 1993).

Battery can occur, without subjective intent, if one evaluates the underlying conduct. For example, a competent adult patient refuses insertion of an intravenous device. The emergency health care provider cajoles, persuades, and encourages the patient to have the procedure done. If the patient continues to refuse, the emergency health care provider knows or should know that restraining the patient to insert an intravenous device is offensive to the patient. Thus intent will be inferred.

Roberson v. *Provident House* (1991) involved the insertion of an indwelling urinary catheter over the nursing home patient's objections. The plaintiff was quadriplegic and resided in a nursing home intermittently. The physician ordered insertion of an indwelling catheter as needed. The physician testified that the patient was not consulted before the order for an indwelling catheter. Approximately 2 weeks after the physician's order, a nurse inserted an indwelling catheter over the objections of the patient. Ten days later, the family reportedly called and insisted the "internal catheter" be removed. Two days later, the catheter was removed but it was reinserted after 5 days—again over the patient's objections. Approximately 12 days later, according to the reported facts of the case, a nurse "jerked the catheter out." The patient had a bloody pus discharge from the penis and required 8 days of in-hospital treatment. The patient sued for damages.

The court stated, "[A] nurse commits a battery upon a patient when she performs an invasive procedure like the insertion of an indwelling catheter over the objections of the patient. There was no emergency situation here" (*Roberson,* 576 So.2d at 994). The plaintiff was awarded $25,000 for mental and physical pain and suffering. The jury award was upheld on appeal.

The Rhode Island Supreme Court addressed the issue of battery in the context of an emergency situation in *Miller* v. *Rhode Island Hospital* (1993). The plaintiff sued the hospital for battery and a jury awarded him $10,000 in compensatory damages and $100 in punitive damages. The hospital appealed the judgment to the Rhode Island Supreme Court.

The reported facts were that the plaintiff sustained injuries in a motor vehicle crash. Upon arrival in the emergency department (ED), he was treated by a trauma team. The patient's serum blood alcohol level was 0.233 mg/dl. The patient resisted when doctors began a diagnostic peritoneal lavage. The patient ultimately was restrained and sedated before the procedure. The patient was admitted to the hospital and left against medical advice the next day.

At trial, the defendants attempted to enter testimony of a physician expert that the combination of intoxication and mechanism of injury constituted a medical emergency. The nature of the plaintiff's accident indicated the possibility of internal injuries that could not be adequately assessed in the patient's intoxicated state. The trial judge ruled that the testimony of three defense experts was inadmissible.

The Rhode Island Supreme Court ruled that the trial judge abused his discretion, vacated the judgment, and ordered a new trial. The court discussed the emergency exception to informed consent. The jury can, and should, hear facts "concerning the existence of an emergency and a patient's competence to consent" (*Miller,* 675 A.2d at 787).

The administration of a blood transfusion was the basis for a battery claim in *Banks* v. *Medical University of South Carolina* (1994). The patient was an

8-year-old girl who had exploratory surgery to determine the source of her infection. She received blood transfusions during the surgery and died from pulmonary emboli. The child's mother, a Jehovah's Witness, argued that no emergency existed to require blood transfusions and that the administration of blood constituted a battery. A physician expert agreed. The court ruled that a genuine issue of material fact existed and reversed the trial court's summary judgment ruling in favor of the defendant.

FALSE IMPRISONMENT

Restraining a person or preventing a person from leaving an area can constitute false imprisonment. Confinement or preventing a patient's freedom of movement may constitute false imprisonment regardless of how long the confinement occurs. Restraining a patient to perform medical procedures could create a false imprisonment situation. The plaintiff, at a minimum, must prove that the conduct of the defendant was (1) unlawful and (2) resulted in deprivation of the plaintiff's liberty and (3) that the defendant confined or detained the plaintiff (Alabama Pattern Jury Instructions, § 16.00, 1993). See Chapter 10 for a more detailed discussion of restraints.

INTENTIONAL INFLICTION OF EMOTIONAL DISTRESS

The tort of intentional infliction of emotional distress is not recognized in all states as a cause of action. Some states have a separate tort of "outrage" rather than intentional infliction of emotional distress. The conduct required to produce outrage or intentional infliction of emotional distress is egregious, atrocious, outrageous, or beyond the bounds of human decency. The plaintiff must prove that the defendant knew or should have known that delivery of information or conduct would lead to mental suffering, shame, humiliation, or significant emotional distress. Significant emotional distress usually requires counseling or treatment before the plaintiff can recover damages. Intentional infliction of emotional distress or outrage legal actions are most commonly seen in cases related to death—misidentification of bodies, autopsy on the wrong body, or burial of the wrong person.

DEFENSES

Affirmative defenses can be asserted by the defendant and should be, in the initial Answer to the Complaint (see Chapter 2). An affirmative defense requires that

---

BOX 16-1   Common Defenses to Intentional Tort Actions

1. Consent
2. Incapacity
3. Self-defense
4. Justification—defense of another
5. Emergency exception

---

the defendant put forth evidence to the trier of fact to show that the plaintiff's claims are not valid. If a lawful, recognized, affirmative defense can be established by the defendant, the plaintiff will probably not succeed in the lawsuit. Some affirmative defenses that may be used in intentional torts are described in the following discussion and listed in Box 16-1.

Consent

A key defense to any intentional tort is **consent.** If, for example, the patient in the ED consents to a procedure, a subsequent claim for assault and battery will probably fail. The defense of consent is best asserted when the documentation in the medical record reflects that the patient consented to the conduct of the emergency health care professional. If a patient initially refuses a procedure but later consents, the change of consent status should be documented in the medical record. Language barriers are a factor in consent. Any language difficulties that create a lack of understanding and comprehension should be identified in the patient's medical record along with the mechanisms used (such as an interpreter) to address the language barrier (see Chapter 5).

Incapacity

A patient's **incapacity** may also be a defense. A patient impaired by alcohol or chemical substances may not have the medical capacity to consent to, or refuse, treatment (see Chapter 5). A prudent approach is to document the patient's behavior, statements, and reactions in the medical record. Such documentation may allow a dismissal of an intentional tort case in the early stages of a lawsuit. In the *Miller* (1993) case described earlier, the patient's capacity was raised as a defense because of the patient's serum blood alcohol level.

Self-Defense

Self-defense may be a defense to a claim of assault and battery. If a patient's behavior is out of control and he or she attacks an emergency health care professional, the emergency health care professional can lawfully repel the attack and defend himself or herself. Key evidence in using self-defense is to demonstrate that the emergency health care professional did not use any more force than necessary to repel the attack or protect himself or herself from injury. As with other defenses, a comprehensive description of the patient's conduct, the means used to deal with the conduct, and the reasons for the force used will probably go a long way in convincing the trier of fact that self-defense was needed.

Justification—Defense of Another

A **justification defense** is used when the emergency health care professional uses the force necessary to protect a third party from injury. If a patient attacks a family member in the ED, the ED staff will probably rescue the family member. In the rescue attempt, it may be necessary to restrain or confine the patient. If the patient later sues for false imprisonment or assault and battery, the circumstances of the situation can lead to a justification defense.

Emergency Exception

The **emergency exception rule** to obtaining consent may also be useful in defending an assault and battery or false imprisonment claim. If the patient is in a life-threatening situation, and delays would lead to significant injury such as death, the emergency health care professional may rely on the emergency exception to the consent rule. The facts and circumstances surrounding the emergency situation should be easily retrieved from the medical records if an attempt is made to use the emergency exception rule.

CONCLUSION

Intentional torts can occur when the emergency health care provider knew or should have known his or her conduct would be offensive or damaging to a patient. The subjective intent related to what the emergency health care provider was thinking or feeling is usually not pertinent. An objective standard that looks at the conduct of the emergency health care provider can lead to an inference of intent. Intentional tort actions such as assault and battery and false imprisonment may arise from common, ordinary, everyday activities in the ED. The documentation of the patient's behavior and the emergency health care provider's response to that behavior is important. Defenses to intentional tort actions include consent, incapacity, self-defense, defense of another, and emergency exception. Recollection of the details of each interaction with each patient is beyond the usual and ordinary ability of emergency health care providers. Documentation is a useful tool to help prevent, defend against, and win intentional tort actions.

References

Alabama Pattern Jury Instructions Committee: *Alabama Pattern Jury Instructions* §§ 5.00, 16.00. New York, 1993, Lawyers Cooperative.

Banks v. *Medical Univ. of So. Carolina*, 444 S.E.2d 519 (S.C. 1994).

Miller v. *Rhode Island Hosp.*, 625 A.2d 778 (R.I. 1993).

Roberson v. *Provident House*, 576 So.2d 992 (La. 1991).

17

Professional Negligence

CHAPTER OUTLINE

Professional negligence, often referred to as *medical malpractice,* differs from intentional torts. Physicians, nurses, and prehospital providers may be subject to professional negligence actions. Professional negligence actions differ from ordinary negligence. One important difference is the standard of care. If an individual does not stop at a red light and strikes another individual's car, perhaps producing property and personal injury, an ordinary negligence action may arise. The jurors probably know that a red light means to stop. Although the facts of the particular case may be in dispute, the jury has common knowledge and experience concerning traffic signals. In a professional negligence case, the decision making and professional judgment involved in treating patients with multiple trauma injuries are beyond the common, ordinary knowledge and experience of the average lay person. Expert witnesses are used to identify, for the jury, what should have been done, what was done, and whether what was done or not done was appropriate for the particular facts of the case.

DEFINITION

Professional negligence is the failure to meet the standard of care that causes damage to an individual. The failure to meet the **standard of care** can be an **omission** or **commission.** *Commission* is the actual conduct of the professional as opposed to *omission,* which is that certain conduct was not present. Administering the wrong drug is an act of commission. Not administering an ordered drug at all is an act of omission.

ELEMENTS

As with most legal causes of action, proving a professional negligence action requires evidence to support the allegations in the complaint. Elements are the component parts of the legal theory used by the plaintiff to allege the defendant's liability. Each element must be proved for the lawsuit to succeed. The burden of proof varies and is determined by state law. The burden of proof in civil cases is generally **preponderance of the evidence,** or it is more likely than not. In professional negligence actions, some states require proof of each element by **substantial evidence.** Alabama (1975) defined substantial evidence as "that character of admissible evidence which would convince an unprejudiced thinking mind of the truth of the fact to which the evidence is directed" (Ala. Code § 6-5-542[5]). The usual elements in professional negligence cases are discussed below and listed in Box 17-1.

Duty

A **duty** must exist before a professional negligence action can occur. The facts that support a duty are the presence of a special relationship. For example, the

BOX 17-1   Elements of Professional Negligence Case

1. *Duty:* relationship between emergency health care provider *and* patient; element that is a question of law decided by judge.
2. *Breach of duty:* standard of care identified and then how the emergency health care provider's conduct met, or failed to meet, the standard of care; breach of duty exists if failed to meet standard of care; question of fact for jury unless minimal legal standards for expert not met.
3. *Causation:* links conduct of emergency health care provider to injury to patient: analyzed as either "but for" or "foreseeability": emergency health care provider knew, or should have known, conduct would lead to injury.
4. *Damages:* physical, mental, and/or emotional injury to patient: compensatory and/or punitive.

patient in an emergency department (ED) has a relationship with the emergency physician or nurse who provides care. Historically, physicians and hospitals had no duty to treat emergencies (Curran, 1997). Determination of a duty to a patient is a question of law and may be determined by a judge early in the case.

One of the first cases to establish the duty of a hospital to its patients was *Darling* v. *Charleston Community Memorial Hospital* in 1965. The Illinois Supreme Court said it is "both desirable and feasible that a hospital assume certain responsibilities for the care of the patient" (*Darling*, 211 N.E.2d at 257). The plaintiff broke his leg and had placement of a cast. The plaintiff suffered swelling, pain, and apparent neurovascular compromise. Over the course of 3 days, the cast was notched, cut, and then split. During the cast-splitting procedure, the plaintiff sustained cuts on both sides of his leg.

The plaintiff remained in the hospital for 14 days before transfer to another hospital. Although his leg wound drained and smelled and was painful, no action was taken to remove the cast or further assess his complaints. After transfer to another hospital, the plaintiff's leg was amputated below the knee. The subsequent lawsuit alleged that the hospital failed to adequately supervise medical staff, hospital nurses failed to report the patient's condition, or the hospital staff was negligent in failing to take action. The appellate court upheld the judgment of $110,000 against the hospital. *Darling* was also the first case to identify nurses' independent action as grounds for liability.

Telephone contact with the public is one area of concern in EDs. It is not uncommon for a member of the public to call the local ED, asking questions as simple as what over-the-counter preparation to use to get rid of lice to complex questions related to symptoms of concern to the individual. State laws typically do not specifically address the duty of an ED physician or nurse to provide telephone advice to members of the public. The important legal question is what duty, if any, exists when an ED physician or nurse provides advice over the telephone (Rothenberg, 1994). Many facilities prohibit, by policy, ED physicians and nurses from giving advice over the telephone. While the policy may serve to somewhat limit the facility's liability, the facts of each case must be explored before ruling out a basis for liability. A blanket policy of prohibition may in fact interfere with appropriate communication such as that for a patient with chest pain. In some circumstances, individuals who call the ED on the telephone should be told to go to an ED for evaluation (George et al., 1995). Whether a relationship exists between a physician, hospital, nurse, and patient may be determined from the circumstances (Heydemann, 1996).

A Washington case related to a patient seen in an ED who later called for telephone advice related to his initial condition. In *Adamski* v. *Tacoma General Hospital* (1978), the plaintiff injured a finger while playing basketball. The plaintiff alleged that an open fracture occurred and that the ED physician sutured the laceration without treating the underlying fracture. A discharge instruction sheet advised the patient to call his personal physician or the ED if particular symptoms occurred (redness, pain, swelling, or bleeding). The patient alleged that he contacted the ED the next day because of swelling and severe pain. The alleged telephone conversation with the on-duty ED nurse was that "pain and swelling were not unusual" after treatment. The patient alleged that he contacted the ED the second day after the injury and was told by an emergency nurse, again, that his symptoms were not unusual and to see his personal physician. The patient attempted to see an orthopedist who was unavailable but referred the patient to a local ED. The patient was seen in the second ED, admitted to the hospital, received treatment with antibiotics, and underwent surgical intervention for a wound infection. The finger eventually healed, and the patient sued the first ED physician and hospital. The hospital and physician moved for summary judgment. The trial court granted summary judgment in favor of the defendants, and the patient appealed. The appellate court reversed the trial court. As to the alleged telephone conversations with the ED nurses, the appellate court said the plaintiff submitted sufficient evidence, not refuted by the defendants, to raise a genuine issue of material fact as to the negligence of the ED nurses.

An attempt to extend a duty to third parties was unsuccessful in the Texas case of *Flynn* v. *Houston Emergicare, Inc.* (1993). The trial court entered summary judgment for the emergency physician, and the plaintiff appealed. The plaintiff attempted to extend the emergency physician's duty to the general public. The plaintiff suffered injuries after her car was struck by an individual en route home from the ED. The patient was not a party to the lawsuit.

The patient, not the plaintiff, came to the ED after using a reported large quantity of cocaine the night before. The ED physician examined and evaluated the patient and prescribed a β-blocker to counter the effects of the cocaine. The patient had a seizure while driving home and rear-ended the plaintiff's car. The plaintiff's lawsuit alleged that the ED physician was negligent in failing to admit the patient to the hospital and failing to warn him not to drive. The appellate court evaluated the ED physician's duty, if any, to the public.

After a review of the facts, the appellate court upheld the trial court's grant of summary judgment in favor of the emergency physician. The court evaluated the emergency physician's conduct and found that the emergency physician did not create the patient's impairment. The emergency physician did not contribute to or cause the plaintiff's injuries. The court also found that the emergency physician had no duty *to the plaintiff* (**duty to the third party**) to warn the patient not to drive.

The case is instructive in that had the injured party been the patient and not a member of the general public, a duty likely would have existed. However, because an emergency health care provider has a legal duty does not mean that the plaintiff succeeds. The other elements require proof in addition to the element of duty.

Breach of Duty

The standard of care and subsequent failure to adhere to the standard of care may be defined in the law. For example, the Alabama Medical Liability Act of 1987 defines the standard of care as "reasonable care, skill, and diligence as other similarly situated health care providers in the same general line of practice, ordinarily have and exercise in like cases" (Ala. Code § 6-5-542[2][1975]). Failure to exercise reasonable care as similarly situated providers is a breach of duty. The breach of duty analysis in a professional negligence action requires that first the standard of care and second how the emergency health care provider's conduct violated the standard of care be identified.

Generally, the identification of a specific standard of care is beyond the common knowledge and experience of an ordinary lay juror. Expert witnesses are used to identify the standard of care in a given set of facts and circumstances. An exception to the use of expert witnesses is the legal doctrine of *res ipsa loquitor.* In general, if the "thing speaks for itself," an expert witness may not be needed or used. For example, the case of a sponge or instrument left in a patient during surgery may not require an expert. The knowledge and experience of most jurors would allow them to decide, without an expert, that a mistake was made in leaving a foreign object in a patient during a surgical procedure (Smith, 1994). *Res ipsa loquitor* requires the plaintiff to prove that the defendant had full management and control of the instrumentality, that the defendant did not exercise proper care in the use of the instrumentality, and that injury to the plaintiff resulted (*Ward* v. *Forrester Day Care Inc.,* 1989).

If an expert is used, the standard of care formulated by the expert may be based on various sources. Hospital, facility, or organizational policies and procedures may provide the expert with expected conduct in certain cases. Individuals involved in writing policies and procedures should use absolute terms cautiously. Absolute terms such as *always, all, never, shall, none,* and *must* leave no room for deviation or professional judgment. Policies and procedures are important because of the voluntary nature of establishing and assuming a standard for the professionals and the health care organization.

Statements of professional associations such as standards, protocols, expectations, and course content may be used by the expert in forming an opinion about the standard of care. If the individual emergency health care provider is certified either by a professional board or association, the expert can use the course materials to establish the expected conduct. Texts, articles, or other published materials can also be used by the expert in establishing the standard of care.

The expert uses available resources and in addition to his or her knowledge, education, and experience, formulates an opinion regarding the standard of care. The expert then identifies how the emergency health care provider met, or did not meet, the standard of care. Usually, the opinion is to a reasonable degree of medical certainty.

Marks v. *Mandel* (1985) demonstrated how a hospital's policy and procedure manual can be used in establishing the standard of care. Michael Marks received an accidental gunshot wound to the chest. Forty minutes after the accident, the on-duty emergency physician instructed paramedics to bring Marks to the closest hospital. Marks arrived 1 hour after the accidental shooting, and the emergency physician attempted to call the on-call thoracic surgeon. The first-call thoracic surgeon was not available and the second-call surgeon was contacted. Approximately 3½ hours after the injury, Marks died. Marks' survivor brought an action against the hospital and physicians.

At the close of the plaintiff's case, the trial judge granted a partial directed verdict in favor of the defendants. The plaintiff appealed. One issue on appeal was the trial court's exclusion of the ED policy and procedure manual. The appellate court agreed with the plaintiff that the policy and procedure manual, which set out a detailed procedure for the on-call system, was necessary evidence. The case was reversed and instructions given to the trial court that the ED policy and procedure manual should be admitted as evidence at the retrial.

Causation

The emergency health care provider can violate the standard of care and not be negligent if causation does not exist. Causation links the omission or commission of the emergency health care provider's conduct to injury to the patient. There are two ways causation is determined in a case analysis: "but for" and "foreseeability." Under the **"but for" analysis,** the injury would not have occurred "but for" the action or inaction of the emergency health care provider. The **"foreseeability" test** is that the emergency health care provider knew, or should have known, that the action or inaction could lead to the injury sustained by the patient.

If the patient died, an autopsy report may be used to establish cause of death. An expert witness qualified to testify about causation is necessary to link the conduct of the emergency health care provider with the injury to the patient. Causation may be established by a pathologist or a similarly situated physician. Nurses generally are not qualified to testify as to causative links between conduct and injury.

In *Crouch* v. *Most* (1967), the patient required distal amputations of two digits after a rattlesnake bite. The patient alleged that the physician's negligent treatment resulted in the amputation of the distal tips of his two fingers. The plaintiff's expert, as well as the defendant's expert, discussed complications that can arise from a snake bite. Neither expert established that the treatment caused the gangrene of the distal two digits. Gangrene was presented as a complication of a snake bite to a digit. Although the plaintiff alleged several errors after a jury finding for the defendant, the appellate court found that causation was not established by the plaintiff.

Damages

Injury to the patient is required in a professional negligence action. Types of damages available to a patient include compensatory and possibly punitive. **Compensatory damages** must be proved by the patient. Medical expenses are a type of compensatory damage. For example, if a hospitalized patient requires prolonged hospitalization because of professional negligence, the additional medical expenses may be recovered if proven. Loss of wages may also be compensatory. Pain and suffering are compensatory although not quantifiable. **Punitive damages** serve to punish or deter conduct. Punitive damages in professional negligence actions may not be allowed or the amount may be capped.

State law determines the types of damages available and any caps that apply. A study of professional negligence litigation cases in New York revealed that the severity of the patient's disability was the best predictor of payment to plaintiffs (Brennan et al., 1996).

DEFENSES

Professional negligence actions are expensive from either the plaintiff's or defendant's perspective. The amount of time and money needed to prepare a case for the plaintiff can overwhelm the resources of a law practice. Defending a professional negligence case consumes a great deal of resources. In addition, the emergency health care provider takes seriously the allegation that negligence occurred in the care of a patient. There are defenses to claims of professional negligence and although the imagination of the defense lawyer is the only limiting factor, common defenses are discussed below and listed in Box 17-2.

BOX 17-2   Defenses to Professional Negligence Actions

1. No duty
2. No professional negligence
3. Statute of limitations
4. Failure to file notice of claim (governmental entities)
5. Failure to provide similarly situated expert
6. Physician-patient privilege
7. Medical or nursing judgment

No Duty

The duty element must be proven by the plaintiff. The determination of a legal duty is a question of law determined by the trial court. Professional negligence cases are often resolved at the summary judgment stage (before trial on the merits of the case) unless the plaintiff can show sufficient evidence early in the case that a legal duty existed between the emergency health care provider and the plaintiff.

No Negligence: Battle of the Experts

As previously discussed, expert testimony is usually necessary in professional negligence actions. The expert witness may testify on behalf of the plaintiff or the defendant. Each side will generally retain the services of an expert witness to testify as to the standard of care, whether or not a breach of the standard of care occurred, and whether the conduct of the defendant(s) caused the injuries claimed by the plaintiff. When experts testify and present competing theories, facts, or standards of care, the jury determines which expert to believe. The credibility of the expert as a witness is critical. An expert witness who testifies routinely for the plaintiff in professional negligence cases will probably be presented to the jury by the defense as a "hired gun" who makes a living from testifying against physicians, nurses, or hospitals. The expert's ability to communicate with the lay jury is critical regardless of who offers the expert as a witness. Sometimes one side or the other will attempt to present a case without an expert. In *Pogge* v. *Hale* (1993), the plaintiff attempted to use the hospital's policies and physician contract, after her expert witness was disqualified, to prove hospital and physician negligence. The court granted the defendants' motion for summary judgment based on plaintiff's failure to provide an expert witness. The appellate court upheld the trial court's summary judgment.

Statute of Limitations

The **statute of limitations** for different legal theories is governed by state statute. The statute of limitations defines the time period, or limits the time, that a lawsuit can be brought. The statute of limitations for a contract action, for example, differs from the statute of limitations for a professional negligence action. If the plaintiff fails to bring suit within the specified time period, the lawsuit is time-barred. In *Bleiler* v. *Bodnar* (1985), the plaintiff filed suit against a hospital, ED physician, and ED nurse for negligent treatment of an eye injury. The case was filed *2 days* after the 2½-year statute of limitation passed. The case was dismissed for failure to comply with the applicable statute of limitations. The plaintiff appealed. The appellate court upheld the dismissal of the professional negligence claims because the plaintiff failed to meet the time deadline established for filing professional negligence claims.

Failure to File a Notice of Claim

Professional negligence actions against governmental entities, such as municipal, county, state, or federal hospitals, may be governed by a notice of claim statute. A time limit usually exists that requires specific notice to the governmental entity before the suit is filed. The failure to file a notice of claim, or filing outside the specified time period, may bar the lawsuit even if the lawsuit is filed within the statute of limitations period.

Failure to Provide Similarly Situated Expert

Jordan v. *Brantley* (1991) demonstrated the significance of an expert witness' qualifications in a professional negligence action. The case related to misidentification of bodies after a motor vehicle crash. Because the emergency nurse was a health care provider, the plaintiff was required to offer expert testimony related to the standard of care. The expert selected by the plaintiffs was a registered nurse who had not worked in a hospital for 3 years before trial, admitted that she never worked in the ED full-time, and was not an expert in ED procedures. The defendant's expert was a current, practicing experienced emergency and trauma nurse. The appellate court found that the plaintiff's expert witness did not provide competent testimony and reversed the trial court. An expert witness who is "similarly situated" mandates someone currently in the field of practice related to the professional negligence action. State statute may define what is required of an expert witness in a professional negligence action.

Physician-Patient Privilege

All states allow some form of physician-patient privilege. A patient who sues his or her physician waives the privilege by virtue of placing the relationship at issue. However, the privilege may be used to prevent access to other patients. In *Dorris* v. *Detroit Osteopathic Hospital Corporation* (1996), the plaintiff sued the emergency physician and staff for allegedly administering intravenous Compazine after she expressly refused it. The patient had an episode of hypotension and required hospital admission. The plaintiff asked the court to compel the defendants to disclose the name of her ED roommate who allegedly witnessed the repeated refusals. The defendant refused, and the trial court ordered the defendant to disclose the information. The defendant appealed the trial court's decision and received a stay in the discovery proceedings. The defendant asserted nonparty physician-patient privilege. The appellate court ruled that the defendant did not have to disclose the name of a nonparty "patient who may, or may not have, overheard a conversation between the plaintiff and medical personnel" (*Dorris*, ¶ 8).

Medical or Nursing Judgment

Physicians and nurses exercise judgment in caring for patients on a daily basis. Patients may fail to understand, particularly if the emergency health care provider does not communicate findings, proposed treatment, and options, the amount of judgment needed to provide emergency care. Hospitals, physicians, and nurses do not ensure or guarantee the outcomes of care. In some circumstances, the physician or nurse's exercise of judgment is a defense to a professional negligence claim.

In *Adams* v. *Cooper Hospital* (1996), the defendants appealed a jury verdict and subsequent judgment against the hospital and individual registered nurse. The defendant argued the jury should have received an instruction related to a nurse exercising her judgment in the care of the patient. The New Jersey appellate court reviewed the medical judgment rule. The rule applies when there are "medically confirmed alternatives." The choice is usually between two alternatives where medical opinions may differ. The medical judgment rule is not a choice between negligent and non-negligent action, but a judgment that must be made given treatment alternatives.

The nurse in *Adams* allegedly failed to monitor the patient. The issue was the nurse's duty to constantly monitor her patient. The plaintiff had been admitted 15 days previously after multiple trauma. On the surgical ward, the plaintiff had increasing sputum production via his tracheotomy tube, a fever, and hypertension. The nurse administered the medication ordered, drew blood for an arterial blood gas analysis, and administered suction. The nurse left the patient alone for at least 30 minutes. The nurse who was the defendant and the trauma surgeon found the plaintiff lying on the floor. The plaintiff had significant sputum production, a comminuted fracture of the left hip, and head trauma. The nursing experts differed over whether the nurse should have "constantly" monitored the patient. The defendant attempted to assert nursing judgment as an issue, but the appellate court held that the trial court did not err in refusing to instruct the jury on the medical judgment rule. The experts focused on the defendant's conduct and not the exercise of judgment between two schools of accepted medical opinion.

The changing complexity of the emergency care environment will probably lead to increased use of medical and nursing judgment as a defense to a professional negligence action. Whether or not to apply restraints on a patient is an area of nursing judgment addressed in at least one jurisdiction (George et al., 1999).

EMERGING ISSUES

The use of practice parameters or guidelines and how those parameters relate to the standard of care in professional negligence actions are worthy of notice (King, 1997). On the surface, practice parameters may appear to be wonderful quality improvement tools. However, in the professional negligence setting, practice parameters and guidelines can be used to help establish the standard of care for a given group of patients.

Claims of negligent hiring, training, and supervision of physicians and nurses are emerging in the professional negligence arena. Another emerging issue is the failure to follow the chain of command and report unsafe practices that can harm patients.

Managed care including the duty owed to managed care enrollees by on-call plan physicians is an emerging issue. A Texas case addressed the relationship between a managed care on-call physician and a patient in *Hand* v. *Tavera* (1993). Hand appealed a summary judgment in favor of Dr. Tavera. The appellate court reviewed the facts and law of the case and reversed the summary judgment. Hand was seen in the ED with a complaint of headache. The emergency physician decided to admit Hand to the hospital and contacted Tavera, the managed care on-call physician who could authorize admissions. Tavera decided Hand could be treated as an outpatient and Hand was discharged from the ED. A few hours later Hand suffered a cerebrovascular accident.

Tavera's summary judgment motion claimed he did not owe Hand a duty as no physician-patient relationship existed. The appellate court said the managed care plan brought Hand and Tavera together and created the relationship. The court held that when a managed care plan patient goes to a participating hospital ED and the plan's on-call physician is consulted about treatment or admission, a physician-patient relationship existed (*Hand,* 864 S.W.2d at 679).

CONCLUSION

Professional negligence cases require that the elements be proved by the plaintiff: (1) duty, (2) breach of duty, (3) causation, and (4) damages. Whether or not a duty exists is a matter of law for the judge to decide. The breach of duty element generally requires expert witnesses to relay the information to the jury in an understandable format. Causation and damages must also be proven before a professional negligence claim succeeds. Defenses to professional negligence claims are only as limited as the defense lawyer's imagination. Emerging issues will continue to surface during the next few years as technologic changes and other societal factors bring about changes in the health care environment. Preparation is key in asserting any claim or defense in the professional negligence arena.

References

Adams v. *Cooper Hosp.,* 684 A.2d 506 (N.J. Super. Ct. 1996).

Adamski v. *Tacoma General Hospital,* 579 P.2d 970 (Wash. App. 1978).

Ala. Code §§ 6-5-542(2), (5) (1975).

Bleiler v. *Bodnar,* 65 N.Y.2d 65, 479 N.E.2d 230 (N.Y. 1985).

Brennan TA, Sox CM, Burstein HR: Relation between negligent adverse events and the outcomes of medical-malpractice litigation, *N Engl J Med* 335:1963, 1996.

Crouch v. *Most,* 432 P.2d 250 (N.M. 1967).

Curran WJ: Legal history of emergency medicine from medieval common law to the AIDS epidemic, *Am J Emerg Med* 15:658, 1997.

Darling v. *Charleston Comm. Memorial Hosp.,* 211 N.E.2d 253 (Ill. 1965).

Dorris v. *Detroit Osteopathic Hosp. Corp.,* No. 183036 (Mich. Ct. App. 1996).

Flynn v. *Houston Emergicare, Inc.,* 869 S.W.2d 403 (Tex. Ct. App. 1993).

George JE, Quattrone MS, Goldstone M: Emergency department telephone advice, *J Emerg Nurs* 21:450, 1995.

George JE, Quattrone MS, Goldstone M: Nursing judgment—is it alive? *J Emerg Nurs* 25:43, 1999.

Hand v. *Tavera,* 864 S.W.2d 678 (Tex. Ct. App. 1993).

Heydemann HW, Macdonald MG, Neely EJ: Medical malpractice. In *Treatise on health law.*

Jordan v. *Brantley,* 589 So. 2d 680 (Ala. 1991).

King JY: Practice guidelines and medical malpractice litigation, *Med Law* 16:29, 1997.

Marks v. *Mandel,* 477 So. d 1036 (Fla. App. 1985).

Pogge v. *Hale,* 625 N.E.2d 792 (Ill. Ct. App. 1993).

Rothenberg MA: *Emergency medicine malpractice,* ed 2, New York, 1994, Wiley.

Smith JW: *Hospital liability,* § 4.03, New York, 1994, Law Journal Seminars-Press.

Ward v. *Forrester Day Care, Inc.,* 547 So.2d 410 (Ala. 1989).

Suggested Readings

De Ville K: Act first and look up the law afterward? Medical malpractice and the ethics of defensive medicine, *Theor Med Bioeth* 19:569, 1998.

De Ville K: Medical malpractice in twentieth century United States. The interaction of technology, law and culture, *Int J Technol Assess Health Care* 14(2):197, 1998.

Gittler GJ, Goldstein EJ: The elements of medical malpractice: an overview, *Clin Infect Dis* 23:1152, 1996.

Koniak-Griffin D, Prepas R: Expanding horizons: from bedside nurse to expert witness, *J Perinat Neonatal Nurse* 10(3):70, 1996.

Levinson W, Roter DL, Mullooly JP, et al: Physician-patient communication: the relationship with malpractice claims among primary care physicians and surgeons, *JAMA* 277:553, 1997.

Majoribanks T, Good MJ, Lawthers AG, Peterson LM: Physicians' discourses on malpractice and the meaning of malpractice, *J Health Soc Behav* 37:163, 1996.

Spiegel AD, Kavaler F: America's first medical malpractice crisis, 1835-1865, *J Community Health* 22:283, 1997.

Spurr SJ, Simmons WO: Medical malpractice in Michigan: an economic analysis, *J Health Polit Policy Law* 21:315, 1996.

Weintraub MI: Medicolegal aspects of iatrogenic injuries, *Neurol Clin* 16:217, 1998.

Suggested Websites

www.findlaw.com	Navigational and search engine from site used to locate statutes, cases, and other legal materials
www.medlaw.com	Site with reports of interesting cases, updates on health-related legal issues
www.nursinglaw.com	Site with updates on nursing-related legal issues

18

Other Torts

CHAPTER OUTLINE

Other legal theories may be used in tort cases brought by patients. Although these torts may not be as common as professional negligence or assault and battery, the emergency health care professional should have a rudimentary understanding of the other torts. Defamation, invasion of privacy, and negligent infliction of emotional distress may be causes of action brought by patients against the emergency health care provider. A wrongful death action may be brought by the survivors of a patient against the emergency health care provider.

DEFAMATION

Defamation involves libel or slander about an individual. **Libel** is the written word and **slander** is the spoken word. Although each state has laws related to defamation, the common elements include (1) communication to another, (2) with some degree of fault, (3) of a false and defamatory statement of fact, and (4) concerning the plaintiff (Alabama Pattern Jury Instructions, 1998). The types of statements that may be considered defamatory include statements, either written or oral, that subject the individual to public hatred, contempt, or ridicule. Statements that relate to moral turpitude offenses such as fraud and dishonesty may be defamatory.

The element of communication requires publication. Publication is communicating the statement to a third party. An exception exists for communication within a business. For example, the statements made to a physician by a nurse about a patient are generally intrabusiness communications because the statements are not published to a third party. A nurse who discusses an individual patient with his or her friends or family is publishing the statement outside the business, and therefore no protection exists. The element "with some degree of fault" refers to either intent or negligence. If the defamatory statement is published with the knowledge that the statement was false or with reckless disregard as to the truth of the statement, fault can be shown by the plaintiff. The element "of a false and defamatory statement of fact" refers to the communication itself. Communication of a statement, whether verbally or in writing, that injures an individual's reputation may be defamatory. Speculation, gossip, and discussion about an individual should be avoided unless one has knowledge of the facts related to the issue. "Concerning the plaintiff" is the element that requires a link between the communication, alleged defamatory statements, and the plaintiff. Using an individual's name links the communication to the plaintiff.

Defamation actions are common in employee-employer lawsuits. The element of publication is significant in employee-employer suits because if the communication or publication only occurred within the facility, the employee-plaintiff will find it difficult to prove the element of publication or communication to another. Employee complaints, discussions, gripe sessions, or gossip can lead to publication outside the facility. Care should be used in discussing any issues of discipline, personal lives, or information about one employee to another. An employee who repeats the statement to an outside third party could be held liable for defamation even though the statement did not originate with him or her.

The damages available to a plaintiff depend to some extent on whether the plaintiff is a private or public figure. Damages compensate for injury to reputation, and no formula exists to guide a jury. Punitive damages may or may not be available. The plaintiff's burden of proof of fault is higher if the plaintiff is a public figure or official. The reasoning is logical as someone who is considered a public figure or official is subject to more public statements about his or her actions.

Defenses

Truth is an absolute defense to a defamation action. The plaintiff has the burden of proving the statement was false. The defendant may assert truth as an affirmative defense. If so, then the defendant must prove the statement was true. Privileged communication is also a defense to defamation. There are varying degrees of privilege. Absolute privilege occurs in legislative, judicial, or quasi-judicial proceedings. Thus, a legislator can make statements on the legislative floor during a legislative proceeding and not be held liable for defamation. Qualified privilege may attach to corporate communications when the publication did not occur outside the corporation. The position of the plaintiff in the community is important as well. A private figure receives more protection than a public figure or public official.

INVASION OF PRIVACY

Common law actions for **invasion of privacy** or violation to the right to privacy existed for years. The right to privacy, even if not codified in state or federal law, at common law related to the rights of an individual to be free from unwarranted publicity, wrongful intrusion into one's private activities, publicizing of an individual's private affairs when the public has no legitimate concern, or unwanted use of an individual's likeness commercially (Alabama Pattern Jury Instructions, 1993).

In the emergency health care setting, inappropriate communication about an individual's health status can lead to invasion of privacy legal action. Patient information stored in a hospital's computer system should be secure. If a hospital employee knows a patient and reads about the patient without a need to know the information, the patient's privacy is invaded even if the patient is unaware the invasion occurred. Access to sensitive information such as human immunodeficiency virus test results, diagnoses related to mental illness, or an individual's personal demographic information should be limited to those with a legitimate purpose. Disclosure of such sensitive information may create legal liability for the facility as well as for the individual.

Patients expect that medical information will be kept confidential. Although the emergency health care professional may have personal values or beliefs that a spouse is entitled to know about a patient's diagnosis of a sexually transmitted disease, disclosure of that information without the patient's consent can lead to liability for violation of privacy. Reportable diseases are an exception to privacy laws because statute and regulations specifically override the individual's concern for privacy in the interest of protecting the public. However, the legal mechanism for reporting should be followed rather than disclosing information without thought as to the legal liability.

Defenses

Consent of the patient for disclosure of the information or mandatory legal reporting requirements are potential defenses for violation of privacy. Without consent or a legal foundation for disclosure, viable defenses may not be readily available. Unauthorized access or disclosure by an employee may be used as a defense by the facility. Such unauthorized disclosure is not within the line and scope of employment.

NEGLIGENT INFLICTION OF EMOTIONAL DISTRESS

Negligent infliction of emotional distress may go hand in hand with an invasion of privacy action, especially if the patient suffered shame, humiliation, or embarrassment. The facility may have failed to exercise reasonable care with a resulting infliction of emotional distress if processes are not in place to protect information, limit access to information, or provide guidance to employees related to disclosure of information. Not all states recognize negligent infliction of emotional distress as a cause of action.

As with other cases, the plaintiff must prove that the emergency health care professional failed to exercise reasonable care and the result was infliction of emotional distress. If the patient received treatment for emotional distress, those treatment records may be used by the defense in establishing a question about the plaintiff's credibility. Damages are generally available if the patient can prove the elements of negligence and emotional distress. A link, or causation, between the conduct of the defendant(s) and the plaintiff's emotional distress must be proven as well.

Defenses

The usual defense in a negligent infliction of emotional distress case is that no negligence occurred. Establishing that reasonable care was exercised in the given set of circumstances may be effective. The investigation and questioning about the extent of the plaintiff's emotional distress is a common, and often effective, defense tactic.

WRONGFUL DEATH

Wrongful death is a legal cause of action *for survivors* in all 50 states. Wrongful death does not have separate elements but relies on the underlying theory of the case. For example, a wrongful death that occurred after professional negligence, is a wrongful death case based on professional negligence. The survivor who brings a wrongful death case must prove the underlying theory of the case. Thus, in a wrongful death case based on professional negligence, the survivor must prove that a duty existed, the duty was breached, and the omission or commission of the emergency health care professional caused the injury (death), and that he or she is entitled to damages (see Chapter 17). Damages are often categorized as punitive because the deceased is not alive to receive compensatory damages. Medical costs, lost earning potential, and expenses may be brought forth. The defenses to a professional negligence action are available in a wrongful death action based on professional negligence.

CONCLUSION

Other torts, although not as common as professional negligence or assault and battery, may be brought by a patient against an emergency health care professional. A rudimentary understanding is necessary to defend against actions such as defamation, violation of the right to privacy, and negligent infliction of emotional distress. Wrongful death is a legal cause of action brought by survivors of the patient. Wrongful death is based on the underlying legal theory such as professional negligence. The survivor brings a wrongful death action to hold the emergency health care professional accountable for professional negligence omissions or commissions that resulted in death.

References

Alabama Pattern Jury Instructions. Defamation. § 23.00 (Supp. West 1998).
Alabama Pattern Jury Instructions. Right of Privacy. §35.00 (1993).

Appendixes

DISCLAIMER

The following forms are samples only. Specific state and federal laws govern how the forms shall look and what the content shall contain.

Appendix A

Summons

IN THE CIRCUIT COURT FOR _____ COUNTY, SOMEWHERE USA

PLAINTIFF,

Vs.   Case Number:

DEFENDANT.

SUMMONS

To any sheriff or any person authorized by either Rules 4.1(b)(2) or 4.2(b)(2) or 4.4(b)(2) of the Somewhere's Rules of Civil Procedure to effect service.

You are hereby commanded to serve this summons and a copy of the complaint in this action upon defendant _____. The summons, complaint and accompanying documents should be personally served on the defendant company at its principal place of business, <u>address, city, state, zip.</u>

NOTICE TO DEFENDANT

The complaint which is attached to this summons is important and you must take immediate action to protect your rights. You are required to mail or hand deliver a copy of a written Answer, either admitting or denying each allegation in the complaint to _____ the lawyer for the Plaintiff, whose address is: <u>LAW FIRM NAME, ADDRESS, CITY, STATE, ZIP.</u> THIS ANSWER MUST BE MAILED OR DELIVERED WITHIN THIRTY (30) DAYS AFTER THIS SUMMONS AND COMPLAINT WERE DELIVERED TO YOU OR A JUDGMENT BY DEFAULT MAY BE ENTERED AGAINST YOU FOR THE MONEY OR OTHER THINGS DEMANDED IN THIS COMPLAINT. You must also file the original of your Answer with the Clerk of this Court within a reasonable time afterward.

Dated: _____   _____
                                 Clerk of Court

* * * * * * * *

_____

RETURN ON SERVICE

Received this summons at _____ on _____ and on _____ at _____ _____ I served it on the within named Defendant by delivering a copy of the process and accompanying documents to the Defendant in person.

Dated: _____, 2000   _____

Appendix B

Civil Subpoena

IN THE CIRCUIT COURT OF _____ COUNTY, ALABAMA

JOHN DOE,	)	
PLAINTIFF,	)	
	)	**CIVIL ACTION NUMBER:**
		CC 2000-XXXXXX
V.	)	
	)	
XYZ MEDICAL CENTER, ALPHA)		
BRAVO, M.D., ECHO HOTEL, RN)		
DEFENDANTS.	)	

CIVIL SUBPOENA

TO: ALPHA BRAVO, M.D.
    5555 River Road
    Somewhere, AL 35XXX

You Are Hereby Commanded to appear in the Circuit Court of _____ County, at _____ Street, courtroom of Judge _____, in the City of Somewhere, on the 26th day of January, 2001, at 9:00 o'clock AM to testify on behalf of the Plaintiff, John Doe, in the above entitled action.

November 15, 2000

_____   _____
Attorney for Plaintiff   Clerk
Law Firm Name
Law Firm Address   BY: _____
Somewhere, AL 35XXX   Deputy Clerk
XXX-XXX-XXXX

RETURN ON SERVICE

Received this subpoena at _____ on _____ and on _____ at _____ I served it on the within named ALPHA BRAVO by delivering a copy of CIVIL SUBPOENA to him.

Dated: _____, 2000.   _____

Appendix C

Civil Subpoena Duces Tecum

IN THE CIRCUIT COURT OF _____ COUNTY, ALABAMA

JOHN DOE,	)	
Plaintiff,	)	CV 2000-XXXXXX
vs.	)	
	)	
XYZ MEDICAL CENTER,	)	
ALPHA BRAVO, M.D., and	)	
ECHO HOTEL, RN,	)	
	)	
Defendants.	)	

CIVIL SUBPOENA DUCES TECUM

TO: Juliette November
Custodian of Records
XYZ Medical Center
P.O. Box XXX
Somewhere, USA XXXXX

You are Hereby Commanded to appear in the Circuit Court of _____ County at Somewhere, City of Anywhere, USA, on the 26th day of January, 2001, at 9:00 A.M. in Judge_____'s courtroom to testify on behalf of the Plaintiff in the above entitled action and bring with you

CERTIFIED COPIES OF MEDICAL AND TREATMENT RECORDS FOR JOHN DOE, DOB: X-XX-XXXX, SSN: XXX-XX-XXXX, from January 1, 1996 – present.

November 15, 2000

_____	_____
Attorney for Plaintiff	Clerk
Law Firm Name	
Law Firm Address	BY: _____
City, State, Zip	Deputy Clerk
Telephone Number	

RETURN ON SERVICE

Received this subpoena duces tecum at _____ on _____ and on _____ at _____ I served it on the within named Juliette November by certified mail to the address listed.

_____
Clerk

Appendix D

Rights of Psychiatric Patients

RIGHTS OF PSYCHIATRIC PATIENTS

Each person voluntarily admitted or involuntarily detained for evaluation or treatment shall have the following rights:

a. To wear his or her own clothes; to keep and use personal possessions including toilet articles; and to keep and spend a reasonable sum of his or her own money for expenses and small purchases.

b. To have access to individual storage space for private use.

c. To see visitors each day.

d. To have reasonable access to telephones, both to make and receive confidential calls.

e. To have ready access to letter-writing materials, including stamps, and to mail and receive unopened correspondence.

f. To refuse shock treatment and any form of convulsive therapy.

g. To refuse psychosurgery.

h. To see and receive the services of a patient advocate who has no direct or indirect clinical or administrative responsibility for the person. The Patients' Rights Advocate may be contacted at _____ _____ [insert address, phone number and times advocates may be contacted].

i. Other rights as specified by regulation.

No person may be presumed incompetent because he or she has been evaluated or treated for a mental disorder or chronic alcoholism, regardless of whether the treatment was voluntarily or involuntarily received.

I hereby acknowledge receipt of a copy of rights of patients and hereby certify that I understand these rights as printed above.

Date: _____   Time: _____ AM/PM

Signature: _____
          [patient]

Witness: _____

A COPY OF THIS FORM MUST BE GIVEN TO PATIENT; PLACE ORIGINAL IN MEDICAL RECORD

Appendix E

Discovery Document

IN THE CIRCUIT COURT OF _____ ALABAMA

JANE DOE,	)	
PLAINTIFF,	)	
VS.	)	CIVIL ACTION NO. <u>CC 2000-XXXXX</u>
XYZ HOSPITAL,	)	
DEFENDANT.	)	

REQUEST FOR PRODUCTION OF DOCUMENTS UNDER RULE XX

Plaintiff requests Defendant produce and/or permit the Plaintiff to inspect and copy each of the following documents at the office of the attorney for the Plaintiff within the time and manner prescribed by law:

1. Any and all records, written or otherwise, maintained by Defendant or anyone on Defendant's behalf, regarding the medical, nursing, diagnostic and/or health care provided to Plaintiff during the past five (5) years.

2. Any and all financial transaction records related to the Plaintiff's services received at Defendant's facilities during the past five (5) years.

3. The disciplinary and/or personnel files of any and all current or former employees of XYZ Hospital, agents or representatives operating on behalf of XYZ Hospital, who participated in the care of Plaintiff at Defendant's facilities over past five (5) years.

4. Any and all reports to state licensing agencies, voluntary accrediting organizations, and annual reports for XYZ Hospital during the past three (3) years.

5. Any and all written statements by any individual to any entity, including but not limited to, insurers, state licensing agencies, or voluntary accrediting agencies regarding the Plaintiff at any time during the past five (5) years.

6. The written minutes of medical staff committee meetings over the past one (1) year.

7. All papers, statements, or written memorandum of every kind and description reflecting any and all monies received from any source by you for services provided to Plaintiff to date hereof for the last five (5) years.

8. Profit and loss statements and balance sheets of any company whatsoever in which you have any interest, legal or equitable, up to and including instant date for the last five (5) years.

9. Any settlements, judicial awards or damages paid by you, or on your behalf, as a consequence of any legal actions undertaken by any recipient of your health care services over the past ten (10) years.

LAW FIRM FOR PLAINTIFF
ATTORNEY FOR PLAINTIFF
LAW FIRM ADDRESS
CITY/STATE/ZIP   BY: _____
TELEPHONE NUMBER   ATTORNEY SIGNATURE

CERTIFICATE OF SERVICE

I hereby certify that I have served a copy of the foregoing pleading on all counsel in this proceeding by forwarding a copy of same to _____ Counsel for the Defendant at (Address, City, State, Zip) by U.S. Mail, properly addressed and First Class postage prepaid on this the _____ day of November, 2000.

_____
OF COUNSEL

Appendix F

Medical Record Release Form

Sample Medical Record Release Form

I, _____, hereby grant authorization to
_____ Medical Center to release my medical records as described
below. The records should be sent to my attorney at the following address:

> XYZ Law Firm
> 555 River Road
> Somewhere, AL 35XXX

The law firm will pay the reasonable cost of duplicating the records as allowed
by state law.

NAME OF PATIENT: _____

DATE OF BIRTH: _____

SOCIAL SECURITY NUMBER: _____

MOTHER'S MAIDEN NAME: _____

DATE(S) OF SERVICE: _____

TYPES RECORDS REQUESTED:

> Any & all records for dates listed above   Laboratory Results only
>
> All emergency department records   Any & all outpatient records

DATE: _____   _____
                         Signature of Patient or Patient's Legal
                         Representative

_____

_____

Witness(es)

_____

Appendix G

Emergency Treatment Physician Certification

EMERGENCY TREATMENT PHYSICIAN CERTIFICATION

_____ is in need of emergency treatment. We, the undersigned treating physicians, consider the treatment necessary to preserve the life or health of _____. The authorities of the hospital have been unable to establish communications with the patient's legal representative(s) within a reasonable time. We certify that, in our professional judgment, any further delay in the performance of medical treatment or an emergency operation on this patient would seriously increase the danger to _____ life or health.

Dated: _____ at _____ [time]. _____
                                                Signature of Physician [1]

                                                _____
                                                Signature of Physician [2]

_____
Signature of Witness

Note: Emergency Treatment Physician Certification is to be used **only** in the event the patient, patient's legal guardian, representative, or other duly authorized person is not available to consent to emergency treatment.

Appendix H

Hospital Standardized Consent Form

_____ HOSPITAL
Somewhere, Alabama XXXXX

CONSENT FOR TREATMENT

I, or my representative whose signature is indicated below, voluntarily authorize and consent to the usual and customary examinations, tests, and procedures as ordered by my physician and his/her associates. For the purpose of advancing medical knowledge, I consent to the admittance of medical students and students of other health care professions in accordance with the ordinary practices of the medical facility.

CONSENT TO SEARCH PERSONAL BELONGINGS AND ACKNOWLEDGMENT OF HOSPITAL RIGHTS TO SEARCH

I or my representative agrees to notify hospital staff and voluntarily surrender any items in my possession that may be considered hazardous to my health or the health or welfare of others on admission. I acknowledge the right of _____ Hospital staff to search the patient's personal belongings and consent to a search of same if it is believed that the patient is in possession of items which may be considered hazardous to the patient or others.

RELEASE FROM RESPONSIBILITY FOR LOSS/DAMAGE OF VALUABLES

I or my representative understand that _____ Hospital is not responsible for the loss or damage of personal property and valuables kept by the patient. _____ Hospital shall not be liable for loss or damage to any personal property, unless deposited with the hospital for safekeeping and shall not in any event be liable in excess of $500.00 for any loss of or damage to any personal belongings.

ASSIGNMENT OF INSURANCE BENEFITS—AGREEMENT TO PAY HOSPITAL

I hereby request and authorize payment for Medicare benefits directly to _____ Hospital for services furnished by the hospital, attending physician, or specialists. I hereby authorize full payment directly to the _____ Hospital and attending physicians of insurance benefits including Medicaid, major medical insurance, surgical, and/or third party benefits. I understand that I am financially responsible to the hospital and physician for charges not covered by this assignment. The hospital may use appropriate means to collect the balance due including referral to an outside collection agency and/or litigation. In the event of default, I agree to pay reasonable attorney fees and court costs, necessitated in order to collect the unpaid balance.

AUTHORIZATION FOR RELEASE OF MEDICAL INFORMATION

The hospital and attending physician are authorized to furnish any medical information requested by Medicare, Medicaid, insurance companies, or other third party payors processing benefits on my behalf or any public agency which may be assisting in payment for my care. A copy of this form is deemed to be valid as the original.

Patient Signature: _____   Date: _____

Patient Representative: _____   Relationship: _____

Witness: _____   Date: _____

Appendix I

Websites for Medical/Nursing Boards by State

STATE/JURISDICTION	MEDICAL LICENSING BOARD	NURSING LICENSING BOARD
Alabama	www.albme.org	www.abn.state.al.us
Alaska	www.state.ak.us/local	www.dced.state.ak.us/occ/pnur.htm
Arizona	Docboard.org/bomex/index.htm	www.azboardofnursing.org
Arkansas		www.state.ar.us/nurse
California	www.medbd.ca.gov	RN: www.rn.ca.gov/
		VN: www.bvnpt.ca.gov/
Colorado	Dora.state.co.us/medical	www.dora.state.co.us/nursing
Connecticut		www.state.ct.us/dph/
Delaware		none
District of Columbia	www.dchealth.com	none
Florida	www.doh.state.fl.us	Www.doh.state.fl.us/mqa/nursing/rnhome.htm
Georgia	Sos.state.ga.us/EBD/	RN: www.sos.state.ga.us/ebd-rn/
		PN: www.sos.state.ga.us/ebd-lpn/
Guam		None
Hawaii	www.state.hi.us	None
Idaho	www.idacare.org	Www.state.id.us/ibnhome.htm
Illinois	www.dpr.state.il.us	www.dpr.state.il.us/
Indiana	www.ai.org/hpb	Www.ai.org/hpb
Iowa	www.docboard.org	www.state.ia.us/government/nursing/
Kansas	www.ink.org/public/boha	www.ink.org/public/ksbn/
Kentucky	www.state.ky.us/agencies/kbml	www.kbn.state.ky.us/
Louisiana		RN: www.lsbn.state.la.us/
Maine	www.docboard.org/me/me_home.htm	Www.state.me.us/pfr/auxboards/nurhome.htm
Maryland	www.docboard.org	www.dhmh1d.dhmh.state.md.us/mbn/
Massachusetts	www.massmedboard.org	www.state.ma.us/reg/boards/rn/
Michigan	www.cis.state.mi.us	Www.cis.state.mi.us/bhser/genover.htm
Minnesota	www.bmp.state.mn.us	www.nursingboard.state.mn.us/

Table continued on following page

STATE/JURISDICTION	MEDICAL LICENSING BOARD	NURSING LICENSING BOARD
Mississippi	www.msbml.state.ms.us	None
Missouri	www.ecodev.state.mo.us/pr/healarts/	www.ecodev.state.mo.us/pr/nursing/
Montana	none	Www.com.state.mt.us/License/POL/index.htm
Nebraska	www.hhs.state.ne.us/	Www.hhs.state.ne.us/crl/nns.htm
Nevada		Www.nursingboard.state.nv.us
New Hampshire	www.state.nh.us/medicine	www.state.nh.us/nursing/
New Jersey	www.state.nj.us	Www.state.nj.us/lps/ca/medical.htm
New Mexico		Www.state.nm.us/clients/nursing
New York	www.op.nysed.gov	Www.nysed.gov/prof/nurse.htm
North Carolina	www.docboard.org	www.ncbon.com/
North Dakota		www.ndbon.org/
Ohio	www.state.oh.us/med/	www.state.oh.us/nur/
Oklahoma	www.osbmls.state.ok.us	
Oregon	www.bme.state.or.us	www.osbn.state.or.us/
Pennsylvania	www.dos.state.pa.us	Www.dos.state.pa.us/bpoa/nurbd/mainpage.htm
Rhode Island	www.docboard.org/ri/main.htm	
South Carolina	www.llr.state.sc.us./me.htm	Www.llr.state.sc.us/bon.htm
South Dakota		www.state.sd.us/dcr/nursing/
Tennessee	www.state.tn.us/health	170.142.76.180/bmf-bin/BMFproflist.pl
Texas	www.tsbme.state.tx.us	RN: www.bne.state.tx.us/
		VN: link.tsl.state.tx.us/tx/bvne/
Utah	www.commerce.state.ut.us	www.commerce.state.ut.us/
Vermont	www.docboard.org/vt/vermont.htm	Vtprofessionals.org/nurses/
Virginia	www.dhp.state.va.us/	www.dhp.state.va.us/
Washington	www.doh.wa.gov	www.doh.wa.gov/hsqa/hpqad/Nursing/
West Virginia	www.wvdhhr.org/wvbom	RN: www.state.wv.us/nurses/m/
		PN: www.lpnboard.state.wv.us/
Wisconsin	Badger.state.wi.us	www.state.wi.us/
Wyoming	www.state.wy.us/director/boards/medicine.htm	Commerce.state.wy.us/b%26c/nb/

Appendix J

Summary of Cases
by Chapter

CHAPTER 4: LAW AND ETHICS IN EMERGENCY CARE

Roe v. *Wade,* 410 U.S. 113, 93 S.Ct. 705, 35 L.Ed. 2d (1973). The U.S. Supreme Court relied on a "zone of privacy" in determining that a woman's decision about whether to terminate a pregnancy is private in the first trimester of pregnancy. *Roe* stood for the proposition that certain aspects of our lives are private and the government must prove a compelling interest to intercede in these private areas (p. 30).

CHAPTER 5: CONSENT

Medeiros v. *Yashar,* 588 A.2d 1038 (R.I. 1991). This case demonstrates that unless a patient is informed of the particular material risks of an operation, the patient cannot intelligently ask questions concerning the procedure, nor can the patient give informed consent. How this communication process occurs can also be important (p. 38).

Belcher v. *Charleston Area Medical Center,* 422 S.E.2d 827 (W.Va. 1992). The court held that procedures, treatment, or withholding of treatment requires the consent of a mature minor. The court recognized that a physician's assessment is subject to later review, and no bright line test exists for determining whether a minor is sufficiently mature to consent to medical care (pp. 55-56).

Miller v. *Rhode Island Hospital,* 625 A.2d 778 (R.I. 1993). The appellate court stated that an assessment of the patient's understanding of the risks and consequences was appropriate where mental capacity was altered by intoxication. The court further stated that whether intoxication impairs a patient's capacity to decide about medical procedures or treatment was a question of fact for the jury (p. 59).

CHAPTER 6: REFUSAL TO CONSENT OR WITHDRAWAL OF CONSENT

In Re E.G., 549 N.E.2d 322 (Ill. 1989). The court ruled the 17-year-old woman a mature minor, thus setting a legal precedent in Illinois requiring proof of maturity by clear and convincing evidence. The court also established direction for future cases to ensure the consideration of the interests of the state in its role as guardian of those who cannot care for themselves (p. 67).

Application of Long Island Jewish Medical Center, 557 N.Y.S.2d 239 (Sup. Ct. 1990). The court recognized the merit of the mature minor doctrine but found that given the facts of this particular case, the minor was not mature. The judge granted the petition of the hospital and authorized the administration of blood transfusions whenever medically necessary (pp. 67-68).

Kirby v. *Spivey,* 307 S.E.2d 538 (Ga. Ct. App. 1983). This case demonstrates the importance of documenting discussions with patients regarding refusal of care. A specific description of the patient's behavior is invaluable should the patient's capacity be an issue (p. 69).

M.N. v. *Southern Baptist Hospital of Florida, Inc.,* 648 So. 2d 769 (Fla. Ct. App. 1994). The appellate court indicated that it was appropriate for a court to override the parent-child relationship when the state's interest is compelling and the least intrusive interference method is used. The court remanded the case to the trial court to balance the competing interests of the state (p. 70).

Matter of Hamilton, 657 S.W.2d 425 (Tenn. Ct. App. 1983). The court ruled that the state's interests in protecting the child from a painful death outweighed the parents' interest in practicing their religious beliefs (p. 71).

Matter of Thomas B., 574 N.Y.S.2d 659 (Fam. Ct. N.Y.C. 1991). The court decided that if a person younger than 18 years of age cannot give consent, that such a person cannot withhold consent either. The court expressed its reluctance to disregard the protests of the 15-year-old but ordered the minor to cooperate (pp. 71-72).

In Re Guardianship of Myers, 610 N.E.2d 663 (Ohio Com. Pl. 1993). The court applied the best interest test, in which a neutral third party (a judge) evaluates the circumstances and renders a decision based on what is in the best interest of the patient. The judge in this case decided the removal of life-sustaining treatment was in the best interest of the minor (p. 72).

In Re Doe, 418 S.E.2d 3 (Ga. 1992). This case demonstrates the difficulty when parents disagree about the treatment of their child. Here, the trial court issued an injunction preventing the hospital from enforcing a DNR order or deescalating treatment *unless both parents agreed.* The Georgia Supreme Court upheld the trial court's judgment (p. 73).

Cruzan v. *Director,* Missouri Dept. Health, 497 U.S. 261 (1990). The case of Nancy Cruzan brought the issue of advance directives to the public. The Missouri Supreme Court reversed the decision of the trial court to allow Cruzan's parents to remove her life support. Missouri law required clear and convincing evidence that Cruzan would refuse the nutrition and hydration if she could (pp. 73-74).

CHAPTER 8: CONFIDENTIALITY AND PRIVACY ISSUES

Estate of Behringer v. *Medical Center of Princeton,* 592 A.2d 1251 (N.J. Super. 1991). Breach of patient confidentiality was a major legal theory in the case. The court held that the medical center and laboratory director breached their duty and obligation to keep the information about the patient's diagnosis confidential (p. 91).

Doe v. *Marselle,* 675 A.2d 835 (Conn. 1996). The trial court ruled that the plaintiff's complaint was insufficient because she did not allege "willful behavior" by the surgeon or his assistant, but the decision was reversed after the Connecticut Supreme Court defined "willful to mean a knowing disclosure of confidential HIV-related information" (p. 92).

Tarasoff v. *Regents of University of California,* 529 P.2d 553 (Cal. 1974) modified 551 P.2d 334. This case established a duty for psychotherapists to warn third parties if a patient made threats toward a specific individual. *Tarasoff* opened the door to imposing liability on psychotherapists for psychiatric patient violent behavior in limited circumstances (p. 93; see also Chapter 10, p. 93-94).

Flynn v. *Houston Emergicare, Inc.,* 869 S.W.2d 403 (Tex. Ct. App. 1993). An emerging legal issue, and often a concern for emergency health care professionals, is the attempt to extend a duty to warn beyond the patient-psychotherapist setting. In *Flynn,* the victim of a car accident sued an emergency physician and hospital and asked the court to extend the physician's duty beyond the patient to the general public. The appellate court held that the defendants did not owe a duty to the plaintiff to warn the patient not to drive (p. 94; see also Chapter 17, p. 213).

CHAPTER 9: FORENSICS IN EMERGENCY CARE

Carroll v. *State,* 1996 WL 549097 (Ala. Ct. App., September 27, 1996). The court found that the suspect's stomach contents were obtained solely for medical purposes and that the analysis of the contents was admissible at trial. Had the physician evacuated the gastric contents at the direction of a law enforcement officer, the outcome might have been different (pp. 105-106).

Rochin v. *California,* 342 U.S. 165 (1952). The suspect was convicted of illegal possession of morphine after a physician retrieved his stomach contents at the direction of police officers. The U.S. Supreme Court reversed the conviction and held that the defendant was denied constitutional rights of due process (p. 106).

Winston v. *Lee,* 470 U.S. 753 (1985). The type of evidence, procedures used to collect the evidence, and risks to the suspect or prisoner will be considered by a court if a court order is sought to obtain evidence over the patient's objections. In *Winston,* the Court weighed the factors and found the proposed surgery would be an unreasonable search and seizure under the Fourth Amendment (p. 106).

Suttle v. *State,* 565 So. 2d 1197 (Ala. Ct. App. 1990). The Alabama Supreme Court of Criminal Appeals reversed the vehicular homicide conviction because the prosecution could not properly establish chain of custody of the defendant's blood sample. The record should reflect direct observation to eliminate questions about the proper identity of the individual providing the specimen (p. 108).

Commonwealth v. *Nixon,* 718 A.2d 311 (Pa. Sup. Ct. 1998). In *Commonwealth,* a teenager died from complications of new-onset diabetes. The parents, who practiced spiritual treatment rather than seeking medical care, were convicted of involuntary manslaughter and endangering the welfare of a child. The appellate court upheld the conviction based on the parents' duty to seek medical treatment for their child's life-threatening condition (p. 112).

CHAPTER 10: PSYCHIATRIC EMERGENCY CARE

Wyatt v. *Stickney*, 325 F. Supp. 781 (M.D. Ala. 1971). The court established minimum constitutional standards for the care and treatment of mentally ill patients. The *Wyatt* standards had a dramatic impact on care of the mentally ill throughout the United States (pp. 118-119).

Montgomery v. *State*, 685 So. 2d 747 (Ala. Ct. App. 1996). The constitutional minimal protection before involuntary commitment of psychiatric patients to inpatient treatment is *clear and convincing evidence.* In this case, the psychiatrist testified that the patient suffered from paranoid psychosis and required inpatient treatment. She was involuntarily committed to the Department of Mental Health, and the probate judge's decision was upheld by the appellate court (p. 119).

Keebler v. *Winfield Carraway Hospital*, 531 So. 2d 841 (Ala. 1988). The court held that there was no duty to the patient because no facts led to foreseeability on the part of the physician or nurses to expect that the patient would commit suicide (pp. 125-126).

CHAPTER 12: EMERGENCY MEDICAL TREATMENT AND ACTIVE LABOR ACT (EMTALA)

Johnson v. *University of Chicago Hospital*, 982 F.2d 230 (7th Cir. 1992). *Johnson* was an early EMTALA case in which an infant died en route to the hospital in an ambulance. The appellate court ruled that the patient had not come to the emergency department for purposes of EMTALA because the patient never arrived on hospital property. The current law is that if a patient is in a hospital-owned ambulance, the patient has come to the emergency department (p. 139).

Cleland v. *Bronson Health Care Group, Inc.*, 917 F.2d 266, 271 (6th Cir. 1990). Cases brought under EMTALA related to "appropriate" are numerous. One measure of appropriateness, for EMTALA analysis, is that all patients with same or similar problems are treated equally. In *Cleland,* the appellate court indicated that reasons other than indigence could lead to substandard attention (p. 141).

Marshall v. *East Carroll Parish*, 1998 FED App. 30592 (5th Cir. 1998). The court reviewed case law and reiterated that an appropriate medical screening examination is judged by whether it was applied equally to patients with similar symptoms, not whether an accurate diagnosis of the patient's illness occurred. The court upheld the judgment in favor of the hospital (p. 142).

Dickey v. *Baptist Memorial,* 1998 FED App. 60681 (5th Cir. 1998). The appellate court overturned the summary judgment, finding a "genuine issue of material fact" in whether the hospital exercised ordinary and reasonable care to ensure that the medical record and reports were sent to the receiving hospital once the patient was transferred (p. 144).

Cherukuri v. *HHS,* 1999 FED App. 0160P (6th Cir. 1999). The focus of the case was the interpretation of "stabilize" under EMTALA. The court indicated that "stabilize" required a "flexible standard of reasonableness that depends on the circumstances." The court set aside the administrative findings, and fine, against Dr. Cherukuri (p. 147).

Bryant v. *Rectors & Visitors of the University of Virginia,* 95 F.3d 349, 352 (1996). The court in the *Cherukuri* case cited *Bryant,* a decision that described "stabilize" as "a relative concept that depends on the situation" (p. 148).

Burditt v. *U.S. Department of Health & Human Services,* 934 F.2d 1362 (5th Cir. 1991). If a patient is injured as a result of an EMTALA violation, he or she may sue the hospital for damages. In *Burditt,* a $20,000 fine was imposed on the physician and upheld by the appellate court (p. 148).

People v. *Anyakora,* 616 N.Y.S.2d 149 (Sup. Ct. 1993). EMTALA is a federal statute that preempts or supersedes state law when a direct conflict occurs between the two sets of law. New York law was the basis for action in *People.* A physician was charged with refusing to treat a patient in need of emergency medical treatment, falsifying a business record, and tampering with physical evidence. EMTALA was also likely violated (p. 148).

CHAPTER 16: INTENTIONAL TORTS

Roberson v. *Provident House,* 576 So.2d 992 (La. 1991). The plaintiff was awarded $25,000 for mental and physical pain and suffering after a nurse inserted an indwelling urinary catheter over the nursing home patient's objections. The court stated that the nurse had committed a battery, the offensive touching of another person in anger, rudeness, or a hostile manner (p. 203).

Miller v. *Rhode Island Hospital,* 625 A.2d 778 (R.I. 1993). This case addressed the issue of battery in the context of an emergency situation. The trial judge ruled the testimony of three defense experts as inadmissible. The Supreme Court ordered a new trial, stating that the jury can, and should, hear facts "concerning the existence of an emergency and a patient's competence to consent" (p. 203).

Banks v. *Medical University Of South Carolina,* 444 S.E.2d 519 (S.C. 1994). The patient's mother, a Jehovah's Witness, argued that no emergency existed requiring blood transfusions and that the administration of blood constituted a battery. The court reversed the trial court's ruling in favor of the defendant (pp. 203-204).

CHAPTER 17: PROFESSIONAL NEGLIGENCE

Darling v. *Charleston Community Memorial Hospital,* 211 N.E.2d 253 (Ill. 1965). This case was one of the first to establish the duty of a hospital to its patients. The lawsuit alleged that the hospital failed to adequately supervise medical staff, hospital nurses failed to report the patient's condition, or the hospital staff was negligent in failing to take action. *Darling* was also the first case to identify nurses' independent actions as grounds for liability (p. 212).

Adamski v. *Tacoma General Hospital,* 579 P.2d 970 (Wash. App. 1978). The case dealt with the important legal question as to the duty, if any, that exists when an emergency department physician or nurse provides advice over the telephone. In *Adamski,* the appellate court said that the plaintiff submitted sufficient evidence to raise a genuine issue of material fact as to the negligence of the emergency department nurses (pp. 212-213).

Ward v. *Forrester Day Care, Inc.,* 547 So. 2d 410 (Ala. 1989). An exception to the use of expert witnesses is the legal doctrine of *res ipsa loquitur.* In general, if the "thing speaks for itself," an expert witness may not be needed or used. As demonstrated in *Ward, res ipsa loquitur* requires the plaintiff to prove that the defendant had full management and control of the instrumentality, that the defendant did not exercise proper care in the use of the instrumentality, and that injury to the plaintiff resulted (p. 214).

Marks v. *Mandel,* 477 So. 2d 1036 (Fla. App. 1985). The case demonstrates how a hospital's policy and procedures manual can be used in establishing standard of care. The appellate court agreed with the plaintiff that the manual, which set out a detailed procedure for the on-call system, was necessary evidence. The case was retried using the manual (p. 215).

Crouch v. *Most,* 432 P.2d 250 (N.M. 1967). The case is an example of how the emergency health care provider can violate the standard of care and not be negligent is causation does not exist (p. 215).

Pogge v. *Hale,* 625 N.E.2d 792 (Ill. Ct. App. 1993). Expert testimony is usually necessary in professional negligence actions. In *Pogge,* the plaintiff attempted to use the hospital's policies and physician contract, after her expert witness was disqualified, to prove hospital and physician negligence. The court granted the defendants' motion for summary judgment based on plaintiff's failure to provide an expert witness (p. 217).

Bleiler v. *Bodnar,* 65 N.Y.2d 65, 479 N.E.2d 230 (N.Y. 1985). This case was filed *2 days* after the 2.5-year statute of limitation passed. The case was dismissed for failure to meet the time deadline established for filing professional negligence claims (pp. 217-218).

Jordan v. *Brantley,* 589 So. 2d 680 (Ala. 1991). This case demonstrates the significance of an expert witness' qualifications in a professional negligence action. The appellate court found that the plaintiff's expert witness did not provide competent testimony and reversed the trial court. An expert witness who is "similarly situated" mandates someone current in the field of practice related to the professional negligence action (p. 218).

Dorris v. *Detroit Osteopathic Hospital Corporation,* No. 183036 (Mich. Ct. App. 1996). A patient who sues his or her physician waives the client-physician privilege by virtue of placing the relationship at issue. However, the privilege may be used to prevent access to other patients. In *Dorris,* the appellate court ruled that the defendant did not have to disclose the name of a nonparty "patient who may, or may not have, overheard a conversation between the plaintiff and medical personnel" (p. 218).

Adams v. *Cooper Hospital,* 684 A.2d 506 (N.J. Super. Ct. 1996). The physician or nurse's exercise of judgment is a defense to a professional negligence claim. The choice is usually between two alternatives where medical opinions may differ. In *Adams,* the appellate court upheld the ruling of the trial court because the focus was on the defendant's conduct and not the exercise of judgment (p. 219).

Hand v. *Tavera,* 864 S.W.2d 678 (Tex. Ct. App. 1993). This case addressed the relationship between a managed care on-call physician and a patient. The court held that when a managed care plan patient presents to a participating hospital emergency department, and the plan's on-call physician is consulted about treatment or admission, a physician-patient relationship existed (p. 220).

Appendix K

Acts

CHAPTER 4: LAW AND ETHICS IN EMERGENCY CARE

Emergency Medical Treatment and Active Labor Act (EMTALA). The failure of the health care delivery system to distribute emergency care resources "fairly" arguably resulted to some extent in the passage of this act, initially known as *COBRA.* EMTALA was passed in response to reports of uninsured and unfunded patients, some in allegedly unstable condition, being transferred to public facilities (p. 29; see also Chapter 7, p. 80; Chapter 11, p. 132; Chapter 12, p. 138).

CHAPTER 5: CONSENT

Louisiana Medical Disclosure Act (1992). Under this act, written consent should specify the nature and purpose of the procedure(s) and the known risks, that disclosures were made, and that all questions were satisfactorily answered. Finally, the patient must sign granting authorization. If the written consent contains all the elements outlined by the statute, the physician receives protection by presuming validity (p. 40).

CHAPTER 6: REFUSAL TO CONSENT OR WITHDRAWAL OF CONSENT

Patient Self-Determination Act (PSDA) of 1991. One of the requirements is that hospital personnel are required to ask on admission whether a patient has an advance directive. The patient's response to the question must be documented according to the regulations. If the patient does not have an advance directive, the facility provides literature to the patient explaining the process (p. 74).

CHAPTER 7: MANAGED CARE AND CONSENT

The Patients Bill of Rights Plus Act. This bill addressed the issue of patient access to emergency medical care. Under the proposed legislation, if the manged care organization plan provides coverage for emergency care, preauthorization is not required for emergency medical screening examinations or emergency ambulance services. The proposed bill specifies that the standard used to evaluate such claims is that of the "prudent layperson." The prudent layperson is one who has "average knowledge" of health and medicine (p. 81).

CHAPTER 8: CONFIDENTIALITY AND PRIVACY ISSUES

Privacy Act of 1974. This law applies only to personal information held by federal agencies. The law also does not address the release of information, without the individual's consent, if needed by federal agencies to meet the agency's statutory mandates. The law does not apply to state or private agencies or facilities (p. 85).

The Health Insurance Portability and Accountability Act of 1996 (HIPAA). This act required the Department of Health and Human Services (DHHS) to issue regulations governing privacy of health records if Congress did not pass statutory protections by August 1999 (p. 85).

The Comprehensive Alcohol Abuse and Alcoholism Prevention, Treatment, and Rehabilitation Act of 1970 and the Drug Abuse Office and Treatment Act of 1972. Both laws provided specific confidential protection for patients admitted to a facility for alcohol or drug treatment. Any facility that receives federal funds is subject to the requirement of maintaining confidentiality of records and other patient information. Before releasing any information about patients treated for alcohol or drug abuse, the patient should provide specific consent for release of that information (p. 94).

CHAPTER 9: FORENSICS IN EMERGENCY CARE

Minnesota Domestic Abuse Act. The statute covers family or household members. The definition included those currently or previously living together and those involved in "significant romantic or sexual relationships" (p. 113).

CHAPTER 10: PSYCHIATRIC EMERGENCY CARE

The Lanterman-Petris-Short Act. The act provides for a 72-hour or "5150" emergency detention. In California, if a patient is a danger to self or others or is gravely disabled resulting from mental illness, inebriation, or the use of narcotics, he or she qualifies for a 72-hour hold. A written application is necessary and the patient must receive oral notice and reason(s) for the detention (p. 120).

CHAPTER 12: EMERGENCY MEDICAL TREATMENT AND ACTIVE LABOR ACT (EMTALA)

Consolidated Omnibus Budget Reconciliation Act (COBRA). Initially known as *COBRA*, the current acronym for the federal patient anti-dumping law is EMTALA (p. 138).

CHAPTER 13: ADVANCED HEALTH CARE PROFESSIONALS IN EMERGENCY CARE

The Balanced Budget Act of 1997. Under the BBA, the federal government mandated reimbursement for nurse practitioners by Medicare. Nurse practitioners are eligible for Medicare reimbursement regardless of location or specialty practice. Extending reimbursement to nurse practitioners encourages practice in remote areas, thus providing health care to those who might have otherwise been unable to obtain any type of health-related services (p. 154).

Title XIX of the Social Security Act. Title XIX authorizes the Medicaid program. Pediatric nurse practitioners (PNP) and family nurse practitioners (FNP) are eligible for Medicaid reimbursement (p. 168).

The Budget Reconciliation Act of 1989. Under this act, states are required to cover services provided by certified PNPs and FNPs. This act became effective July 1, 1990, and requires states to provide reimbursement whether or not the nurse practitioner is practicing under direct supervision of, or associated with, another physician or provider (p. 168).

CHAPTER 14: PREHOSPITAL CARE: EMERGENCY MEDICAL SERVICES (EMS)

The National Highway Traffic Safety Act. Passed in 1966, this act provided federal funding for equipment, training, and communications in prehospital care (p. 182).

The Emergency Medical Services (EMS) Systems Act of 1973. This act identified 15 components of a prehospital EMS system (p. 182).

CHAPTER 17: PROFESSIONAL NEGLIGENCE

The Alabama Medical Liability Act of 1987. This act defined the standard of care as "reasonable care, skill, and diligence as other similarly situated health care providers in the same general line of practice, ordinarily have and exercise in like cases" (p. 214).

Glossary

advance directive Document that allows the individual to preplan and state decisions about future health care.

allegation An accusation made against the defendant in a lawsuit.

AMA "Against medical advice"; process a patient may use to refuse treatment; usually involves patient's voluntary removal of self from the facility, with or without signing a refusal form.

answer Defendant's response to the plaintiff's allegations in the complaint.

appeal Request for a change in a verdict or judgment.

assault Intentional, immediate threat of harm to another with the ability to carry out the threat.

attorney-client privilege Protection of communication between attorney and client to encourage complete disclosure.

autonomy Right of independent control; in health care, a fundamental, ethical right to control decisions about one's own body.

battery Offensive touching of another person (including clothing the person is wearing) in anger, rudeness, or a hostile manner.

beneficence Concept of doing good.

breach of duty Element of professional negligence case that, if proved, establishes failure of defendant to meet standard of care.

burden of proof Expectation that the plaintiff must prove that the defendant is guilty of the allegations made through preponderance of evidence, substantial evidence, or clear and convincing evidence.

"but for" analysis Assertion that an injury would not have occurred "but for" the action or inaction of the defendant.

capacity Assessment of individual; may be established by laws such as minors, judicial determination of mental competence, or mental status.

case manager Facilitator and gatekeeper in delivery of health care services assigned to monitor quality and cost containment over a continuum of care, particularly for complex patient cases or those involving long-term medical care.

causation Element of professional negligence case that links conduct of defendant to injury of plaintiff.

chain of custody Principle of emergency care forensics used to establish to a reasonable probability that there has been no tampering with evidence.

clear and convincing evidence Burden of proof required for involuntary commitment of a psychiatric patient to inpatient treatment; the constitutional minimal protection required before such commitment.

clinical nurse specialist (CNS) Nurse with special licensure and education (usually including a master's degree) who focuses on five roles of nursing: clinician, teacher, consultant, researcher, and manager, usually focusing on a specific patient population as well.

commission Type of failure in meeting the expected standard of care by virtue of incorrect professional conduct.

common law Law that develops as cases are determined by judges, using accepted societal principles, customs, and prior case decisions (precedents) to make a just decision.

compensatory damage Damages (usually expenses incurred or wages lost) that a plaintiff must prove to win. Element of professional negligence action.

complaint First document in a civil lawsuit, identifying the facts of the case, proposing legal theories of liability, and asking for damages or an equitable determination of interests.

confidentiality Ethical concept of the right of fidelity; also, management or nondisclosure of private information provided by the patient or patient's family.

consent (1) Key defense to any intentional tort in that it establishes that the patient (plaintiff) had agreed to the conduct of the defendant. (2) Process of communication between health care provider and patient requiring fulfillment of certain established elements (usually, competence, sufficient disclosure, understanding, and voluntariness) before patient's agreement to treatment can be considered "informed."

consent for aeromedical transport Patient's or family's consent to allow aeromedical as opposed to ground transportation to a treatment facility. This is usually a time-critical decision and is *one of two* forms of consent to be considered in this treatment environment; not to be confused with **consent for treatment by aeromedical crew.**

consent for treatment by aeromedical crew Patient's or family's consent for actual therapeutic intervention in the aeromedical environment; this is *one of two* forms of consent to be considered in this treatment environment; not to be confused with **consent for aeromedical transport.**

damages Element of professional negligence case that demonstrates physical, mental, and/or emotional injury to patient. May be compensatory and/or punitive.

defamation Spoken or written damage to an individual's reputation. Usually must include the following elements: is communicated to a third party, is a falsehood concerning the plaintiff, and subjects the plaintiff to public ridicule or contempt.

default judgment Decision made in favor of the plaintiff when the defendant fails to plead, answer, or otherwise defend against the allegations in a complaint.

defendant Person or company being sued; also, the defendant's attorney.

deposition Oral testimony recorded under oath, usually before the actual trial; the questions and answers are recorded, either in written or video-taped form, and a transcript of the testimony is available to both sides for use as evidence in the trial.

direct medical control   Immediate and concurrent communication with the EMS provider either at the scene or via electronic communication devices.

disclosure   Revelation of facts of the case; such communication is generally protected when it occurs between client and attorney. Also, a component for measuring and ensuring informed consent.

discovery   Process of investigating the other side's evidence and the identity of their witnesses; this process takes place from the time of the complaint up to and including the duration of the trial.

DNR   Acronym for "do not resuscitate" order, which is a withdrawal or refusal of consent should a patient suffer a cardiopulmonary arrest.

durable power of attorney   Type of advance directive that allows a competent individual to appoint another, known as a proxy or surrogate, as the health care decision maker should the patient be unable to decide.

duty   Essential element that must be established in any professional negligence action; responsibility or obligation to an individual, particularly a client or patient, established by the presence of specific elements that constitute a special relationship.

duty to warn the third party   Requirement for a psychotherapist to warn a third, identifiable individual when a serious threat is made against that individual by a patient.

emancipation   Legal recognition of adulthood, even if the chronologic age is below the age of majority; also called *removal of disability of nonage.*

emergency detention   Emergency holding period designed to keep an individual under protection while procedures are initiated for an involuntary commitment.

emergency exception   Possible defense against charges of assault and battery or false imprisonment claim, if it can be shown that the patient was in a life-threatening situation and that delays would have led to significant injury.

emergency exceptions consent   Concept requiring a physician's signature to certify that there is no time to obtain consent from the patient or anyone else before instituting lifesaving treatment.

emergency medical condition   Acute symptoms of sufficient severity such that the absence of immediate medical attention would reasonably result in serious jeopardy to the health of the individual, serious impairment of bodily functions, or serious dysfunction of any bodily organ or part.

EMTALA   Emergency Medical Treatment and Active Labor Act (42 U.S.C.A. 1395dd 1996) mandating that any individual who comes to the emergency department seeking emergency care or in active labor is entitled to receive a medical screening examination, within the hospital's capability, to determine whether an emergency medical condition exists.

ethics   Study of decisions and the bases of those decisions.

expert witness   Witness used in both civil and criminal cases who, because of education, experience, and/or training, is qualified to testify as to the professional standards that apply in a particular case, particularly of a scientific or technical nature.

express consent   Verbal or written agreement, particularly in regard to treatment.

fact witness   Witness called by either side in a legal case because he or she has personal, firsthand knowledge of the facts of a case.

forensics   Study of evidence used in legal cases.

"foreseeability" test   Determination of whether a defendant knew, or should have known, that an action or inaction could lead to the injury sustained by the plaintiff.

Good Samaritan laws   State statutes that prevent liability for individuals who assist at the scene of an emergency.

impairment   Reduced mental or decision-making capacity, whether temporary or permanent.

implied consent   Legal fiction used to protect health care professionals, which presumes that, in certain cases, the patient would consent to treatment if capable of doing so.

incapacity   A possible defense against charges of intentional tort if it can be established that the patient (plaintiff) did not have the medical capacity to consent to, or refuse, treatment.

incompetency   See **legal incompetency.**

informed consent   Legal and ethical concept requiring recognition and respect for the individual's autonomy; patient authorization for treatment or procedure after full disclosure of risks and benefits.

intent   An objective standard under the law. Differentiates subjective standard (what the defendant was thinking) from objective standard (actual conduct and what the defendant knew or should have known regarding likely damage or injury resulting from that conduct).

intentional tort   Objective standard examined by law in tort cases that looks not at the subjective standard, but at the actual conduct and what the defendant knew or should have known regarding how this conduct could likely cause injury to the plaintiff.

interrogatories Written questions directed to a party or witness, generally answered under oath and within a specific time limit.

invasion of privacy Legal term for unwarranted publicity, wrongful intrusion into one's private activities, publicizing of an individual's private affairs when the public has no legitimate concern, or unwanted use of an individual's likeness for commercial purposes.

involuntary commitment Enforced admittance into psychiatric inpatient treatment either against the patient's will or outside the patient's awareness (as in the case of a disoriented patient). Although this is usually a judicial process, involuntary confinement can take place in emergency departments in response to obvious immediate need.

jurisdiction Legal authority or power of a court to render a decision.

justice Ethical concept of fairness; in health care, this applies in particular to the distribution of health care resources.

justification—defense of another Defense used when a defendant (e.g., an emergency health care professional) uses the force necessary to protect a third party from injury.

legal incompetence Legal proceeding in which a judge determines that an individual is unable to manage his or her daily affairs and may need assistance in decision making.

libel Written damage to an individual's reputation; printed form of **defamation.**

living will Type of advance directive that allows a competent patient to decide that should a terminal illness, injury, or persistent vegetative state exist, treatment should or should not be rendered.

LWBS "Leaving without being seen"; a way for a patient to withdraw consent for treatment.

medical forensics Collection, analysis, and interpretation of medical evidence presented in legal cases.

medical screening examination (MSE) Comprehensive evaluation to determine whether an emergency medical condition exists. Not to be confused with triage.

motion Effort by either side of a lawsuit to try to resolve the case or specific issues before trial.

motion for a new trial Motion filed by either party unhappy with the outcome of a trial.

motion for directed verdict Motion made at the close of the opposing party's case, asking for a ruling in favor of the motioning party.

motion for judgment notwithstanding the verdict Posttrial motion asking the judge to set aside the verdict of a jury.

motion for protective order   Pretrial motion to protect confidential information during the discovery process.

motion for sanctions   Pretrial motion filed if the opposing side fails to comply with a court order.

motion for summary judgment   Pretrial motion to have a judge rule on a matter of law; the opposing party can file an opposition to this, with both sides arguing the law applied to the specific facts.

motion in limine   Effort by one side of a lawsuit to keep out information about a party or witness that is considered not relevant, prejudicial, or of questionable value to the case.

motion to compel   Pretrial motion to ensure that the opposing side responds to discovery requests for interrogatories, documents, depositions, and so on.

motion to dismiss   Effort by the defendant to dismiss a case before or along with the answer, usually on the grounds that the court does not have jurisdiction over the particular case.

nonmaleficence   Principle of avoiding harm.

nurse practitioner   Advanced practice nurse prepared by a master's program with a broad scope of practice involving nursing and medical management.

offline medical direction   Development of protocols establishing standards, education, and quality-improvement activities for EMS providers.

omission   Type of failure in meeting the expected standard of care by the absence of an expected professional conduct.

online medical control   Direct communication with the EMS provider via radio or telephone.

parens-patriae   Role of the state as guardian for those who cannot care for themselves.

physician assistant (PA)   Graduate of accredited physician assistant program who is licensed by a state or credentialed by the federal government to practice medicine as delegated by, and with supervision of, physicians.

plaintiff   Person or company suing another; also, the plaintiff's lawyer.

pleadings   General category of documents that sets forth claims and defenses for specific parties, providing notice to the opposing side of the facts and legal theories of the specific case.

preponderance of the evidence   Burden of proof in civil cases.

privacy   Right to be free from invasion and left alone.

professional negligence   Failure to meet the standard of care (SOC), causing damage to an individual.

psychiatric advance directive   Patient-generated document stating (in a period of clarity) preferences for treatment or refusal of treatment for mental illness in the future.

punitive damage   Damages that serve to punish or deter conduct.

rationing   Limiting available resources.

res ipsa loquitur   Knowledge common to the average person; literal translation is "the thing speaks for itself."

respiratory therapist   Practitioner trained and accredited in both emergency airway clearance procedures and also in long-term treatment meant to aid in patient breathing exercises and self-care relief therapy.

right of fidelity   Ethical concept of an expected level of privacy or confidentiality.

SANE   "Sexual assault nurse examiner" program used in emergency departments to ensure more consistent and reliable "rape kit" evidence collection.

self-defense   Possible defense to a claim of assault and battery, if it can be documented that the patient's (plaintiff's) behavior was out of control and the defendant simply lawfully repelled an attack to defend himself or herself.

slander   Spoken damage to an individual's reputation; verbal form of **defamation.**

stabilize   Provision of medical treatment for the patient's condition to ensure "within reasonable medical probability" that the patient's condition will not materially deteriorate as a result of or during transfer.

standard of care (SOC)   Expected professional conduct (in a specific situation) that would reasonably be expected of any professional in the same situation (often established through the use of expert witnesses).

statute of limitations   The time period in which a lawsuit can be brought for an action.

subpoena   Documented, enforceable requirement for the recipient to appear as a witness in a case either at a trial or deposition to offer testimony.

subpoena duces tecum   Requirement that recipient bring specified documents or records to a deposition or trial.

substantial evidence   Proof required in some states for any charge of professional negligence.

summons   Notice of a lawsuit given to the defendant (person or company being sued), delivered along with the complaint.

telemedicine   Assessment, treatment, and evaluation of a patient via communication lines, such as telephone, facsimile, computer, or Internet.

threshold elements   Category of conditions that must be present before informed consent is valid; these conditions are *competence* and *voluntariness.*

tort law   Cases based on injury to a person or property.

transfer   Movement of an individual outside hospital facilities, including discharge of an individual, but excluding patients declared dead or who leave without permission of the hospital staff.

triage   An emergency center's process of sorting patients based on complaint, assessment, and initial evaluation of acuity.

truth   Provable fact; the only absolute defense to a defamation action.

venue   Legal authority associated with the geographic location of a lawsuit; venue requirements determine which courts (e.g., state versus federal) have jurisdiction over a specific case.

wrongful death   Legal cause of action for damages to be paid to a survivor when it can be proved that professional negligence caused a death and that the survivor is entitled to damages.

wrongful life   Theory of liability concerning a physician's alleged refusal to follow a patient's living will.

Index

Page numbers in italic indicate illustrations; *t* indicates table.

ISBN 0-7216-8324-X

9 780721 683249